Constitütion *is* Born

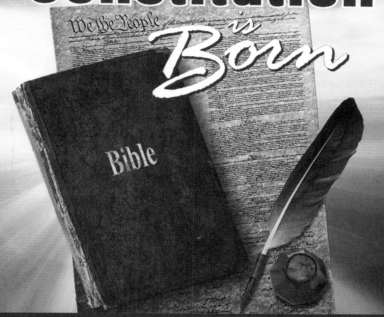

We The People

Bible

A Brief History of the Constitution of the United States of America, Tracing the *Hand of God*

By

Norma Swanson *and* Barbara Aud

Includes writings, quotes, landmark court decisions, fascinating facts and historical documents.

AB ASPECT Books
www.ASPECTBooks.com

Copyright © 2016 Norma Swanson

Copyright © 2016 Aspect Books, Inc.

ISBN-13: 978-1-4796-0645-0 (Paperback)

ISBN-13: 978-1-4796-0728-0 (Hardback)

ISBN-13: 978-1-4796-0646-7 (ePub)

ISBN-13: 978-1-4796-0647-4 (Mobi)

Library of Congress Control Number: 2016914395

Printed in Canada

ASPECT Books
www.ASPECTBooks.com

INTRODUCTION

Why this book? - A different agenda!

While we stand, pledging allegiance to the flag and lustily singing our national anthem, a tidal wave of anti-Americanism is rising and threatens the very core of our existence. America is drifting rapidly from its Biblical foundation and — our nation's greatest document is under the microscope of revisionists. Our citizens, particularly our youth, appear to be stampeding in the direction of declining patriotism and even hostility towards our present form of government. We are living on the shifting sands of uncertainty and appear to have lost our moral compass.

There's a rustling in the winds, perhaps indicating that America may be awakening to the realization that, as a people, we know little regarding the foundation of our government — **who we are, where we came from, how we got here, what we stand for, what it cost, and that God orchestrated the whole process**! The Christian roots of our nation are historically evident. Religious faith was central, pervasive and indispensable in the founding of our Nation, the most powerful nation on earth — but power without God's control is the formula for disaster.

In a recent poll of 1000 tourists at a national mall, 70% could not answer the question, "What is the supreme law of the land?" 61% did not know the length of a senator's term, 63% did not know the number of Supreme Court Justices, and 86% did not know the number of representatives in the House of Representatives, or the freedoms granted by the Bill of Rights. Most knew only the 1st and 5th Amendments.

Now, as never before, basic knowledge of our governmental heritage is essential if we want to be empowered to keep elected officials accountable and defeat the forces that would destroy our freedoms. The truths of the Constitution must be embedded in our hearts — (not blocked out by social media or minds captured by electronic devices) as it is the only way to a guarantee of freedom. Since the celebration of the 200th anniversary of our Constitution, all three departments of government have, to a large degree, ignored the Constitution. Neglect of the principles contained in our Constitution has been responsible for the loss of many of the freedoms it guaranteed.

Our Constitution has blessed the people of this nation as well as people throughout the world, and we have been the recipients of the greatest blessings of any people who have lived on this earth. Millions of people have risked their lives to come to America to enjoy the freedom offered by our constitutional republic.

***A Constitution is Born* was written to be a clarion call, loud and clear, for renewed patriotism, a love for country and above all a realization that our direction comes from God, not from man, and we are responsible to Him, our Maker.** This brief history of the U.S. Constitution with relevant information is to be a sword of the Lord, piercing the heart and soul, invoking action to carry out His plan as He makes it known to us — until the battle is over and we are safe with Him.

Our continuing prayer is that *A Constitution is Born* will find a special place in the hearts of Americans and that they will read it to their children to provide insight, and understanding as to what it means to be a free, courageous American with increased faith in our God who has brought us this far. **With His help and wisdom, we will NOT be defeated — our God is marching on.**

ACKNOWLEDGEMENTS

When the idea for *A Constitution is Born* was conceived, we were totally unaware of the perils and pluses we would encounter on the path to a published book. The many hours of research, writing, editing and yes, a computer that would not always cooperate, were beyond comprehension. Now that we have emerged from a labyrinth of books and papers, the pluses far outweigh the perils.

Our eyes have been opened as never before to our magnificent spiritual heritage, and our hearts are filled with a deeper sense of gratitude for our great God who has made our freedom possible. There were others who joined us on this path with interest and expertise, and for them we are extremely grateful. Barbara is especially grateful for the patience of her husband, Joe and daughter Hannah who put up with her lack of sleep, lack of home-cooking, and their constant support though these many months of writing and research.

Historians Ronald Mann and Lawrence Yandell took time from their busy schedules for the ever important task of checking the document for accuracy and providing suggestions for inclusions. We are especially grateful for the generosity of Ron Mann and Herbert Shuck for allowing us the use of original lithographs and steel engravings dating back to 1755.

We thank Pam Pencola, Diana Samuelson and Judy Nusbaum for their professional editing. How often we needed the technical assistance provided by Debbie Pearse, Michael Hamner and Paul Pencola. For their prayers and encouragement, we thank Sarah Patterson, Charlotte Bendell, Sue Dickson, Gary and Shelby Hooper and Norma's son Dane and daughter-in law Karen. We are especially grateful for the inspiration and encouragement from our long-time friends, Joe and Gladys Grimaud. Without their encouragement and support there may never have been *A Constitution is Born*. And how can we ever sufficiently thank The National Center for Constitutional Studies for the abundance of quality reference material they provided?

Then there is our publishing team at Aspect Books. We thank them sincerely for their patience and wise counsel through the long and tedious process of putting this book together.

Our prayers will continually ascend to our Lord who has answered our prayers for wisdom, guidance, and for strength when we were weary. We trust now that *A Constitution is Born* will be read and will accomplish the purpose for which it was written — to invigorate the soul of the American with the inspiration to keep freedom alive and to bring glory to our God who made this nation possible.

Authors, Norma and Barbara

A word from the authors...

The inspiration for "A Constitution is Born" came as a response to a clarion call from patriotic Americans across the land as they saw cultural and spiritual erosion in America. That was nearly five years ago. Their cry was "Stand firm and hold on to the Biblical principles that God laid down for us through our Founding Fathers and His Word". Standing tall among them was a Methodist preacher from Tupelo, Mississippi, Donald E. Wildmon, whose voice for many years was heard as one crying in the wilderness. We heard that cry, our hearts were moved, and we have tried, to the best of our ability and dependence upon God, to carry that word through the pages of "A Constitution is Born."

FOREWORD

During the celebration of the Bicentennial of the United States Constitution, several national surveys were taken of adults and student's knowledge of the Declaration of Independence and the United States Constitution. The results were appalling. In response to most questions, the answers revealed the vast majority of those surveyed bordered on gross ignorance. Since that time I am sure that any surveys taken would reveal a worsening of the results.

Repeatedly, our Founding Fathers warned us if our system of government a "Constitutional Republic," was to continue, it would be necessary for the citizens of the United States to maintain it. Thomas Jefferson wrote to his friend Chas Yancey (1786): *"If a nation expects to be ignorant and free, in a state of civilization, it expects what never was and never will be."*[1] The Virginia Declaration of Rights written in 1816, also addressed this subject. *"That no free government or the blessings of liberty cannot be preserved to any people, but by a firm adherence to justice, moderation, temperance, Frugality and virtue, and by frequent recurrence to fundamental principles."*

The members of Congress dutifully take the Oath of Office (see Article II, Section 1 and Article VI) and then almost immediately proceed to ignore it by passing legislation which is not authorized by the Constitution. The President and Judiciary give lip service to the Constitution, but like the Congress, ignore it. Perhaps it has reached the point that it may be necessary to start impeachment proceedings (see Article II, Section 4 and Article I, sections 2 & 3) against some of our elected officials in order to force them to do their work in accordance with the Constitution.

---

[1] Jefferson Quotes and Family Letters – http://1ref.us/bv

Have we forgotten or ignored what James Madison warned? *"Because it is proper to take alarm at the first experiment on our liberties, we hold this prudent jealousy to be the first duty of citizens, and one of the noblest characteristics of the late Revolution. The freemen of America did not wait till usurped power had strengthened itself by exercise, and entangled the question precedents. They saw all the consequences in the principle, and they avoided the consequences by denying the principle."* (Memorial and Remonstrance, James Madison, 1785) We dare not wait any longer to start addressing the numerous violations of our Constitution.

Our Founders provided us with the greatest Constitution in the world. It has provided us with the best form of government on earth but it must be maintained, and the best way to accomplish that is to continually elect moral and righteous men, and to educate our youth with a goal of deep respect and love of our Constitution.

> *Our Founders provided us with the greatest Constitution in the world. It has provided us with the best form of government on earth but it must be maintained, and the best way to accomplish that is to continually elect moral and righteous men, and to educate our youth with a goal of deep respect and love of our Constitution.*

And lastly, to remember that our Constitution was written only for a moral and righteous people. President John Adams said: *"We have no government armed with power capable of contending with human passions unbridled by morality and religion.*"[2] President George Washington wrote to his dear friend Lafayette: "*Though, when a people shall have become incapable of governing themselves and fit for a master, it is of little consequence from what quarter he comes.*"[3] For this reason and others, we must elect a moral and righteous president as well as representatives, individuals who will truly live up to their oath of office.

George Washington said: "*Let (the people) persevere in their affectionate vigilance over the precious depository of American happiness, the Constitution of the United States. Let them cherish it, too, for the sake of those who from every clime are daily seeking a dwelling in our land.*"[4]

President Abraham Lincoln said of our Constitution: "*Let every American, every lover of liberty, every well-wisher to his posterity support the Constitution. Let it be taught in schools, in seminaries and colleges. Let it be written in primers, in spelling books and in almanacs. Let it be preached from the pulpit, proclaimed in legislative halls, and enforced in courts of justice. In short, let it become the political religion of the nation, and in particular, establish a reverence for the Constitution.*"[5]

Perhaps one of our most favorite quotes on our Constitution was a statement written by Frances Grund in: *Aristocracy in America*, Harpers, 1959, *pp. 212-213:*

"The American Constitution is remarkable for its simplicity; but it can only suffice a people habitually correct in their actions, and would be utterly inadequate to the wants of a different nation. Change the domestic habits of the Americans, their religious devotion, and their high respect for morality, and it will not be necessary to change a single letter in the Constitution in order to vary the whole form of their government."

The authors of this book are of the conviction that one of the best ways to address the problems confronting this nation is through an educational process dedicated to our people, particularly our youth. Via this process they hope and pray that our youth will learn to drink from the sources of our Constitution – our Fathers, and thereby develop the understanding and knowledge necessary to maintain the source of their freedoms – our Constitution.

I believe our Constitution was inspired by God. It took centuries to prepare and locate a people that could bring it into being and then at a terrible cost in

---

2   John Adams – http://1ref.us/bw

3   Founders Online – http://1ref.us/bx

4   Sixth Annual Message of George Washington – http://1ref.us/by

5   Abraham Lincoln's Lyceum Address – http://1ref.us/bz

personal sacrifice. We are its caretakers, responsible to ensure its continuance. If we allow it to be destroyed at this point in history, there is no doubt in my mind that we will never again live to see the blessing of freedoms we have enjoyed. This nation and the world at large will have lost the greatest beacon of liberty ever built.

Ronald M. Mann, *former Director and Deputy Director of*
The Commission on the Bicentennial of the United States Constitution.

COMMENTS ABOUT
A Constitution is Born...

"The importance of educating our youth about the principles set forth in our Constitution has always been high on my list of priorities. I am pleased and excited to recommend the work of Norma Swanson and Barbara Aud through <u>A Constitution is Born</u>. The book provides a brief history of the Constitution and what it means in layman's terms."

> **Ronald M. Mann,** *Former Director and Deputy Director of the Commission of the Bicentennial of the Constitution, Special Advisor to President Ronald Reagan*

"Norma Swanson and Barbara Aud's new book, <u>A Constitution is Born</u> is a must-read for every American citizen. In this fascinating book, they trace the invisible hand of God in formulating the foundational guiding document for our nation. This book is essential reading for everyone who wants to know the truth of the founding of our country."

> **Dr. Robert Jeffress,** *Senior Pastor, First Baptist Church, Dallas, Texas and Fox News Contributor.*

"Our children must understand the freedoms that the Declaration of Independence and the United States Constitution guarantees for all Americans if our republic is to survive.

<u>A Constitution is Born</u> is a vital tool available to all parents, teachers, and all who love liberty. Read this book, teach it to your children, share

it with your students, tell your neighbors about it. This is something you can do to light freedom's way for generations to come.

> **Dr. Robert Sweet, Jr.** *Professional Staff Member, Committee on Education and the Workforce, United States House of Representatives*

"As you become aware of today's political and social climate and the attack on our freedoms, you can't help but think *A Constitution is Born* could not have been published in a timelier manner. Citizens both young and old, now more than ever, need to understand the sacrifice and principles that were so thoughtfully crafted in the Constitution by its designers. Every household, school and church should have this book and integrate the principles and truths into their lives."

> **Rose Gamblen, Ph.D.** *Educational Specialist and Published Author, Professor, Penn State Producer and Co-Host of My Home School Companion, radio network*

"I APPLAUD Barbara Aud and Norma Swanson for their many hours of research and labor in producing this very timely book, *A Constitution is Born*. Never before have we needed to provide for our youth a basic understanding of how they received the freedom by which they live, and how the hand of God moved in the forming of the nation as we know it today. As an educator, I highly recommend that every home and parent make this book a "must" in the education of their children."

> **Dr. Arthur Nazigian** *Board Chairman Emeritus, Association of Christian Schools, International Published Author, Charter member ACSI Board*

"*A Constitution is Born* should be distributed to every teacher in the land, to their teachers' rooms, school libraries and homes, so future generations of young Americans will have knowledge of the world's greatest document of freedom passed intact to them, and hopefully to all future generations. It is the responsibility of every true American to pass it on. Bravo to the authors, Barbara and Norma!"

> **Sue Dickson** *Teacher and curriculum designer, Author Sing, Spell, Read & Write, Songs that Teach, Learning Systems L Pearson, Published author*

" '*The road to hell is paved with good intentions*' is a saying that was popular in my youth. I think of this saying frequently when talking to many of my friends in the Congress or listening to their comments on the floor of the House or Senate. They genuinely believe that the larger and more controlling the Federal government is, the better off we will be because government always makes better decisions than people do and always spends money more wisely. They really do have good intentions, but they have no sense of where this will lead. They desperately need to read *A Constitution is Born*. In clear layman's language, the authors detail the origin of the Constitution and why the 'original intent' interpretation is crucial to the preservation of our liberties and indeed to the preservation of our status as a premier world power."

Roscoe Bartlett *Maryland Representative of the United States House of Representatives (26 years)*

"Patriotism (love of what is noble in one's country) is a neglected virtue in character education. At the heart of what is noble about our country is the U.S Constitution and its moral framework, the Declaration of Independence. But we can't love what we don't understand. Norma Swanson's and Barbara Aud's *A Constitution is Born* will help our young citizens in-the-making grasp and cherish the crucial foundations of our democracy."

Dr. Thomas Lickona *Director, Center for the 4th and 5th R's (Respect and Responsibility) New York University. Author, Educating for Character, Bantam, 1992*

"Authors Swanson and Aud have completed a 'trifecta' with *A Constitution is Born.* They have (1) written on a topic that is relevant and necessary for these times, (2) provided in-depth and comprehensive information on the subject of the Constitution as it relates to God's working in the process and (3) presented the material in a well written, readable narrative. This is a publication that will be an invaluable resource for anyone interested in understanding the background and creation of the Constitution."

Lawrence Yandell *Historian and homeschool educator*

As a longtime friend of Norma Swanson, I am intimately aware of her love for God, America, and the Constitution. In her collaboration with Barbara Aud, _A Constitution is Born_, gave me a far greater understanding of why our Constitution is so unique and why we are so blessed as a nation to have had forefathers with the wisdom and willingness to sacrifice so much that we may live in freedom.

Joseph A. Grimaud Jr. *Two-time candidate for the United States House of Representatives and former CEO and President of the international franchisor Precision Tune, Incorporated*

"_A Constitution is Born_ is a real gem. It is wonderful exposure to our United States founding documents as our youth and adults know little about their origins. This book is useful as a textbook or resource for personal information. With lifetime certification as an Administrator for the Association of Christian Schools International, and Association of Secondary Schools and Colleges, I highly endorse this book."

Sarah Patterson, *Administrator Emeritus, The King's Christian Academy, Callaway, Maryland*

DEDICATION

It is with gratitude and admiration that this book is dedicated to the Reverend Don Wildmon whose life has embodied the essence of Christian principles and the spirit of a true American.

Reverend Wildmon founded the American Family Association in 1977 and the American Family Radio network in 1991. AFA and AFR were created to give leadership to the Christian community in addressing the great moral issues of our time. His leadership on these issues has resulted in millions of patriotic Americans becoming the salt and light in the culture that the Bible commends Christians to be. Like many of the Founding Fathers, Rev. Wildmon has given his life to promoting the values of faith, family and freedom.

CONTENTS

Part I

A BRIEF HISTORY OF EVENTS IN THE DEVELOPMENT OF THE UNITED STATES CONSTITUTITON

Blessed is the nation whose God is the Lord. Psalm 33:12

MY COUNTRY 'TIS OF THEE

"We can best honor the Constitution by giving ourselves a civics and history lesson on its origin and meaning. "
Warren E. Burger, *Chief Justice of the United States Supreme Court*

"SWEET LAND OF LIBERTY" … *"Where the Spirit of the Lord is, there is Liberty" (II Cor. 3:17).* What is liberty? Is it something we can touch or feel? A state of mind? A philosophy? Why do we sing about it, talk about it and pray about it? Where do you get it? Where does it come from? Is it for everyone or just a privileged few? Why do we desire it?

The Founding Fathers considered liberty (freedom) so important that they pledged their lives, their fortunes and their sacred honor just to secure and keep it.

Webster's dictionary states that liberty is the *"quality or state of being free"* (freedom). The Founding Fathers considered liberty (freedom) so important that they pledged their lives, their fortunes and their sacred honor just to secure and keep it. They fulfilled their pledge and liberty (freedom) was won.

Liberty is ours today, not given to us by them alone but by the multitudes that have come after them subscribing to the same basic concepts that made freedom possible. What then is liberty?

Liberty or freedom is the legal right not to be enslaved by government. It means possessing the power to act, think, or speak within established boundaries and norms. It is the right and capacity of people to self-rule. It is the absence of subjection to domination by government.

The Founding Fathers recognized the impossibility of maintaining freedom unless those who govern are able to exercise self-restraint. They gave to the Nation, through the Constitution, sufficient authority to complete the tasks assigned to it. They created within the document built-in reserves with a system of "checks and balances." They built a system of government while incorporating Christian principles and the recognition of God, the true Giver of liberty and freedom. However, liberty is never free. America's freedom is still being paid for every day, by those who wear the uniform of our country, and by others who willingly sacrifice all to safeguard our liberty.

The Declaration of Independence of July 1776 stated that we are endowed by our Creator with certain "unalienable" rights. The moral state of our Nation, then and now, is directly tied to this single phrase in the Declaration. Our American form of government has its roots in God's word, the Bible. The first two commandments of our Lord are the basis upon which our dual form of government was established. The first commandment represents one's duty to God: *"You shall love the Lord your God with all your heart, and with all your soul, and with all your mind" (Matthew 22:37).* The second commandment is the basis for the relation of the individual states to each other—our relation to our neighbor: *"You shall love your neighbor as yourself" (Matthew 22:39).* The concept of representation began in the Old Testament. It is interesting that in the first chapter of the book of Deuteronomy, Moses was instructed by the Lord to: *"Take you wise men, and understanding, and known among your tribes, I will make them rulers over you… captains over thousands, and captains over hundreds, and captains over fifties, and captains over tens, and officers among your tribes."*

The Reverend Thomas Hooker, on May 31, 1638, chose this text for a sermon on liberty that planted the seeds for the first written constitution in America—The Fundamental Orders of Connecticut. The colonists were very explicit in instruction to individuals to whom they had given the power of representation. They made sure men of integrity were elected, men who would manifest integrity and character in the selection process.

Samuel Adams wrote of liberty speaking of *"this gift from Heaven."* *"The perfection of liberty therefore, in a state of nature, is for every man to be free from any external force, and to perform such actions as in his own mind and conscience he judges to be rightist; which liberty no man can possess whose mind is enthralled by irregular and inordinate passions; since it is no great privilege to be free from external violence if the dictates of the mind are controlled by a force within, which exerts itself above reason."*[6]

The colonists were very explicit in instruction to individuals to whom they had given the power of representation. They made sure men of integrity were elected, men who would manifest integrity and character in the selection process.

John Quincy Adams said, *"Posterity! You will never know, how much it cost the present Generation, to preserve your Freedom! I hope you will make a good Use of it."*[7]

In addressing liberty, Thomas Paine said, *"What we obtain, too cheap, we esteem too lightly:--'Tis dearness only that gives every thing its value. Heaven knows how to set a proper price upon its goods; and it would be strange indeed, if so celestial an article as Freedom should not be highly rated."*[8]

William Prescott wrote to the men of Boston, *"... Our forefathers passed the vast Atlantic, spent their blood and treasure, that they might enjoy their liberties, both civil and religious, and transmit them to their posterity. ... Now if we should give them up, can our children rise up and call us blessed? ...."*[9]

---

[6]   National Center for the Development of Constitutional Strategies – http://1ref.us/c0

[7]   Massachusetts Historical Society – http://1ref.us/c1

[8]   Library of Congress – http://1ref.us/c2

[9]   WorldNetDaily.com, Inc. – http://1ref.us/c3 /

In 1779 in a letter to James Warren, Samuel Adams stated ... "*A general dissolution of principles and manners will more surely overthrow the liberties of America than the whole force of the common enemy...*"[10]

This collective vision culminated in a document born of men, not perfect men, but men who put their trust in the Providence of God. It has served us well. Beginning with the Declaration of Independence and the signing of the U.S. Constitution, Americans rested in the confidence of chartered waters and the Providence of God. It appears, however, in the twenty-first century we have, in part, relinquished our liberties to an encroaching government and moral decline. It is encouraging that some in Congress have begun to recognize a general falling away from these principles and the lack of emphasis given to the teaching of the U. S. Constitution.

While some among us would argue that our present Constitution is not adequate in a global society, is it not possible that if God scripted the Document through the minds and hands of 55 men who sought His guidance, will God not take care of all our tomorrows?

In 2005 Congress entered an amendment in *Public Law* 108-447, Sec. 111 (b) that stated: "*Each educational institution that receives federal funds for a fiscal year shall hold an educational program on the United States Constitution on September 17 of such year for the students served by that institution.*" This action further showed that Congress understood Supreme Court Chief Justice Warren Earl Burger's intent when they passed and sent this bill to President George W. Bush who signed the act into law. Although the intentions were good, this mandate has not been taken very seriously; and for reasons unknown to us, school districts have not implemented the law and most teachers are not prepared to comply. Unfortunately, today most communities do not celebrate this special day. This amendment pleased Christians who already recognized a moral mandate to develop in the next generation a love for liberty, equality for all people, and a deep faith in the Almighty, the foundational values established for us by the Founding Fathers.

Through the years, most Americans have been proud of their country and for what it stands. In 1952 President Harry S. Truman signed a bill that moved "*I Am an American*" day from the third Sunday in May to September 17. This was done to coincide with the day the U. S. Constitution was signed in 1787. This day would later be renamed "*Citizen's Day.*"

---

[10]   The Writings of Samuel Adams, Harry Alonzo Cushing, Putman: 1908 – http://1ref. us/c4

After looking at our pluralistic, sometimes almost socialistic society, we ask, "What has happened?" Is it possible we could see an actual attempt to overthrow our constitutional liberties? We look to our elected officials or even to the media and receive no answers to our questions. April 1, 2010, Michigan Supreme Court Justice Stephen J. Markman said in a speech delivered in Washington, D.C., *"Proponents of a '21st century Constitution' or a 'Living Constitution' aim to transform our Nation's supreme law beyond recognition—and with a minimum of public attention and debate."*[11] It appears today that they have made considerable progress toward their goal.

Have we lost our way? Do we not know our own Christian heritage? Do we know the "why" and "how" our liberty is protected? Do we understand why some in our midst (even in Congress) strive to change it? Are we aware of the dangerous interpretations of the Constitution? A recent poll revealed the following:

- Of the four specific rights guaranteed by the First Amendment of the U.S. Constitution, only *Freedom of Speech* could be identified by more than 20% of the respondents.

- 16% could identify *Freedom of the Press.*

- 19% could name *Freedom of Religion.*

- Only 3% could identify the *Right to Petition the Government for a Redress of Grievances.*

- Most American homes do not have a copy of the U. S. Constitution. (Although during the celebration of the Bicentennial of our Constitution, more than 50,000 copies of the Constitution were given out by the Commission.)

In the book, *The Sum of Good Government,* by former U.S. Representative Phillip Crane (August 2001), he quotes Dr. Roger Freeman, *"By its massive entry over the past two decades into the field of domestic public services, the national government has decisively altered the nature of the American federal system. In establishing a federal structure with an intricate system of checks and balances, the Founding Fathers aimed to disperse authority so widely that no branch or level of government –and no one man could prevail over the others. They concluded from history that concentration of power corrupts and sooner or later leads to abuse and tyranny...American society has strayed far from its beginnings. Instead of desiring freedom from governmental interference, instead*

---

[11]   The Coming Constitutional Debate – http://1ref.us/c5

of looking to the government primarily as a source of protection from foreign or domestic enemies and not the provider of services and benefits, Americans have embraced the very centralized government the Founding Fathers urged them to fear and to hold in check.[12]

Some have asked "Have we exchanged freedom for perceived security?" Government controls have not only restricted our freedom to use our economic resources, they have also affected our freedom of speech, of the press, and of religion. We have been brainwashed to believe that it is the responsibility of the government to take resources from some and give them to others. Why have we allowed this to happen? The late Senator Jesse Helms had the answer, *"When you have men who no longer believe that God is in charge of human affairs, you have men attempting to take the place of God by means of the Superstate. The Divine Providence on which our forefathers relied has been supplanted by the Providence of the All-Powerful State."*[13]

How much do we value our freedom and our liberties? At this time, America faces gigantic crises on several fronts, the results of which could be a very real loss of liberty. If freedom is to prevail, we must embrace the valor, determination and the faith of our Founding Fathers. In view of available information, how can we be prepared to defend our liberties if we do not know the rights guaranteed to us through the Constitution?

In the following chapters of this book the authors have attempted to present America's greatest document, The Constitution of the United States, with explanations of what it means in laymen's terms. It includes other interesting facts as well as background information and articles to expand the readers' understanding of our Christian heritage. Reasons for the preservation of our liberty are clearly set forth.

We will walk through the colonial period, view the colonists' lifestyle and their struggles as they faced what seemed insurmountable odds in their determination to build a new and free nation. As these historic documents are read, the reader will see how fifty-five brave men committed themselves to preserving freedom for us and our posterity while they sought guidance from a Sovereign God. Religious liberty was so important to them that it was placed in the First Amendment of the Constitution. While we still have freedom to speak out in defense of our liberty, may we as Christian soldiers pick up the drumbeat of our Founding Fathers and proclaim the message as we march on singing lustily, "Then conquer we must, for our cause, it is just…"

---

[12]   January 1998 Newsletter, NavSource – http://1ref.us/c6

[13]   The Authenic Jesse Helms (The one I knew and loved) – http://1ref.us/c7

(See Appendix: *How the Bible Helped Shape the Constitution*, Bill Bright, *Campus Crusade for Christ*)

"*A nation which does not remember what it was yesterday, does not know what it is today, nor what it is trying to do. We are trying to do a futile thing if we do not know where we came from or what we have been about.*"[14] —Woodrow Wilson

---

[14]   http://1ref.us/c8

THE STRUGGLE TO BUILD A NEW NATION

Things were not going well for the American colonists. They had reached a population of nearly three million people in thirteen separate colonies, each with its own form of government. These colonies were: New Hampshire, New Jersey, Connecticut, Massachusetts, Rhode Island, New York, Maryland, Pennsylvania, Delaware, Virginia, North Carolina, South Carolina, and Georgia. The colonists' hope for peace and freedom from British oppression had not yet been fully realized. Operating as thirteen independent colonies with taxes and duties on goods imported from other states was cumbersome. There were debts that had to be paid. Printing money without any type of backing created unbearable inflation.

Central to the thinking of the colonists at that time was the issue of Laws of Nature and of Nature's God. This phrase to them meant God's law revealed to man through the Holy Scriptures.

A revolutionary idea had been developing over the past 140 years through the Great Evangelical Awakening in 1738. It was spurred on by the popular Englishman, William Blackstone, an expositor of law and government, and the Reverend George Whitefield. There were other great thinkers as well whose views were in agreement with Blackstone and Whitefield. Central to the thinking of the colonists at that time was the issue of *Laws of Nature and of Nature's God*. This phrase to them meant God's law revealed to man through the Holy Scriptures. The laws of nature are God's laws given to man at creation. These truths are self-evident and unalienable. The unalienable right to life is a gift from God and the person who holds that right cannot give it away. The word "equal" meant we are all equal before God.

Hence, the central idea behind the Declaration of Independence was to set forth the conviction by the colonists that the authority of the government comes from God down through the people. This was a revolutionary idea coming from people who had been governed by monarchies for hundreds of years. Thomas Jefferson won great acclaim when he declared that the authority of King George III came from God through the people and that governing the colonies was not the King's birthright. Samuel Adams of Massachusetts was the first person to call for a meeting of the colonists to discuss what action could be taken to address the oppression from the British King.[15]

It had become clear that the king was not going to be a conciliator. It was then that Thomas Paine's *Common Sense*, a rather small pamphlet, was published advocating republicanism as an alternative to monarchy rule. It was significant because it stimulated public debate on a subject that was not openly discussed.

In 1774 the Massachusetts Provincial Congress, in an effort to be ready to fight at a moment's notice, reorganized the state militia, one-fourth of which would be "Minutemen." Their charge would be:

"You…are placed by Providence in the post of honor, because it is the post of danger…The eyes not only of North America and the whole British Empire, but all of Europe, are upon you. Let us be, therefore, altogether solicitous that no disorderly behavior, nothing unbecoming our characters as Americans, as citizens and Christians, be justly chargeable to us."[16]

---

[15]   The Committees of Correspondence: The Voice of the Patriots –http://1ref.us/c9

[16]   American's God and Country: Encyclopedia of Quotations, William Joseph Federer 1994 - Literary Collections – http://1ref.us/ca

The First Continental Congress

On September 5, 1774, the thirteen English colonies began meeting together at Carpenter's Hall in Philadelphia as a confederation of colonies or as a "Congress of States." All of the colonies were represented except Georgia. They had done this without national authority from England and without any formal constitution. English policy was forcing the colonies to unite and to establish themselves as a free and independent people with some sort of formal charter. However, this "Congress of States" appeared to be ineffectual and was making poor decisions in foreign affairs that caused some strained relationships with the other colonies. There was no strong central government. The country's need for restructuring had become apparent as was a strategy for dealing with England. Although a war had already been fought (The French and Indian War) dealing with problems, they had not received help from England with the Native American problems on the frontier.

THE BRITISH FLEET IN THE LOWER BAY.

They adopted a Declaration of Rights, and they also called for a repeal of the tax laws they opposed, and agreed to boycott English-made goods. This initiative was in response to the passage of the *Intolerable Acts of the Colonial Americans* by the British. These *Acts* punished the colonists for the Boston Tea Party. The British had stormed Boston to arrest those who publicly voiced their opposition to the Crown. Fights at Concord and Lexington had become bloody. It was not the purpose of the delegation to declare independence but to come up with a way to address their grievances. They adopted a resolution *"that these United Colonies are, and of right, ought to be free and totally dissolved."*

There were concepts, as well, that had been handed down to them through the ages. First, and perhaps the most important concept was the principle of popular sovereignty: The people are the source of government power, and the people consent to a constitution and delegate powers to the government. The second concept involves the separation of powers in the three branches of government. Each branch has a limited and specified charter over which they are never to overstep. The third concept involves the division of powers between the states and the Federal Government. The states must not allow the Federal Government to deprive them of any of the powers granted to them through the Constitution. The fourth concept is the rule of law and not man. Allegiance is to be given to the Constitution and to the principles it embodies, not to individuals or political parties.

Early on, the Founders thought of a president instead of a king. They agreed with John Locke who said, *"As men, we have God for our King, and are under the Law or Reason: as Christians we have Jesus the Messiah for our King, and are under the law by Him in the Gospel."*[17]

Second Continental Congress

On May 5, 1775, the Second Continental Congress convened in Philadelphia with 56 delegates to organize the defense of the colonies. In spite of the efforts of the colonists, Britain was unmoved. There was still no authority for Americans to pass laws. Also, they had no powers to enforce any of the measures they adopted, and no means of raising revenue. Congress appointed a committee of five members to draft a resolution. Congress approved a Resolution of Independence on July 2, 1776, and attention was turned to forming a formal Declaration of Independence.

The 33-year-old Thomas Jefferson composed the original draft of the Declaration of Independence while his fellow committeemen Benjamin Franklin and John Adams did some revisions. John Hancock, President of the Congress, signed the Document. It was then sent to Congress for a final editing. Once these things were accomplished, the Second Continental Congress ended. All 56 delegates signed the Declaration of Independence.

This document represented much more than just a birth certificate for a new nation. It contained a magnificent preamble that revolutionized the principles and policies of government. Other revolutions had taken place, but they signaled only a change in the rule of men. The Declaration affected a change in principles.

After it was adopted, the Declaration of Independence exerted an incalculable influence upon later history. With its democratic principle that *all men are created equal,* it stimulated humanitarian movements of various kinds in the United States. This action of the Congress resulted in the beginning of a new nation.

---

[17]   The Works of John Locke: The Reasonableness of Christianity– http://1ref.us/cb

The Declaration of Independence

Published by Samuel Walker, Boston

On July 4 a statement was issued by the Congress that they were no longer a part of the British Empire but they now were to be regarded as independent states. They were now a new Nation—THE UNITED STATES OF AMERICA. The original document is now on display at the National Archives in Washington, D.C.

The Declaration of Independence is considered the official and unequivocal affirmation by the American people of their belief and faith in God. It affirms God's existence as a "self-evident" truth that requires no further discussion or debate. The Declaration contains five references to God: God as Supreme, God as Creator of all men, God as the Source of all rights, God as the world's Supreme Judge, and God as our Protector on whom we can rely.

Articles of Confederation

The Continental Congress appointed another committee to draft a plan of union. After much debate and many revisions, the Congress on November 15, 1777, adopted the committee's plan, The Articles of Confederation. The Articles provided no legitimacy for the Revolutionary War or to conduct diplomacy with Europe as well as to deal with issues involving Native Americans.

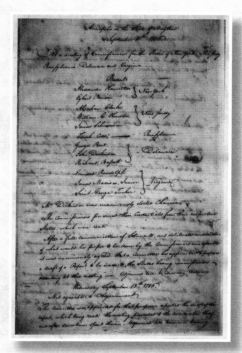
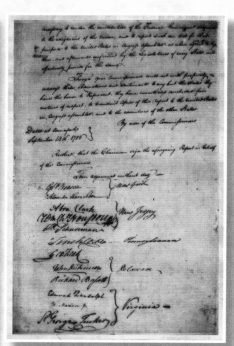

Annapolis Convention, September 11, 1786

As chairman of the committee, John Dickinson (Pennsylvania and Delaware) wrote a draft of the Articles of Confederation. It was not to be a "people's Constitution" but simply a compact among the states. Much haggling ensued and a watered down version of Dickinson's draft was agreed upon. The Congress operated under the Articles of Confederation all through the Revolutionary War even though the Articles were not formally ratified until the war was nearly over in 1781. Moreover, the Articles were inadequate and nearly caused the failure of the War for Independence.

The Articles were internally flawed because they created a weak central government and did not allow taxation of the people. Also, they had no power over the states and led to no enforcement of trade agreements. Therefore, they could not regulate trade between the states. Also, there was no provision to protect an individual's property rights. However, one of the few good things in this document was the provision for each state to have an equal vote in Congress. The states were, hereby, to retain sovereignty over all government functions not specifically assigned to the National Government. The Articles were approved for ratification by the signatures of 48 of the 55 delegates but the process was not completed until March 1, 1781. There was now a guide for the government to operate and the official name for the new nation became The United States of America.

During this time George Washington moved back to his farm at Mount Vernon but continued to work for ratification by the states. On April 30, 1789 he was unanimously elected as President of the new United States of America.

Mount Vernon Trade Conference

Since the Articles of Confederation allowed the states to pursue their own trade policies, conflict was inevitable. On March 28, 1785, representatives from Maryland and Virginia met in Alexandria, Virginia. The plan was to discuss a trade dispute involving fishing rights in the Potomac River. Because they were not making progress, George Washington suggested they meet at his Mt. Vernon estate on the Potomac River. This meeting concluded successfully with a contract being ratified by both states. Encouraged by the results of this meeting, the General Assembly of Virginia, and at the urging of James Madison, proposed on July 21, 1786, a broader trade conclave to be held in Annapolis, Maryland the following year.

WASHINGTON'S HEAD-QUARTERS AT NEWBURGH.

Washington's headquarters at Newburgh.

Annapolis Trade Conference

In September 1786, although all thirteen states were invited, only five sent delegates to meet in Annapolis to discuss commerce and establish standard rules and regulations. But with so few in attendance, a quorum could not be met to conduct any substantive business. Most delegates in the group were *"Nationalists"* who desired a stronger national government. It was decided that another meeting was necessary to address the deficiencies in the Articles of Confederation. The report of the Annapolis Conference was the first step toward the Constitutional Convention that would lead to the Constitution of the United States.

Significant Concerns

Serious problems in the birth of our nation presented themselves. The cost of food was of great concern. The veterans of the Revolutionary War were losing their farms because they could not pay their taxes and the currency was nearly useless. Merchants could not pay their debts, and farmers were losing their land. States were arguing with each other and in some instances, the debate became intense. An uprising led by Captain Daniel Shay called "Shay's Rebellion" grew to a force of eleven hundred men, the majority of them farmers, to capture the state arsenal in Springfield, Massachusetts and to take possession of the arsenal's muskets. They were defeated by a determined state militia. Hostility, leading to the taking up of arms, coupled with economic chaos, was not what the states had anticipated. All agreed that something had to be done. The people had not learned to govern themselves as a united republic. These problems finally convinced the Continental Congress to agree to a Constitutional Convention, which later convened in Philadelphia on May 25, 1787.

The Constitutional Convention

Eventually, fifty-five delegates from twelve states convened in Philadelphia on May 25, 1787 (Rhode Island boycotted the Convention.). The average age was 42, and almost seventy-five percent of them had had political experience. At 29, Charles Pinckney of South Carolina was the youngest delegate. Benjamin Franklin, one of the most prolific of the delegates, was the oldest at 82 years. Their goal was to give the national government sufficient power to perform its assigned duties within established limits. Knowing man's fallen nature, Madison said, *"There is a degree of depravity in mankind which requires a certain degree of circumspection and distrust."*[18] Although the original intent of the Convention was to amend the Articles of Confederation, they began by drawing up a new plan for their government. Their idea of self-governance was to be rooted in a respect for the rights with which we are endowed, and a respect that shapes society where everyone may benefit. They gave Congress power to legislate for the common good, and three branches of Government that would control each other. It was a blueprint for a free society.

Divisions arose over apportionment of representation. Roger Sherman and Oliver Ellsworth proposed what is sometimes called the "Great Compromise," a bicameral (2 houses) legislature with proportional representation in the lower house and equal representation in the upper house. That compromise was approved on July 16, 1786. A Committee of Detail met during the July recess and produced a draft, most of which can be found today in the final version of the Constitution.

---

[18]   The Federalist #55 Constitution Society – http://1ref.us/cc

A Committee of Style completed the final version to be voted on and presented it to the states. Thirty-nine of the fifty-five delegates supported the adoption of the new Constitution. There was a signing ceremony on September 17, 1786.

On December 7, 1786 it was ratified by five states: Delaware, Pennsylvania, New Jersey, Georgia, and Connecticut. Massachusetts ratified the Constitution in February 1788 followed by Maryland and South Carolina. New Hampshire ratified it on June 2, 1788 followed by Virginia on June 21 and New York on July 26, 1788. It was agreed that the new government would begin on March 4, 1789. North Carolina ratified the Constitution after her Second Convention in 1789. Rhode Island squeezed into the Union on May 29, 1790, after the Constitution had been functioning for 2 years.

It is significant to note that this Convention was not without the recognition of a Sovereign God. The endeared Benjamin Franklin stood before the Convention reminding them of how at the beginning of the war with England, The Continental Congress had voiced prayers for Divine protection. "*Our prayers, Sir,*" he said, "*were heard and they were graciously answered…. I therefore beg leave to move that henceforth prayer imploring the assistance of heaven and its blessing on our deliberation be held in this assembly every morning…*"

The Northwest Ordinance

The Continental Congress met on July 13, 1787 and passed the Northwest Ordinance. This expressed the desire of the United States to settle the region north of the Ohio River and east of the Mississippi River. It also provided a method whereby new states with the same rights and powers that other states had could be added to the Union. Significantly, this included the freedom of religion.

The Framers

Who were these men who were to change history? Did they have the kind of experience to write a constitution that would pull a nation together? What influenced them and how was this displayed in their public service? These fifty-five men were undertaking a seemingly impossible task — to have a country where they could live and die as free men. They had lived under tyranny and felt the results of a monarchy — a monarchy that had controlled the thirteen colonies with an iron hand.

Most of the Framers were experienced in governmental affairs. Almost four-fifths of them had served in the Congress. Several were leaders in their

state governments, and many had played important roles in the Revolutionary War. Thirty-five were either lawyers or had an education in law. Some had
become judges. They were men of intellect, responsibility and dedication. All
were well educated in political philosophy and brought with them ideas and
inspiration from French and English philosophers.

Several had been involved in other founding documents of our country.
Roger Sherman and Robert Morris helped write the Declaration of Independence and the Articles of Confederation. Eight of the fifty-five delegates including George Clymer (Pa.) Benjamin Franklin (Pa.) Elbridge Gerry (Mass.) Robert Morris (Pa,) George Read (Del.) Roger Sherman (Mass.) James Wilson (Pa.)
and George Wythe (Va.) had signed the Declaration of Independence. Five
others, Dickinson, Gerry, Gouverneur Morris, Robert Morris, and Sherman
had signed the Articles of Confederation.

However, of the fifty-five delegates, few were long to survive. Five were
captured by the British and tortured before they died. Twelve had their homes
sacked and looted, occupied by the enemy, or burned. Two lost their sons in the
army. One had two sons captured. Nine of the fifty-five died in the war from

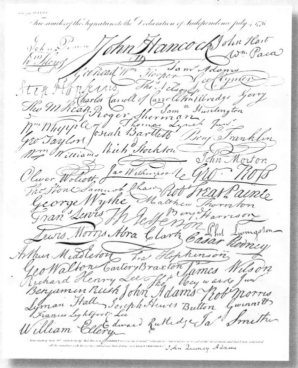

A copy of the signatures on the Declaration of Independence,
verified by John Quincy Adams

its hardship or from its bullets. They were not wild-eyed radicals or poor men. They were men of means, rich men, most of them. They were wealthy, prosperous landowners and highly respected in their communities.

Today, Thomas S. Winter, Editor-in-Chief of *Human Events* magazine[19], reminds us:

- The Founders were conservatives by today's standards; they were for gun rights, limited government, and religion in public life.

- George Washington fervently believed that God himself saved the Revolution.

- Thomas Jefferson would have vetoed all federal domestic programs of the last 100 years.

- John Adams considered virtue, morality, and religion to be the bulwark of a free republic.

- Alexander Hamilton did not believe in direct taxation or a large government debt.

- John Taylor of Caroline County, Virginia, predicted the problems of modern state capitalism and central banking.

---

[19]   Limbaugh, David – The U.S. Constitution and Religious Liberty – http://1ref. us/cd

CREATING A CONSTITUTION —
A Closer Look

Inspiration and Initiative

Although all fifty-five signers of the Constitution played significant roles, as in every major governmental issue, some emerge as we would say today "movers and shakers." They were sensitive to the Providence of God in all their endeavors and were giants in love and dedication for their God and country.

George Washington (1732-1799)

Was elected unanimously as president of The Constitutional Convention in 1787. He was highly respected and admired for his leadership in the Revolutionary War and had become an early advocate for separation from England. Washington was anxious that a formal charter be established to clearly state the position of the colonies. He encouraged the governors of every state to send a delegate to a special meeting to consider organizing the states under some form of formal charter. Because, as president, he could not join in the debate, during the evenings he would visit the various taverns and encourage various delegates to take a different position or encourage others to do the same. His presence made it easier for the people to accept the document.

His faith: Washington rarely expressed his religious views but was clearly a believer in the Christian faith, often referring to God in his letters and public speeches as "Providence."

Washington rarely expressed his religious views but was clearly a believer in the Christian faith, often referring to God in his letters and public speeches as "Providence."

James Wilson (1742–1798)

Was a strong believer in a central government and spoke with fervor for it. In 1775 he signed the Declaration of Independence breaking the deadlock of the Pennsylvania delegation at the Second Continental Congress. As an influential figure, his ideas were incorporated into the Constitution. He was ranked as the second most influential member of the Convention, behind James Madison.

His faith: Wilson was an Episcopalian by church membership but later became a Presbyterian. He was known as a devout Christian.

John Adams (1735–1826)

As a lawyer, statesman and diplomat from Massachusetts, he became a leader in the American Revolution. He helped draft the Declaration of Independence in 1774, became the first Vice President of the United States and later became the second President of the United States.

John Adams

His faith: Was raised a Congregationalist but later became a Unitarian. He had a strong faith in God encouraging his fellow Americans to humbly ask God for His favor and benediction.

Charles Pinckney (1757–1824)

Was a former governor of South Carolina, and at age 29, was the youngest delegate and signer of the Constitution. He presented the Pinckney Plan portions of which were incorporated into the Constitution.

CHARLES COTESWORTH PICKNEY
Nat-1746 — Ob-1825.
From the Original Painting in the Trumbull Collection Yale School of Art.

His faith: He was an Episcopalian by affiliation. As a strong supporter of the separation of church and state in general, he strongly believed in guaranteeing religious freedom. He presented a proposal that "the legislature of the United States shall pass no law on the subject of religion." It was apparently dropped at the time but reappeared in the First Amendment of the Bill of Rights.

Gouvenor Morris (1752–1816)

Was considered one of the most important and vocal participants in the 1787 Convention. He argued for granting veto powers to Congress over state laws, and proportional representation to Congress based on taxation. He organized the writing of the Constitution and worked towards language clarification.

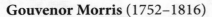

His faith: He was an Episcopalian by affiliation and believed that God gives every man the right to liberty, and felt strongly that morality had to be taught through religion.

Benjamin Franklin (1706–1790)

A man of many talents and accomplishments, his opinion was sought on many matters. He was a printer, writer, inventor, scientist and best known for his experiments with electricity. As the oldest of the Founding Fathers he

Benj. Franklin.

was highly respected and yielded great influence. He was the only member to have signed three documents, the Declaration of Independence, the Peace Treaty with Britain and the Constitution.

His faith: In a letter to Ezra Stiles, then President of Yale College he wrote: "Here is my creed. I believe in one God, Creator of the Universe. That He governs it by His Providence…."

James Madison (1751–1836)

Was a co-author of the influential Federalist Papers, writing over 15 of them. Recognizing the weaknesses in the Articles of Confederation, he initiated a meeting in Annapolis, Maryland (1786) to address the concerns. He was known for his copious notes and attention to detail. He created the foundation for the Bill of Rights and because of his pivotal role in drafting the Constitution, he is hailed as the "Father of the Constitution." He later became the fourth president of the United States.

His faith: History records that he was outspoken about his Christian beliefs and convictions. An example is that he encouraged his friend, William Bradford to be sure of his own relationship to God.

Thomas Paine (1737–1809)

Is remembered as a strong advocate of separation from the British Monarchy. His views were expressed in *Common Sense*, a pamphlet that had wide circulation. He possessed outstanding writing skills. His first book sold over 100,000 copies. Because of his influence, he is referred to as "The Father of the American Revolution." Although he wrote the most successful publications, he never accepted any compensation for his work.

His faith: Although a firebrand of the Revolution, there is little written about his personal faith in God. It is generally understood that the faith of our Founding Fathers was Christianity, and that would include Thomas Paine.

Roger Sherman (1721–1793)

Was a drafter and signer of the Declaration of Independence and helped draw up the Articles of the Confederation. He was the only member to have signed all four of our nation's significant documents: the Continental Association from the first Continental Congress, the Declaration of Independence, the Articles of Confederation and the U.S. Constitution.

His faith: He held a high reverence for the Bible and studied it with deep attention. He was intensely acquainted with the doctrine of the Gospel. His dedication to Christ as a youth continued and was expressed in his public service.

Robert Morris (1734–1806)

Was considered by many to be, next to George Washington, the most powerful man in America. He possessed a profound understanding of finances and became the master financier of the Revolution and the early republic. He was responsible for the establishment of the Bank of the United States. He signed all three of the principal documents: the Declaration of Independence, the Articles of the Confederation, and the Constitution. He died in the poor house having given all of his money to win the war.

His faith: He was a constant worshiper and supporter of the Anglican church.

Thomas Jefferson (1743–1826)

Was the principal author of the Declaration of Independence, the nation's first Secretary of State and the third president of the United States. Although he was not present at the signing of the Constitution, he had a profound influence in the creation of the document.

His faith: He believed Christianity to be the highest expression of faith and took a public stand

for religious freedom by drafting a Virginia resolution calling for a day of fasting, humiliation and prayer as British ships blockaded Boston's harbor. Historians record numerous expressions of his faith in a sovereign God.

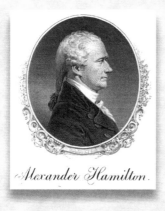

Alexander Hamilton

Alexander Hamilton (1755–1804)

As a staff aid to General George Washington, he became an influential promoter and interpreter of the Constitution. He was the founder of the Federalist Party, the nation's financial system and the first U.S. Secretary of the Treasury. He is credited with authorship of over 50 of the *Federalist Papers*.

His faith: The pronouncement of his faith appears in a number of his quotes but most notably as he neared death. He is said to have remarked, "I have a tender reliance on the mercy of the Almighty, through the merits of the Lord Jesus Christ."

The Perils and Pluses

George Washington, having just retired from the Continental Army, was anxious that a formal charter be established to clearly state the position of the colonies. He encouraged the governors of every state to send a delegate to a special meeting to consider organizing the states under some type of formal charter. James Madison of Virginia, Alexander Hamilton of New York, and others wrote letters to Congress urging Congress to call a convention of delegates from each state.

Many were experienced in writing constitutions as each state had written its own state constitution. Seventy-four delegates from twelve states were appointed to a Constitutional convention in Philadelphia. Rhode Island, the smallest of the thirteen states, refused to participate. They assumed that being small, they would lose control to the larger states.

A Constitutional Convention was scheduled to begin on May 14, 1787. However, because of bad weather the necessary majority was not reached until May 25. Altogether, seventy-four delegates had been appointed by the states, but in the end only fifty-five actually participated. Many of the states had not provided any travel or expense money, and this accounted for much of the absenteeism. In fact, many who came, including James Madison, had to borrow money for living expenses before the convention was over. Some members were late due to heavy rains making muddy roads impassable.

Congress had indicated previously that the convention was for the sole and express purpose of revising the Articles of Confederation.[20] Little did the delegates suspect that before it was over, this convocation of delegates would come up with a whole new system of government under a completely unique constitution.

Several important decisions would be made at this first meeting. Perhaps the most important decision was the election of George Washington as president of this Constitutional Convention. Another important decision was that each state was to have one vote. A member could not be absent from the Convention sessions unless he had been granted permission from his fellow members, especially if his absence would prevent his state from having a vote. The delegates also decided to facilitate a free and open exchange of ideas. However, none of these exchanges were to be made public, lest the people should lose faith in what the Framers were doing and vote against their work. Each state had to have a majority in place before a "yea" vote could be cast.

Although the weather was warm, the delegates met behind closed doors and windows. They all pledged secrecy. People were curious and gathered outside the hall but were not allowed entrance. George Washington, as president of the Constitutional Convention, presided as moderator; and James Madison, as well as several others, kept records over the proceedings.

From May 25 through September 1787, they discussed and argued their ideas for the document. Many speeches were made and different points of view were heard. There was not only a thorough discussion of the important issues but a willingness to make compromises so an agreement could be reached. The Framers had seen the weaknesses in the Articles of Confederation, which nearly cost the loss of the war, and they also witnessed the failings of many European governments in that day. Their desire for their country to succeed was first and foremost in their minds and discussions. This led to a new constitution, which would both strengthen and limit the federal government.

Some of the most prolific Founding Fathers were not a part of the writing or signing of the Constitution. Thomas Jefferson was in France serving as a U.S. minister and John Adams served as a U.S. Minister to Great Britain at the time of the Convention. Other Founding Fathers who did not attend or sign the document included Richard Henry, Patrick Henry, Samuel Adams, and John Hancock. However, they were kept apprised of what was going on by a friend who did attend.

---

[20]   The Founders' Constitution, Volume 4, Article 7, Document 1 – http://1ref.us/ce, The University of Chicago Press; 1987; accessed January 16, 2016

The Preamble

By July 26 the principle issues had been sufficiently settled to put the Constitution into rough form. A Committee on Detail was appointed with instructions to have the report completed by August 6. It was decided that the opening words of the Constitution should spell out the reasons for the Constitution and the intent of the law. By September 8 there were still many details to be refined, and the amended rough draft was then submitted to the Committee on Style for a final re-write.

Gouvernor Morris, a delegate from Pennsylvania, a skilled lawyer and perhaps the best writer was designated to do the rewrite. Gouvernor Morris not only wrote the Preamble but organized the entire Constitution as it now exists, a significant and incredible accomplishment. The rewriting done by the Committee resulted in the Preamble we know today.

"We the People of the United States, in Order to form a more perfect Union, establish Justice, insure domestic Tranquility, provide for the common defense, promote the general Welfare, and secure the Blessings of Liberty to ourselves and our Posterity, do ordain and establish this Constitution for the United States of America,"

Fundamental Points

The debates were heated, and adding to this the humid temperature outside and the confinement to space without open windows or doors only added to the challenges. During the debate Benjamin Franklin advised a daily prayer before each session. Thanks to Benjamin Franklin, his wisdom kept the conflicts from becoming too quarrelsome or intense. He suggested during an especially tenuous session that the members stop everything and pray. His strong emphasis on the fundamental points of religious belief was recognized and respected by the other Founders. They included:

- There exists a Creator who made all things, and God should be worshiped for it.
- The Creator revealed a moral code of behavior that distinguished between right and wrong.
- The Creator holds man accountable for the way man treats others.
- There is a life beyond this one.

- Man will be judged in the next life based upon what he did in this one.[21]

Issues of Concern

If any progress was to be made, the Framers were going to have to exercise a "give and take" position on some issues, and many of the issues were not going to be easily resolved. The issues causing the most dissension included how representatives would be elected and the allocation of representatives to states. The smaller states which included New Jersey, feared the larger states such as Pennsylvania would have more votes and thus gain more power than the smaller states.,

> *If any progress was to be made, the Framers were going to have to exercise a "give and take" position on some issues, and many of the issues were not going to be easily resolved.*

There were other issues that had to be hammered out, such as the role and selection of a national leader. Would he be a governor or president? Would he be appointed by the Congress or elected by the people? What powers should he have? And what should he be called? What powers should be given to a national government?

Of significant concern was the issue of slavery. They knew well that slavery was wrong but they recognized they could not resolve it there and still hold together a national Constitution. Northerners thought that slaves, most numerous in the southern states, should be counted in determining a state's share of taxes (to be levied on the state in proportion to its population). These represented only a few of the issues that had to be resolved before a Constitution could be sent to the states for a vote. Eventually the sectional differences were adjusted by means of Constitutional provisions.

(See Appendix.... The Issue of Slavery)

---

[21]   Letter from Franklin to Ezra Stiles, 9 March 1790 – http://1ref.us/cf

Plans for Representation in Congress

In response to the concern of the elections of representatives, several plans were presented. Edmund Randolph, the governor of Virginia offered the *Virginia Plan* which suggested two houses of Congress, one elected by the people and the other by the state legislators. This plan created much debate. Shortly after the presentation of the *Virginia Plan*, William Patterson of New Jersey offered the *New Jersey Plan*. This plan suggested one house representing the states but not the people. However, the *New Jersey Plan* was soundly rejected, which disappointed the smaller states. There were weeks when both sides argued and debated the issue.

Later, Alexander Hamilton presented another plan based on the British system of government. He explained that, personally, he would like to see the state governments extinguished entirely, or at least reduced to the status of mere administrative units and a single "general government" substituted for them. Recognizing the beauty of the British Constitution, he urged his fellow delegates to imitate it as closely as they could. It was said that the British plan actually descended from the Ten Commandments given to the Hebrews by God. However, this plan was not even considered.

Another plan was the *Pinckney Plan*, presented by Charles Pinckney of South Carolina. This plan advocated the counting of all slaves as a basis of representation and opposed the abolition of the slave-trade. He opposed the election of representatives by popular vote, and also opposed the payment of senators, who, he thought should be men of wealth.

James Madison was a proponent of the *Virginia Plan*, the main component of which was a strong central government that would make laws and collect taxes. The people would be ruled by a state government and a strong federal government. Since both houses were proportional in nature, the larger states strongly favored this plan, whereas the smaller states were in fear of it. The smaller states felt that they would no longer have an equal voice in the legislature.

Comparison of the Virginia and New Jersey Plans

	The Virginia Plan	The New Jersey Plan
Branches of Government	• Two branches for the legislature. The legislative powers derived from the people. A single executive (President). A majority of the legislature can act. • Removal of President by impeachment. • Allow the establishment of inferior federal courts.	• A single legislative body. Legislative powers derived from the states. • More than one executive. A small minority can control the legislature. • Removal of President upon application of a majority of the states.
Legislative Duties	• Two Houses – the Senate elected by the State legislators. • The House of Representatives elected by the people. • Both houses to be represented in proportion to state's population.	• One house. States would have equal representation. All states would have equal power.
Other Powers and Duties	• The legislature could put down laws which they felt were unconstitutional. • They could also use the military to enforce the law. • They could also regulate the trade between states.	• The national government could impose taxes on its citizens and tariffs on imports. • Another duty would include regulating trade. • State laws would fall in line with national laws. • National laws would take precedence over state laws.

Finally, another plan, the *Connecticut Compromise* was drafted and it included parts of both the *Virginia* and *New Jersey* plans. The *"Compromise"* included having a two-house Congress which included the Senate and the House of Representatives. Both houses would be elected by the people. The

House of Representatives would be proportional and the term would be 2 years. The Senate would have equal representation for all the states and its members would serve 6 years. As President of the Convention, George Washington was invited to join in the debate. On some of the thorny or critical issues he would, in the evenings, talk with the delegates in the taverns (taverns were a combination of a hotel and restaurant). He was a vital and important influence on the proceedings.

After much debate and compromise, the delegates finally were ready to present a document for signing. On September 17, 1787, in the east room of Independence Hall in Philadelphia, Pennsylvania, the Constitution was read aloud to forty-one of the original fifty-five delegates. Some delegates still had some reservations. Their main objection was that the Constitution did not include a Bill of Rights. After the Constitution was read, it was signed by thirty-nine of the forty-one delegates.

It has been said that as the delegates went forward to affix their names to the document, Benjamin Franklin followed and wept as he affixed his own name. He had gazed many times at the painting of a sun on the back of General Washington's chair and wondered if it was a rising sun or a setting sun. On this day, as he gazed on it, he said, "*I have the happiness to know that it is a rising sun.*" As he left the convention a lady asked him what they had created. He answered, "*A republic, if you can keep it.*"[22]

Appeal for Ratification

Congress was informed that the Framers had completed their work. George Washington sent a copy of the Constitution to the Continental Congress meeting in New York for their consideration. Now it was the Congress' role to submit the Constitution to each of the states for ratification The Constitution stipulated that nine out of the thirteen states had to ratify the Constitution. The Constitution was subsequently submitted to the states.

As the Constitution was introduced to the various states there was still more debate and compromise about various points in the document. The state conventions were to notify the people in their states of the issues, giving them an opportunity to reflect on the issues and come up with an informed basis for ratification.

---

[22]   Benjamin Franklin Quotes – http://1ref.us/cg

Anti-Federalists

Even though the Framers were unified in their support of the Constitution, it was questionable whether the Constitution would be ratified by all the states. There were those who opposed the Constitution, called "Anti-Federalists." They were against the Constitution because they felt the Framers exceeded their authority when they replaced the Articles of Confederation. Their views were spread through newspapers, pamphlets and town meetings.

Others felt the delegates, with their status and financial standing, did not represent them. One of the biggest arguments came from those who felt the national government had too much power and authority and there would be nothing to protect the rights of the individual. Among the Anti-Federalists were: Governour George Clinton from New York, James Monroe and Patrick Henry from Virginia. Over time, many of the arguments made by the Anti-Federalists (in the *Federalist Papers)* have proven to be valid.

The Federalist Papers

Despite opposition, the Federalists, which included James Madison, John Jay and Alexander Hamilton, during the period of October 1787 and May 1788 wrote a series of eighty-five articles (essays) defending the Constitution. They were published under the pen name *Pubilius* in the state of New York. The essays were written primarily to help convince the delegates from New York to support the Constitution. They explained particular provisions of the Constitution in detail, thus providing a strong defense for the Constitution. They proved to be invaluable in getting the Constitution ratified by all the states.

Because both Hamilton and Madison were members of the Constitutional Convention, the Federalist Papers are considered to be the most valuable literature available today in determining the intent of the Founders. These three men, John Jay, James Madison and Alexander Hamilton analyzed every phrase of the Constitution so it could be better understood by the people. They pointed out how defective the Articles of Confederation had been and the necessity of restructuring the framework of the Government.

Ratification

On December 7, 1787, Delaware became the first state to ratify the Constitution. Although it required only nine of the thirteen states to ratify it, the Framers wanted a unanimous vote from the states. Massachusetts and New York were the states where the strongest debates occurred. Their major concern was a Bill of Rights.

Most of the criticism of the Constitution was subsequently resolved with the promise of a Bill of Rights. However, after much debate, the Constitution was approved on June 21, 1788, by New Hampshire, the ninth state to ratify thus putting the Constitution into force.

When a proposed Bill of Rights was presented by Congress, North Carolina voted for ratification of the Constitution. On May 29, 1790, Rhode Island ratified the Constitution by the narrowest of margin, but their vote made the ratification of the Constitution unanimous.

THE ORDER OF STATES TO RATIFY THE CONSTITUTION

State	Date Ratified	Votes for Ratification	Votes Against Ratification
Delaware*	December 7, 1787	30	0
Pennsylvania	December 12, 1787	46	23
New Jersey*	December 18, 1787	38	0
Georgia*	January 2, 1788	26	0
Connecticut	January 9, 1788	128	40
Massachusetts	February 6, 1788	187	168
Maryland	April 28, 1788	63	11
South Carolina	May 23, 1788	149	73
New Hampshire	June 21, 1788	57	47
Virginia	June 25, 1788	89	79
New York	July 26, 1788	30	27
North Carolina	November 21, 1789	194	77
Rhode Island	May 29, 1790	34	32

*The three states that voted unanimously for the Constitution

Birth of the Bill of Rights

When the first Congress met in 1789, James Madison took upon himself the task of drafting a Bill of Rights. Most of the opposition to the Constitution as presented was that it contained nothing to ensure individual rights. Some states had already included individual rights for their citizens in their state constitutions. Maryland and Massachusetts had developed individual rights in special documents. Massachusetts had experienced certain privileges provided to them through the 1641 Massachusetts Body of Liberties. They included freedom of speech, the right to petition the colonial government, and the right to a trial by jury. Maryland was a colony founded on religious tolerance, and it developed An Act for the Liberties of the People. This document granted its citizens the same "rights, liberties, immunities, privileges and free customs" as those of native English subjects.

Several states had debated the merits of the Constitution, and the opponents of the Constitution charged that the government could become like the British who had tyrannized the Americans and trampled individual rights. These opponents felt that a "bill of rights" would provide needed protection to the citizens. Some states ratified the Constitution with the understanding that these rights would be added in additional amendments.

> *Several states had debated the merits of the Constitution, and the opponents of the Constitution charged that the government could become like the British who had tyrannized the Americans and trampled individual rights.*

Amendments were developed by George Mason that would later establish the personal liberties in the Bill of Rights. He had been an advocate for the rights and freedoms of the individual and was experienced in this area as he was responsible for writing these rights into the Virginia state constitution in 1776. One of the tenets he affirmed was the principle of *"unalienable rights,"* which meant these rights could not be infringed upon or taken away by the government.

James Madison from the Virginia House of Representatives, although previously against a Bill of Rights, subsequently changed his mind to believe that without an agreement to include a Bill of Rights the Constitution would not be approved. He sponsored a bill of twelve amendments to be added to the Constitution.

The amendments included:

- The right to freedom of speech, press and worship,
- The people's right to keep and bear arms,
- The right for individuals to own and maintain private property,
- Fair treatment of those accused of crimes (which included the right not to incriminate one's self).
- The right to a speedy and impartial jury trial,
- Representation from counsel during any and all criminal proceedings,
- Protection from the government using unreasonable search and seizure.

Mason had wanted one item in the Bill of Rights which was not included in the original ten amendments, — putting a stop to the slave trade in the colonies. The Founding Fathers had proposed a compromise that would have allowed the slave trade to continue through 1808. Because that issue had not been thoroughly resolved, years later the Civil War caused much bloodshed on both sides.

In the two centuries since its ratification, many amendments have been added to the Constitution and these additions have served to refine and safeguard our personal freedoms. Some of the most groundbreaking amendments include the 15th Amendment, which in 1870 ensured the right to vote to African American male citizens. The 19th Amendment finally gave those same voting rights to women in 1920.

THE BILL OF RIGHTS

First Amendment:

Freedom of religion, speech, the press, the right to assemble peacefully and to register complaints directly to the Government.

Second Amendment:

The right to bear arms, weapons, and to establish a militia.

Third Amendment:

No one has to house a soldier in times of peace. (Had this amendment not been included, it is likely the southern states would not have ratified the Constitution.)

Fourth Amendment:

The government may not search citizens' homes or take their property without permission. Permission must be granted by a judge.

Fifth Amendment:

A person is innocent of a crime until proven guilty. A person cannot be tried twice for the same crime.

The government can take no property without payment. A right to refuse to testify in court.

Sixth, Seventh, and Eighth Amendments:

The right to a speedy trial, and the right to a jury, the right to a lawyer, and a fine must be suitable to the crime.

Ninth and Tenth Amendments:

Americans have more rights than those stated in the Bill of Rights.

The Federal Government has only the rights given to it by the Constitution.

Part I, Chapter IV

INSPIRATION AND INFLUENCES

Evidence of God's Hand at Work

Although the Constitution was a collaborative effort by different men, the ideas were by no means original with them. Many concepts were inspired by documents of other countries and cultures. As the Framers began to develop the Constitution, they sought wisdom from God and other governments that had been somewhat successful. They sought different ideas that might help form a new and completely different government from the ones they had witnessed in Europe. Consequently, they produced a blueprint for a free society and a set of principles that would never change. They upheld a gratitude to God for their rights.

Obviously their perspective was building a framework of government that would last indefinitely, depending upon the morality of future generations. Many of the participants to the convention recognized and acknowledged the hand of God behind this perspective. James Madison wrote in the Federalists Papers (#37): *"It is impossible for the man of pious reflection not to perceive in it a finger of that Almighty Hand which has been so frequent and signally extend to our relief in the critical stages of the revolution."*[23] James Wilson made an interesting observation. *"... I am lost in the magnitude of the object. We purest patriots and wisest statesmen that ever existed, aided by the smiles of a benign Providence;*

it almost appears a Divine interposition in our behalf." (From the works of Daniel Webster, 1851)[24]

Charles Pinckney of South Carolina wrote: *"When the great work was done and published, I was struck with amazement. Nothing less than the superintending Hand of Providence, that so miraculously carried us through the war... could have brought it about so complete, upon the whole."*[25]

The Influence of Christianity-Evidence of God's Hand at Work

The "Great Awakening" was the name given to a period of heightened religious activity in Great Britain and in the American colonies in the 1730s and 1740s. A great revival began with Jonathan Edwards, a well- educated Congregationalist minister from North Hampton, Massachusetts. He emphasized the importance of a personal experience with Christ. His most famous sermon was *Sinners in the Hands of an Angry God,* and an essay, *A Faithful Narrative of the Surprising Work of God.* It has been told that he fasted and prayed for twenty-two hours prior to preaching that famous message. It was common for political leaders in many New England villages to call for a fast when they faced a crisis.

His messages rocked the Protestant world, both in America and Europe. The "Great Awakening" had begun, and it would unleash forces that would have a lasting impact on American theology, church life and politics. Edward's work was carried on by a young man from England named George Whitefield. The "boy preacher" as he was called, preached in hundreds of towns and villages. It has been said that he could hold an audience spellbound with his messages.

It is difficult for today's readers to fully comprehend the power of the "Great Awakening" in 18th-century America, in part because religious passion is no longer so central a component of mainstream American life. As a result of the "Great Awakening" many colonists came to know and believe in the reality of a relationship with Christ, which is believed to have helped forge a new national identity that consequently served as a backdrop to the American Revolution.

The story is told that the skeptic Benjamin Franklin provided this account of a Whitefield sermon in Philadelphia. *"I happened soon afterwards to attend one of his sermons, in the course of which I perceived he intended to finish with a collection, so I silently resolved that he should get nothing from me. I had in my*

---

24   Liberty Park, USA Foundation – http://1ref.us/ci

25   Infoplease – http://1ref.us/cj

pocket a handful of copper money, three or four silver dollars and five in gold. As he proceeded, I began to soften and concluded to give the copper, another stroke of his oratory made me ashamed and determined me to give the silver. He finished so admirably that I emptied my pocket into the collection dish, gold and all.[26]

Contrary to the view of many today, the vast majority of the Framers were Christians. It is certain that they were influenced by the Bible and its teachings. It is also apparent that they understood the sinfulness of man and how absolute power could bring havoc to a nation. They chose to deal with man's depravity through practical means — by establishing a sense of "checks and balances" on each segment of government.

The Influence of the Bible

The influence of the Bible on our Constitution has been documented by a thorough study by Kirby Anderson who noted this in his article *"The Declaration and the Constitution: "Their Christian Roots."*[27] The influence of the Bible on the Constitution was profound. Although the Framers did not make specific references to the Bible in the Constitution, it was clear they felt government's role was to espouse civic virtue. This was evidenced by their efforts to bind the people together with checks and balances in civil law. James Madison made it perfectly clear that virtue was to be held in high esteem when he argued for this in *The Federalist* No. 55. In *Federalist No. 55* he examines the size of the United States House of Representatives, (65 members) and notes that the size of the House will increase as the population increases. He stated that the small size does not put the public liberty (civil law) in danger because of the "checks and balances" relationship the House of Representatives has with the state legislatures, as well as the fact that every member is voted in by the people every two years.[28] John Jay further added that the individual needed a means of internal checks to counter poor behavior. In *Federalist No. 64*, he emphasized the importance of internal checks on individual behavior.[29] The Framers clearly understood the rule of law.

---

[26]   Benjamin Franklin on Rev. George Whitefield – http://1ref.us/ck

[27]   Anderson, Kerby. The Declaration and the Constitution: Their Christian Roots, May 2003 – http://1ref.us/cl.

[28]   James Madison, Federalist, no. 55, 372–74

[29]   John Jay, The Federalist Paper #64 – http://www.1ref.us/fw

> *Two decades ago, Constitutional scholars and political historians assembled 15,000 writings from the Founding Era (1760-1805). They counted 3154 citations in these writings, and found that the book most frequently cited in that literature was the Bible.*

The influence of the Bible on the making of the Constitution has been confirmed through many instances. Kerby Anderson noted this most fascinating statistic in his article "The Declaration and the Constitution: Their Christian Roots". The influence of the Bible on the Constitution was profound but often not appreciated by secular historians and political theorists. Two decades ago, Constitutional scholars and political historians assembled 15,000 writings from the Founding Era (1760-1805). They counted 3154 citations in these writings, and found that the book most frequently cited in that literature was the Bible.

BIBLICAL PRINCIPLES: BASIS FOR AMERICA'S LAWS[30]

PRINCIPLE	LEGAL DOCUMENT	BIBLICAL
Sovereign authority of God, not sovereignty of the state, or sovereignty of man.	Mayflower Compact, Declaration, Constitution, currency, oaths, mention of God in all 50 state constitutions, Pledge of Allegiance	Ex. 18:16, 20:3, Dt. 10:20, 2 Chron. 7:14, Ps. 83:18, 91:2, Isa. 9:6-7, Dan. 4:32, Jn. 19:11, Acts 5:29, Rom. 13:1, Col. 1:15-20, 1 Tim. 6:15
Moral absolutes, Fixed standards, Absolute truth, Sanctity of life	Declaration ("unalienable" rights—life, etc., "self-evident" truths)	Ex. 20:1-17, Dt. 30:19, Ps. 119: 142-152, Pr. 14:34, Isa. 5:20-21, Jn. 10:10, Rom. 2:15, Heb. 13:8

[30]   www.faithfacts.org – The Bible and Government – http://1ref.us/cm

PRINCIPLE	LEGAL DOCUMENT	BIBLICAL
Rule of law rather than authority of man	Declaration, Constitution	Ex. 18:24, Dt. 17:20, Isa. 8:19-20, Mat. 5:17-18
All men are sinners	Constitutional checks and balances	Gen. 8:21, Jer. 17:9, Mk. 7: 20-23, Rom. 3:23, 1 Jn 1:8
All men created equal	Declaration	Acts 10:34, 17:26, Gal. 3:28, 1 Pet. 2:17
Judicial, legislative, and executive branches	Constitution	Isa. 33:22
Religious freedom	First Amendment	1 Tim. 2:1-2
Church protected from state control (& taxation), church to influence state	First Amendment	Dt. 17:18-20, 1 Kgs. 3:28, Ezra 7:24, Neh. 8:2, 1 Sam. 7:15-10:27, 15:10-31, 2 Sam. 12:1-18, Mat. 14:3-4, Lk. 3:7-14, 11:52, Acts 4:26-29
Democracy/Republic	Constitution	Ex. 18:21, Dt. 1:13, Jud. 8:22, 9:6, 1 Sam. 8, 2 Sam. 16:18, 2 Kgs. 14:21, Pr. 11:14, 24:6
Importance of governing self and family as first level of governance	First, Second, Ninth, and Tenth Amendments	Mat. 18:15-18, Gal. 5:16-26, 1 Cor. 6:1-11, 1 Tim. 3:1-5, Tit. 2:1-8
Establish justice	Declaration	Ex. 23:1-9, Lev. 19:15, Dt. 1:17, 16:19-20, 24:17-19, 1 Sam. 8:3, 2 Sam. 8:15, 1 Kings 3:28, 10:9, Mic. 6:8, Rom. 13:4
Fair trial with witnesses	Sixth Amendment	Ex. 20:16, Dt. 19:15, Pr. 24:28, 25:18, Mat. 18:16
Private property rights	Fifth Amendment	Ex. 20:15,17
Biblical liberty, Free enterprise	Declaration	Lev. 25:10, Jn. 8:36, 2 Cor. 3:17, Gal. 5:1, James 1:25, 1 Pet. 2:16

PRINCIPLE	LEGAL DOCUMENT	BIBLICAL
Creation not evolution	Declaration	Gen. 1:1
Biblical capitalism not Darwinian capitalism (service and fair play over strict survival of the fittest)	Anti-trust laws	Ex. 20:17, Mat. 20:26, 25:14-30, 2 Thes. 3:6-15, 1 Pet. 2:16
Importance of the traditional family	State sodomy laws, few reasons for divorce	Ex. 20:12,14, Mat. 19:1-12, Mk. 10:2-12, Rom. 1:18-2:16, 1 Cor. 7:1-40
Religious education encouraged	Northwest Ordinance	Dt. 6:4-7, Pr. 22:6, Mat. 18:6, Eph. 6:4
Servanthood, not political power	Concept of public servant	Ex. 18:21, Rom. 13:4, Php. 2:7
Sabbath day holy	"Blue laws"	Ex. 20:8
Restitution	Restitution laws	Lev. 6:1-5, Num. 5:5-7, Mat. 5:23-26

Bibles had been shipped to the colonies from England but in 1777 supplies were shut off. Realizing that the power of the Bible was so great, Congress resolved to import 20,000 copies. However, because that resolution was not acted upon, Robert Aiken of Philadelphia published a New Testament. In 1781 he petitioned Congress and gained approval to print the entire Bible. This first Bible of 1782 was called, "The Bible of the Revolution."[31]

Separation of Church and State

The early clergymen were especially grateful for the First Amendment which stated that, *Amendment I, "Congress shall make no law respecting an establishment of religion, or prohibiting the free exercise thereof; or abridging the freedom of speech, or of the press; or the right of the people peaceably to assemble, and to petition the Government for a redress of grievances."*

They felt that the First Amendment prohibited the establishment of a state religion. Congregationalist Joseph Lathrop said: *"The foundation of all social*

---

[31]   Wall Builders – Historical Documents - Aiken Bible – http://1ref.us/cn

virtue is a belief in the existence and government of a Deity. A regard to the Deity cannot be maintained without some public exercises of religion.[32]

In 1801, a group of Baptists in Danbury, Connecticut wrote a letter to Thomas Jefferson voicing their concerns that they were a religious minority in their state, and complained that their religious liberties were not seen as immutable rights but as privileges granted by the legislature — as "favors granted."[33] Jefferson's reply addressed his beliefs about Federalism and the Establishment Clause but did not address their concerns about problems with state establishment of religion. It only addressed the establishment of religion on a national level. "Separation of church and state,"[34] which is used today, was within the letter.

President Jefferson was concerned that the words would not be misconstrued as the "establishment of religion." That section of the letter to the Danbury Baptists was actually blocked off for deletion but it was not deleted in Jefferson's draft of the letter.[35] Much to the dismay of Christians, the phrase has been used and misused, thus creating in the minds of many Americans that a "wall of separation" exists between the state and religion. The Establishment Clause in the First Amendment was intended to prohibit the Federal Government from declaring and supporting a national religion. It should be noted that Thomas Jefferson was not a delegate to the Constitutional Convention and could not speak with the authority of those who attended the Convention. The "wall of separation" was never expressed by any delegate. The intention of the First Amendment was to restrict any state or the Federal government from establishing a state religion.

Many of the delegates came from states or countries where there was a state religion and they were strongly against it. Our original founders of this nation came to America for freedom of religion and would never have agreed to such a concept as "separation of church and state." For this reason, the wordage was not included in the Bill of Rights.

---

[32] God's Hand in the Founding of America, Wisdom of the Founders, The center for Constitutional Studies. Michael Loyd Chadwick (Editor)

[33] Jefferson's Letter to the Danbury Baptist Heritage Foundation – http://1ref.us/co

[34] Thomas Jefferson's Letter to the Danbury Baptist – http://1ref.us/cp

[35] Jefferson's Wall of Separation Letter – http://1ref.us/cq

> *Our original founders of this*
> *nation came to America*
> *for freedom of religion*
> *and would never have*
> *agreed to such a concept as*
> *"separation of church and state."*
> *For this reason, the wordage was*
> *not included in the Bill of Rights.*

As noted, the Constitution does not specifically mention the words "God "or "Bible," but does mention that the government is not to espouse one religion above another. The government is not to prevent its citizens from worshiping in the way of their choice. For the first 150 years of our country's history there was almost no mention of "separation of church and state." Contrary to common belief, that phrase is not mentioned in the Constitution. However, in 1947, change came with the case of Everson v. Board of Education. It was in this case where the phrase "separation of church and state" was first used. The Justices declared that the First Amendment calls for a wall between church and state. This wall must remain high and invincible and there must not be the slightest "chink" in the wall to allow anything or anyone to tear it down.[36]

(See Appendix… Separation of Church and State, Thomas Jefferson's letter to the Danbury Baptists)

It is obvious that the Founding Fathers did not believe in this "wall of separation," or they would not have allowed scripture or Biblical influences to be obviously displayed. Two of the most notable examples of this are the Liberty Bell and the Great Seal which contain Bible quotes or references. The Liberty Bell contains the words, *Proclaim liberty throughout the land and to all the inhabitants thereof* from Leviticus 25:10. The Great Seal is a depiction of Moses lifting up his staff and parting the Red Sea.

From the base of the Washington Monument to its aluminum capstone, the memorial to our first president is filled with references to our Creator. This is not coincidence, as George Washington was a profoundly religious man. When Washington took the oath of office on April 30, 1789, he asked that the

---

[36]   Everson v Board of Education (1947) – http://1ref.us/cr

Bible be opened to the Book of Deuteronomy, chapter 28. Immediately following the oath, Washington added, *"So help me God"* and then bent forward and kissed the Bible before him.[37] (Excerpted from *Rediscovering God in America*, by Newt Gingrich)

The early Founders recognized their dependence upon God. They also felt it was important to seek God's guidance in the establishment of a new nation. No clearer example of this is seen than in the contrast between the French Revolution and the American Revolution. In the years following 1776 Americans realized that without the intervention of God they would face defeat by the British. It appeared that the French followed Voltaire's philosophy which espoused the reasoning that man was sovereign over Biblical Christianity. The end results were quite obvious with the Americans winning over the British and establishing their own Constitution and government. The French lost their bid for independence and continued their chaotic and tyrannical government. This new French government summarily executed 40,000 people.[38] Their new constitution lasted only two years. America has kept her Constitution for over 230 years compared to the French with over seven different Constitutions in that same period.

America, A Christian Nation?

If so, what are the elements in our form of government that are distinctly Biblical? The answer lies in the fact that our nation was founded on the Christian view of man and government that prevailed at that time. The Framers understood that every nation has a theological and philosophical basis. Post-modern critics who assert that America is not a Christian nation fail to give any explanation or definition of what "Christian nation" means.

A Christian nation is not one in which all citizens are Christians, or that the laws require everyone to adhere to Christian theology. Founding Father and U.S. Supreme Court Justice John Marshall states: *"A Christian nation as demonstrated by the American experience is a nation founded upon Christian and Biblical principles, whose values, society, and institutions have largely been shaped by those principles."*[39] This definition has been reaffirmed by American legal scholars and historians for many years. Obviously, it has been ignored by current revisionists.

---

[37]   What 'So Help Me God' Meant to George Washington – http://1ref.us/cs

[38]   The Reign of Terror – http://1ref.us/ct

[39]   Is President Obama correct: Is America No Longer a Christian Nation? – http://1ref.us/cu

Prior to the Revolution it was illegal to print English-language Bibles in America. After the final victory over the British at Yorktown, Robert Aiken a local Philadelphia printer approached Congress requesting permission to print an English-language Bible, particularly for schools, on his presses. Congress approved his request and appointed a committee to oversee the project. On September 12, 1782, Congress officially approved that Bible. This was the first English-language Bible ever printed in America. In the front of the Bible was an endorsement: *Where upon, Resolved, That the United States in Congress assembled... recommend this edition of the Bible to the inhabitants of the United States.*[40]

In Church of the Holy Trinity v. United States, (1892) the U.S. Supreme Court held "this is a Christian nation."[41] They meant that this nation was founded on Biblical principles, and that those who brought these Biblical principles to this land and who implemented these principles that made up our system of government, were for the most part, professing Christians who were active in Christian churches. Justice David Josiah Brewer stated that the United States was a "Christian nation." The Court had already demonstrated the country's religious character with eighty-seven examples of pre-Constitutional documents, historical practice, and colonial charters that reveal religious roots.[42]

The United States Supreme Court in 1931 ruled that the United States is a Christian nation. In a mid-Atlantic summit with British Prime Minister Winston Churchill in the darkest hours of World War II, President Roosevelt, who had described America as *the lasting Concord between men and nations*, founded upon the principles of Christianity—asked the crew of an American warship to join him in a rousing chorus of the hymn, "Onward Christian Soldiers."

In 1947, writing to Pope Pius XII, President Truman said flatly, "This is a Christian nation." No one argued with that statement.[43] In 2009 President Obama said, "We do not consider ourselves a Christian nation or a Jewish nation or a Muslim nation."[44]

---

[40]   Teach Our History, The First Congress and the First Bible – http://1ref.us/cv

[41]   Church of the Holy Trinity vs United States 143 U.S. 457 (1892) – http://1ref.us/cw

[42]   The Christian Nation Debate and the U.S. Supreme Court – http://1ref.us/cx

[43]   In Letter to Pope Pius XII in 1947 – http://1ref.us/cy

[44]   Joint Press Availability With President Obama and President Gul Of Turkey – http://1ref.us/cz

The Role of the Clergy

According to James Hutchinson Smylie's *American Clergy and the Constitution of the United States of America* 1781-1796[45], the early clergymen's main concerns were first theological, then political, economic and social. It is important to recognize that the colonial clergymen were deeply involved in the development of American national life. Many of the clergymen were patriotic propagandists before the outbreak of hostilities, and remained ardent supporters of the American cause as citizens or chaplains during the conflict.

Many churches fired the cause of liberty by convincing the colonists that the British government was usurping the rights given to them by God and this was in violation of the laws of God. Hence, the Founding Fathers considered it their duty to uphold the law of God even if it meant a revolution. This fight was considered a sacred responsibility because civil liberty is an inalienable right, according to God's natural law.

Many of the clergy were heavily involved in the struggle with England and held key positions. Joseph Willard was at Harvard, Ezra Stiles, and later Timothy Dwight, presided over Yale. James Madison was at William and Mary. They were not only preachers set over congregations, but superintended the education of many of the nation's leaders in colleges spread across the country.

Jedidiah Morse (1761-1812) was an educator, clergyman, geographer, and father of Samuel Morse, inventor of the Morse code, stated: "*Our dangers are of two kinds, those that affect our religion and those that affect our government. They are, however, so closely allied that they cannot, with propriety, be separated.... Whenever the pillars of Christianity shall be overthrown, our present republican forms of government, and all the blessings which flow from them, must fall with them.*"[46]

Where did the early clergy of America obtain their political ideology? The clergymen rested the case for their political opinions and decisions upon the three keys to political knowledge: reason, revelation, and experience. The Bible was the most important single source of political knowledge cited. They felt the adoption of the Constitution by representatives of the people was the beginning of a glorious period in the development of the American nation.

The clergy was especially supportive of the First Amendment to the Constitution which stated that "*Congress was to make no law respecting the establishment of religion, or prohibiting the free exercise thereof...*" They felt the First

---

[45]   American Clergy and the Constitution of the United States of America, Was Frankenstein Really Uncle Sam? – http://1ref.us/d0

[46]   Jedidiah Morse – http://1ref.us/d1

Amendment prohibited the establishment of a state religion. They never felt it was to be utilized to divorce government from a formal recognition of God. Congregationalist Joseph Lathrop stated: "*The foundations of all social virtue is a belief in the existence and government of a Deity.*"[47] The early clergy felt that the American people not only had rights guaranteed by the Constitution, but certain obligations. It was the duty of the people to elect men of wisdom, virtue, and experience. Clergyman David Parsons quoted: Proverbs 29:2 "*When the righteous are in authority the people rejoice; but when the wicked beareth rule, the people mourn.*"

The clergy was united in declaring the Constitution, although formulated by wise and noble men, was inspired of God.

The Black Robe Regiment

So involved was the clergy at this time in America's history that many were involved in what was called "The Black Robe Regiment." This was not a term applied to a regiment of soldiers but rather to the clergy who were indeed "Soldiers of the Cross." They supported the military struggle against Britain by encouraging the patriot cause and building support through their congregations.

From their pulpits, wearing their black robes, they reassured their congregations that the revolution was justified in the sight of God. Winning support from the people for the War for Independence was critical especially because the war effort relied heavily upon volunteers.

The Influence of Israel

Although rarely acknowledged today, the influence of Israel on the founding of this nation was significant. The earliest Jewish immigrants settled in New England in the early 17th century as refugees escaping religious persecution. They viewed their immigration to the New World as a re-enactment of their history, escaping the cruel treatment by the pharaoh in Egypt and they saw the crossing of the Atlantic as a parallel to the crossing of the Red Sea. It is interesting that at the time of American independence, Benjamin Franklin proposed that the new nation's Great Seal should feature Moses parting the Red Sea and Thomas Jefferson proposed images of the Israelites journeying

---

[47]   1786 A Miscellaneous Collection of Original Pieces – Joseph Lathrop – http://1ref.
       us/d2

through the wilderness.[48] Even in the legal system of the new commonwealth, they sought to incorporate the Law of Moses.

The Hebrew language was taught in the schools and universities. Hebrew words appear on the seals of Yale University, Dartmouth College[49], and Columbia University.

Haym Salomon (1740-1785) a Jewish immigrant who came to America during the American Revolution is credited with aiding the Continental Army as one of the prime financiers of the American side. Prior to the Battle of Yorktown, George Washington's war chest was empty and in dire need of $20,000 ($250,000 today) to finance the campaign. He gave a simple order *"Send for Haym Salomon."* Haym provided the needed funds and the final battle of the Revolution was fought and won.[50] A statue of George Washington flanked by Haym Salomon and Robert Morris stands today in Chicago, Illinois at the corner of Wabash and Wacker Drive.

The Influence of Rome

Many of the delegates of the Constitutional Convention were impressed with the way Rome provided its citizens with basic freedoms. Few countries had given these freedoms to their residents before the time of the Romans. The other ideas that these delegates espoused in their meetings was how the Roman government was run.

One of the ideas from the Romans was to combine two forms of government, a democracy and a republic, and combine them into one. Also, the thought was to take the best ideas of both forms of government and fuse them into one form of government. By combining these ideas, they established a new type of government that had not been seen before this time, a Constitutional Republic. The Founders had transformed the role of government and the new nation would prove that it was possible for the people to create something new under the sun.

The Influence of Britain

Even though America was at odds with England during the Revolutionary War, England still had a profound influence on America's Framers. England had a rich history of lords and peasants. However, despite the fact that peasants had little materially, they were given unwritten rights that could not be denied

---

48 First Great Seal Committee–July/August 1776 – http://1ref.us/d3

49 Seal of Dartmouth College - Wikipedia, the free encyclopedia – http://1ref.us/d4

50 Revolutionary War-Haym Saloman – http://1ref.us/d5

by rich and powerful lords and barons. The peasants were given the right to a trial by jury and the right to have nothing taken through unlawful search and seizure. All British citizens were considered loyal subjects of the British Crown. Although the rights and laws were not clearly written into a British Constitution, many of them were based on tradition.

It was in 1215 that these rights were finally clearly defined through the institution of the *Magna Carta*. It not only referred to the rights of barons, towns and churches, but it also made frequent reference to the rights of English "freemen." Another change introduced by the *Magna Carta* was how the British government was run; the parliament was separated into two different houses – the House of the Lords and the House of Commons.[51] Because of this change, many segments of the population were allowed to take part in the governmental process.

Another change observed in the British government was the concept of a limited government. The power of the monarchy was limited. This was a big difference from the absolute control that the rulers had before that time. In fact, had it not been for a group of barons forcing King John to sign the *Magna Carta*, the monarchy would have been completely different — rich, powerful and most likely corrupt. The rich, powerful feudal lords were not allowed to violate the freedoms of the common man.

One of the ideas foremost in the minds of the American colonists derived from the *Magna Carta* was the concept of "no taxation without representation." This was the "lynch-pin" upon which the American Revolution was based. It caused the Americans to go to war with the British. Americans thought they were unjustly taxed and were without representation in the British government.

Another influential British governmental document was the *1628 Petition of Rights*- a document the British monarchy was forced to sign. Parliament succeeded in forcing King Charles I to sign the *Petition of Rights*. He had tried to raise money illegally, and to force British citizens to house and provide for British soldiers in their own homes. When the *Petition of Rights* was signed, the king was denied the right to raise taxes without the consent of Parliament, and British citizens were no longer forced to house and give accommodations to British soldiers. Unfortunately, the British did not learn from this issue. They forced American colonists to house and keep British soldiers against their will. This became another issue to divide the American colonists and the British.

The "*Habeas Corpus Act of 1678*" was one more important piece of legislation that influenced the American Framers. This act denied the trying of

---

[51]   Magna Carta: Cornerstone of the U.S. Constitution – http://1ref.us/d6

someone unlawfully. Cases would have to be tried in a court of law. It established that the arrested person must know what they were accused of, and enough evidence had to be presented to determine guilt. If not enough evidence was presented, the person would be set free. The *English Bill of Rights of 1689* also influenced the Framers. This bill prohibited the king from taking away some of the freedoms already given to the people. However, it did not give them freedom of speech, religion or of the press. Soon after this, the *Glorious Revolution* of 1688 revealed the need for an *Act of Toleration,* that gave religious freedom to the Protestants as well as Roman Catholics.

Influence of the Mayflower Compact (1620)

Before the Pilgrims stepped foot on Plymouth Rock, it was understood by the leaders that there needed to be a means of governing and protecting the people. It was religious persecution that sent the first successful colonizers on freedom's freeways to America during the fall of 1620. On November 9 the Pilgrims sighted land. They had originally intended to land on the coast of Virginia, where they had a land patent from England. However, because of violent storms, which proved to be Providential, they were driven off course and forced to enter Cape Cod Bay (Massachusetts). Two days later a document was agreed upon by all the Pilgrims and was signed by the men of the group. The significance of this document was the provision it granted to the group to appoint leaders and to make laws. This was the first document of its kind in the New World.

The Mayflower Compact was our first American document of self-government with unity. It was the mustard seed transplanted to the shores of America... It was the seed of American Federalism, of voluntary principles of government derived from the Word of God, and the consent of the governed.[52]

The Colonists were disturbed with the way they were treated by the British. The British placed trade limitations on the Colonists and did not give them representation in the government. This was critical. Soon groups like the *Sons of Liberty* were formed and began to rebel against the various trade restrictions placed on them by the British. The *Tea Act of 1773* was answered by the *Sons of Liberty* with the Boston Tea Party. Tension increased between the British and the Colonists. In response, the fledging group of colonies started to bind together and form a militia to fight the British. This led to the drafting of a *Declaration of Independence.* This document was sent to the British.

---

[52] The Bible and the Constitution of the United States of America, Verna M. Hall and Rosalie Slater, San Francisco, Ca., 1983, pg. 15 (The New Revolutionary War)

The British sovereignty was challenged by this document in which the colonies totally rejected British rule. Distrust and disenchantment between the two parties came to a head with the Revolutionary War, that was ultimately won by the colonies.

Influence of the Articles of Confederation (1781)

After the Revolutionary War was fought and won, ratification of *The Articles of Confederation* was needed. However, the charter was internally weak and flawed because it created a weak central government and did not even allow taxation of the people. Also, it had no power over the states and led to no enforcement of trade agreements. This meant they could not regulate trade between the states. In addition, there was no provision to protect an individual's property rights. However, one of the few good things in this document was the provision for each state to have an equal vote in Congress. (See Appendix… Articles of Confederation)

Influence of Fundamental Orders of Connecticut

On January 14, 1639, the Council of the Connecticut Colony adopted the *Fundamental Orders of Connecticut.* The orders described the government set up by the Connecticut River towns of Windsor, Wethersfield, and Hartford. It was a constitution, written by Thomas Hooker, a Puritan minister who came to America in 1620 as a direct result of religious persecution in England. It is believed to be the first written constitution, thus earning for Connecticut the nickname, *The Constitution State.*

It was a short document but included principles applied later in creating the Constitution of the United States. It addressed the rights of the individual, and how those rights are insured by the government. It states the powers and limitations of the government. It provides that all free men share in the election of their magistrates, and the use of secret paper ballots. The official document began with the words,

For as much as it hath pleased the Almighty God by the wise disposition of his divine providence so to Order and dispose of things that we the Inhabitants and Residents of Windsor, Hartford and Wethersfield are now cohabiting and dwelling in and upon the River of Connecticut and the lands thereunto adjoining; and well knowing where a people are gathered together the word of God requires that to maintain the peace and union of such a people there should be an orderly and decent Government established according to God, to order and dispose of the affairs of the people at all seasons as occasion shall require do therefore associate and conjoin ourselves to be one public state or commonwealth and do, for ourselves and our

successors and such as shall be ajoined to us at anytime hereafter, enter into com-
bination and confederation together, to maintain and preserve the liberty and
purity of the gospel of Jesus Christ which we now profess, as also the discipline of
the Chapter churches, which according to the truth of the said gospel is now prac-
ticed among us; as also our civil affairs be guided and governed according to such
laws, rules, orders and decrees as shall be made, ordered or decreed as follows:

Today, the individual rights in the *Orders*, with others added over the years, are still included as a "Declaration of Rights" in the first article of the current Connecticut Constitution, adopted in 1965.

Influence of Shay's Rebellion

In 1786 Daniel Shay led a revolt in Massachusetts with several hundred farmers. They were losing their farms because the money they were paid was worthless and as a result they could not make payments on the farms they had created out of the wilderness. These farmers were angry and afraid because of the economic losses they were facing. Their response was to attack the state government and take weapons from the state arsenal in Springfield, Massachusetts. Eventually, Shay's Rebellion was stopped by a determined militia, but there was a fear that other groups would spring up and there would be nothing to stop them. This action greatly influenced the Congress as to the urgency of unity and forced Congress to support the Constitution created in Philadelphia.

It made the people keenly aware of the need for a strong central government. In a letter to James Madison, George Washington wrote, "*We are either a united people or we are not. If the former, let us act as a nation. If we are not, let us no longer act a farce by pretending to it.*"[53] Without Shay's Rebellion it is questionable whether Congress would have approved the Constitution and sent it out to the states for ratification.

Without Shay's Rebellion it is
questionable whether Congress
would have approved the
Constitution and sent it out to
the states for ratification.

---

[53]   Letter to James Madison, Teaching American History – http://1ref.us/d7

The Influence of Significant Writers and Clergymen

John Locke (1632-1704)

John Locke was an Oxford scholar, medical researcher, physician, political operative, economist, and an ideologue for a revolutionary movement. Locke believed in the existence of God, but he also believed that God gave man the ability to use logic and reason. Thus this allowed man the ability to establish government and keep it accountable to its principles and purposes. He was a prolific writer and his works were well- known by many of the Framers.

He was, perhaps, the most inspiring of the early philosophers, primarily because of his belief in natural rights. He believed there were certain rights that were given by nature and they couldn't and shouldn't be denied by the government. They included the right to life, liberty and property. Locke further believed that some of these rights might have to be forfeited in order to be protected from criminals and persons who sought to take advantage of others. He proposed that the government and the people enter into a "social contract" whereby the government would protect its citizens while the citizens would give up some of their rights. The laws would be designed to protect the law-abiding citizens.

Charles Louis de Secondat, Baron de la Brede et de Montesquieu (1689-1755)

Charles Louis de Secondat, Baron de la Brede et de Montesquieu, was a French social and political philosopher whose ideas about laws and government had great influence on the leaders of the American Revolution and the Framers of the Constitution. He believed the best way to protect the rights of citizens was for government to have separate powers. This would prohibit one group from attaining more power than another. For citizens to maintain their liberty against the encroachment of oppressive rulers, a government would have to be composed of separate and balanced powers that would check and moderate each other, thus leaving the people a maximum degree of freedom under the laws. The Framers liked the idea of separation of powers, with a system of checks and balances.

Jonathan Edwards (1703-1758)

Jonathan Edwards, a native of Massachusetts is considered the grandfather of modern Protestant missions in America, and perhaps the last and the greatest of the great New England Puritan preachers. Historians account him as the greatest intellect of the Western Hemisphere before 1900. He entered

Yale University at 13 and was later known as a theologian and historian. At age 27 he was ordained a minister in the Presbyterian church in Northampton, Massachusetts.

His dedication to God and his preaching ministry encouraged many across New England to turn to Christ and played a critical role in "The Great Awakening," a religious revival that swept New England and reached as far as Scotland and England in the 1730's-1740's and which ultimately influenced the Framers of the Constitution. He stressed the importance of a personal rebirth, the unworthiness of man and the grace of God. He wrote that ...*in the spring and summer following (1735) the town seemed to be full of the presence of God; it was never so full of love, nor of joy, and yet so full of distress, as it was then.*[54]

Jean Jacques Rousseau (1712-1778)

Jean Jacques Rousseau, a Swiss philosopher, continued the ideas of Locke and built upon them. His political philosophy influenced the French Revolution and the development of modern political and educational thought. In common with other philosophers of his day, he looked to a hypothetical "State of Nature" as a normative guide. He affirmed the necessity of religion. He saw the presence of God in creation, including mankind, which apart from the harmful influence of society, is good, because God is good. He accepted the argument of Intelligent Design. His works were of interest and great influence to the Framers.

George Whitefield (1714-1770)

The stirring messages of George Whitefield, a Methodist minister-evangelist, reverberated throughout the colonies with power and influence, carrying on the power and influence of "The Great Awakening." He was born in England, educated at Oxford, and was ordained a priest in the Church of England.

He voyaged to the New World seven times when a one-way trip took two months. He was equally at home on both sides of the Atlantic. Benjamin Franklin, who heard him preach many times in Pennsylvania, declared he had a voice like an organ.[55] He preached the Gospel of Jesus Christ from Georgia to New England and is recognized as a key figure in the" Great Evangelical Awakening" in America. He gave his heart and soul to the "Great Awakening".

It is believed that because of the influence of Jonathan Edwards and George Whitefield, Americans who had drifted away from their Christian beliefs

---

[54] Jonathan Edwards, A Faithful Narrative of the Surprising Work of God – http://1ref. us/d8

[55] Geeorge Whitefield (1714-1770) – http://1ref.us/da

repented. Christianity was revived and God blessed America in her efforts to remove herself from the authority of England. This was a time of significant religious advances leading to the reinforcement of the concept that God's laws are the supreme law by which government should govern. The "Awakening" built up interest and faith in God's direction and increased the opposition to the Anglican church. Many historians agree that it sparked a spirit that led to a strong desire for political freedom. The "Awakening" was perhaps one of the first significant movements against slavery.

John Witherspoon (1723-1794)

The influence of the Reverend John Witherspoon and his emphasis on Biblical principles impacted government and was felt in the colonies during the foundation of America. He was a signer of the Declaration of Independence and served in over 100 Congressional committees. He became a famous educator, clergyman and President of Princeton College. He spiritually mentored three Supreme Court Justices, a president and seventy-seven members of America's early Congress.

He said, "*It is in the man of piety and inward principle, that we may expect to find the uncorrupted patriot, the useful citizen, and the invincible soldier—God grant that in America true religion and civil liberty may be inseparable and that the unjust attempts to destroy the one may in the issue tend to the support and establishment of both.*"[56]

(Interesting note: Until 1902 every president of Princeton University was a minister of the Gospel of Christ.)

William Blackstone (1723-1780)

Sir William Blackstone was an English judge, a professor and jurist. He produced the historical treatise on the common law, *Commentaries on the Laws of England*. It consisted of four volumes and was an extraordinary success. Four volumes of the Commentaries were published in Oxford, England from 1765 to 1769. An American edition was published in 1771.

His works are considered by many scholars to be one of the most complete and consistent expositions of the Judeo-Christian worldview of law ever written. Blackstone's Commentaries were well known to the Framers including Thomas Jefferson, and Alexander Hamilton. His works are often quoted by U.S. courts as a pre-Revolutionary War source of common law. It is believed that Blackstone's Commentaries were the basis for the United States Constitution. The Ten Commandments were the heart of his philosophy. The Found-

---

[56]   John Witherspoon – http://1ref.us/d9 /

ing Fathers referred to Blackstone more than any other English or American authority. He stated that man's law must be God's law. He explained: *"Man, considered as a creature must necessarily be subject to the laws of his Creator, for he is entirely a dependent being... And consequently... it is necessary that he should in all points conform to his maker's will."*[57]

Francis Asbury (1745-1816)

As Americans moved westward, preachers braved the obstacles to bring the Gospel to the pioneers among whom was Francis Asbury, a Methodist circuit rider who traveled nearly 300,000 miles and preached more than 16,000 sermons between 1771 and 1816. His message was one of repentance and salvation through the blood of Christ. He is considered the "Father" of the present Methodist denomination.

---

[57]   Constitution Society, Section the Second. Of the Nature of Laws in General – http://1ref.us/db

Part II

The United States Constitution and What It Means

"This matter is by the decree of the watchers, and the demand by the word of the holy ones; to the intent that the living may know that the most High ruleth in the kingdom of men, and giveth it to whomsoever he will, and setteth up over the basest of men." Daniel 4:17

AN INTRODUCTION TO THE CONSTITUTION AND OVERVIEW OF THE PREAMBLE

"The basis of our political systems is the right of the people to make and to alter their constitutions of government."

George Washington

America's Constitution is one of the oldest living constitutions in the world. Many countries older than the United States have gone through several radically altered constitutions. Even after over 225 years our Constitution still provides all the basic freedoms the Framers intended for its citizens. It is essential that all Americans know what the Constitution says and what it means.

There are three basic parts to the Constitution: — the Preamble, the Articles, and the Amendments. The Preamble identifies the purpose of the document, while the Articles give the structure of the government and how the Constitution can be changed. The amendments list the changes that have been made including the *Bill of Rights*.

The Framers designed the Constitution originally without the Bill of Rights, but after several states debated the feasibility of having a written statement of rights for the citizens, George Mason and James Madison put together a statement containing these rights. Soon after the ratification of the Constitution, the Bill of Rights was introduced to the Congress by James Madison. They were voted on and accepted as part of the Constitution.

Two hundred years later, 11,000 amendments have been proposed, but only 33 were sent to the states for ratification. Through the entire struggle for these 33 proposed amendments to become amendments, only 27 of them made it through the states and were later ratified by the Congress. In fact, in every session of Congress, new amendments are proposed, but very few become amendments. Interestingly enough, most of these proposals do not even make it out of committee.

Although changes to the Constitution have occurred through the years, the Constitution still remains the standard for our government. In 4543 words, it not only gives the plan for our government, but guarantees rights for its citizens. It is the strongest document in the land and its power supersedes that of any state constitution or state government. Yet, despite its strength, it provides opportunity to be changed.

Although changes to the Constitution have occurred through the years, the Constitution still remains the standard for our government. In 4543 words, it not only gives the plan for our government, but guarantees rights for its citizens.

The Constitution is the overall plan for our government, but it goes beyond that. It imposes limitations to the government's power, but at the same time gives rights to the citizens. The Constitution also states how the government will protect the rights of its citizens and the resources it provides for them.

AN OVERVIEW OF THE PREAMBLE

"*We the People of the United States, in Order to form a more perfect Union, establish Justice, insure domestic Tranquility, provide for the common defence, promote the general Welfare, and secure the Blessings of Liberty to ourselves and our Posterity, do ordain and establish this Constitution for the United States of America.*"

The Preamble was the work of Gouvernor Morris, who was an accomplished lawyer, author and perhaps the greatest writer at the Convention. It was decided by the Committee on Detail that the opening words of the Constitution should spell out the reasons for a Constitution and the intent of the law. A rather modest preamble was written but it was unacceptable to the committee. As chairman of the committee, Gouvernor Morris assumed the responsibility of writing a preamble. He was quite sure that very few people would actually read the entirety of the Constitution; thus it would be important to set forth the seven objectives the Founders intended this government to attain. Surprisingly, controversy over the Constitution induced thousands to read the Constitution. Political scientists through the years have been amazed at the insight of Gouvernor Morris and have declared his work extraordinary in listing the seven objectives of the Founders.

It appears that Thomas Jefferson's words, "*I consider the people who constitute a society or nation as the source of all authority in that nation*"[58] carried significant importance as the *Preamble* begins with, "*We the People of the United States....do ordain and establish this Constitution...*"

Most documents have an introduction that states the author's intent and the reasons for developing his written work. The Preamble was no exception to this. The Preamble did not give or define the law, but simply stated, it provided the purposes for this document. There are actually seven purposes to the Constitution. They are:

1. To form a more perfect union

2. Establish justice

3. Insure domestic tranquility

4. Provide for the common defence

5. Promote the general welfare

6. Secure the blessings to ourselves and our posterity

7. Ordain and establish this Constitution

We the People is a phrase that has been used in a variety of ways, but when the Framers wrote it, they were clearly saying it was "about the people," not about government. The Framers knew the dangers of an overactive government when they were British colonists. They wanted this document to protect the citizens from an intrusive, controlling government. Also, the document

---

[58]   Jefferson on Politics & Government – http://1ref.us/dc

begins with "We the people" to let the common man know that this was not an edict passed down from a king. This was a document created for the good of all citizens.

In order to form a more perfect union

The Framers had distinct goals in mind for this new American government, and they made sure they were clearly stated. There could be no debate over what they meant. The first purpose, *"In order to form a more perfect union,"* lets the reader know that the Framers felt the country was doing well, but they wanted to build and enhance its foundations. The *Articles of Confederation* had not proven to be in the best interest of the country and had failed to unite the states. This weakness was one of the major reasons the Constitution was written. A strong, central government to unite the states was needed.

To establish justice

The Framers had seen abuses of power through England's system of government and it was extremely important to them to establish a "fair and balanced" system of justice. Another issue was unfair trade practices. The Framers once again wanted it stated clearly that courts would have a uniform measure of justice and that trade inside and outside the country's borders would be handled fairly. America still strives to provide justice where all citizens have the same rights and all are afforded the same punishment for their crimes. Because of the wisdom of the Framers, and their concern for equal justice, our Constitution is recognized as one of the best in the world. The writ of *Habeas Corpus* and a guarantee of a trial by jury ensured citizens they would not be unlawfully arrested, tried, convicted and sentenced.

Insure domestic tranquility

After the Revolutionary War, the Framers wanted to live in peace and chose to affirm it through their Constitution. The time of peace after the war was short-lived, shattered in part by Shay's Rebellion. This caused Americans to stand in opposition to the state government. The phrase "domestic tranquility" was written to assure the citizens that the government would quell future revolts. In fact, the Framers hoped that the new government would be able to keep small rebellions from turning into major battles. Another purpose was to establish a unity among the states for peaceful existence and cooperation.

To provide for the common defence[59]

This was one of the most important components of the document. The Americans had just defeated the British and had to quell the armed attacks of Shay's Rebellion. Citizens were concerned and needed assurance of protection from internal forces of hostile Indians, and outside forces such as the British and Spanish that were waiting for the new government to fail, providing them the opportunity to subjugate and take over the new republic.

To promote the general welfare

This was the culmination of all the previous concerns and it summed them up by stating that each citizen, in each of the states, would benefit by having justice, security, tranquility, and defense. The Framers were forward thinking men who desired to see their country expand in land and holdings and develop to its fullest potential. They felt a strong "federal" government would accomplish this if the people would work together for the welfare of the common good.

Secure the blessings to ourselves and our posterity

Many of the Framers had children, and like all parents they wanted a legacy of equality and freedom for not only their children, but for their descendants. That is the meaning of the phrase, "secure the blessings to ourselves and our posterity." The intent was to develop a nation where tyranny from a king or an intrusive and invasive government did not exist. Some of the Framers had fought in the Revolutionary War (which was less than a decade from the time they established the Constitution). They did not take the sacrifices of freedom lightly and they looked forward to many years of liberty not only for themselves, but for all who would follow.

Do ordain and establish this Constitution

Several important thoughts are seen here. The document was given a name as well as restating that this Constitution was for the United States of America. Also, the Framers gave their approval for this document by repeating that it was they who established it. That established the connotation that this particular document would replace any previous documents. Finally, the word "ordained" seems to indicate that the Framers wanted it known that this was not the work of a king or his council, but it was drawn up for and from the

---

[59]   United States History - Proclamation of Neutrality – http://1ref.us/dd

people themselves. Other goals the Framers wanted were addressed through a *Bill of Rights* and the seven *Articles of the Constitution*.

In summary, the *Preamble* to the Constitution is not law; it represents the intent and purpose of the document. It implies that although the union has been in place, the document is intended to perfect that union. Because it is dated in the twelfth year of the United States, that date takes us back to the *Declaration of Independence* and reminds us of the foundational principles of the earlier document which were based on a recognition of the laws of a sovereign God.

THE ARTICLES

In addition to the seven purposes listed in the *Preamble*, there were also other measures of protection set forth by the Constitution. They were designed to keep each branch of government from exceeding established limits. The goals outlined a separation of powers which included a system of checks and balances between the powers and the rule of law.

"Separation of powers" meant the government's power was divided among three branches of government – the Legislative, the Executive and Judicial. Each branch was responsible to the law in the following ways: The Legislative branch made the laws, the Executive branch signed bills into law and enforced the law, and the Judicial branch interpreted the law. James Madison is responsible for our three-part government. His inspiration came from Isaiah 33:22.

For the Lord is our Judge (Judicial branch)
The Lord is our Lawgiver (Legislative branch)
The Lord is our King (Executive branch)
He will save us.

The Framers had seen the abuses of powers as a British colony and wanted safeguards in the Constitution to prevent this from happening again. The separation of powers and a system of checks and balances were devised to prevent one branch from seizing power over the other two. Each branch could challenge the other two, but whatever was done in one branch of government had an impact on the other two. The following paragraphs outline the way each branch can check the other two and keep the powers balanced among the three branches.

Legislative Branch

The Legislative branch is bicameral, which means it contains two distinct houses. The chief role of the Legislative branch is to propose bills which are carefully crafted, researched and discussed. These bills are sent to the President who decides to sign the bill into law or reject it and return it to the Legislature with comments.

This system of checks and balances is an important aspect of the Constitution. The Legislature can check the Executive and the Judicial. It can also check itself in that there are two houses. Checks by the Legislative and Judicial branches on the Executive branch include the power of impeachment. The House of Representatives may impeach elected officials who are not properly discharging the duties of their position. The Senate may hold trials of impeachment and can officially remove elected officials from the Executive or Judicial branches. Military officers are excluded.

The Constitution provided for an electoral college designed to select the President. It is based on the population of the districts within a state. Usually, the "electors" vote based on the way the general population votes. If there is no majority of electoral votes, the House of Representatives can select the President and the Senate can select the Vice President.

Also, should the Vice President be unable to complete his duties within the term of his service, the Congress may vote for a replacement. The Executive branch may nominate ambassadors and heads of departments. The Senate confirms or disallows candidates to these positions. The Senate also ratifies all treaties.

Congress may override a veto with a two-thirds vote, which would enact the bill. If a two-third's vote was not received, the bill would not become law. Congress has impeachment power over the Executive and Judicial branches. If a judge or an official is not properly discharging his duties, he can be impeached by the House of Representatives and tried by the Senate.

Congress may initiate amendments to be added to the Constitution. Congress has proposed hundreds of amendments, but only the *Bill of Rights* and seventeen other amendments have been added to the Constitution. Congress may check the appointments and the setting up of lower courts and jurisdictions by the Judicial branch. Congress approves all federal and Supreme Court Justices.

Each house of Congress provides a check on the other. Both houses must pass a proposed bill before it is submitted to the President. Only the House of

Representatives can originate revenue bills. Both houses must give consent to each other if they adjourn for more than three days. All legislative proceedings must be recorded and published.

The Executive Branch

The Executive branch also exercises checks on the Judiciary. The President has the power to appoint federal and Supreme Court judges. Since the Supreme Court Justices are appointed for life, it becomes essential for the President to make wise appointments. The Executive branch can check itself. This is done mainly through the appointment of cabinet members. However, the Framers did place an additional check in place for the President. If the President was deemed unfit either mentally or physically to carry out his duties, the Vice President and the Cabinet could vote to discharge him.

Other checks the President has over Congress include his power to call both houses back in session if there is an emergency. The converse of this can also happen. If one or both houses cannot reach an agreement, the President may force them to adjourn. The Vice President is the President of the Senate and presides over their meetings.

Judicial Branch

The Judicial branch of the government is not just the Supreme Court, but includes all federal judges. Because these are life-time appointments, each candidate is reviewed carefully before confirmation. The Executive branch makes the appointments and the Legislative branch votes for or against confirmation. The Chief Justice of the Supreme Court shall serve as President of the Senate in the event of the impeachment of the President.

Supreme Court judges review laws made by Congress and interpret them by using the Constitution as its guide. Justices can deem a law unconstitutional. However, Congress may, by a two-thirds majority, propose amendments to the Constitution to override a Supreme Court decision (Article V). A check on the Executive branch by the Judicial branch includes a judicial review of the legislation that has been signed into law by the President.

Another principle set forth by the Constitution is that of "Constitutional Supremacy." That means the Constitution is superior to any state's law or state constitution. No city or state can make a law that supersedes the Constitution. One final principle found in the Constitution is the "Rule of Law." This means that all citizens, including the President and all elected officials must obey the same laws. The President included in his Oath of Office, promises to uphold the Constitution.

A BRIEF DESCRIPTION OF THE ARTICLES
AND WHAT THEY COVER

Article Number	Issue	Description
I	Legislative Branch	Longest of articles with 10 sections; Authorizes Congress to make laws; establishes a bicameral legislative body of the Congress; develops rules for the election of members; lists the responsibilities and limits of Congress.
II	Executive Branch	Establishes President and Vice President to inforce laws; Gives rules for elections; lists powers and responsibilities of the President; lists procedures for impeachment.
III	Judicial Branch	Establishes a Supreme Court as the highest court in the country; lists the powers and responsibilities of the Supreme Court and other federal courts; establishes the power of judicial review; defines treason.
IV	The States	Sets rules and guarantees for states to cooperate and work together; rules for a new state's admittance into the United States.
V	Making Amendments	Gives the procedures for adding new amendments to the Constitution.
VI	Supreme Law of the Land	Makes the Constitution the highest law of the land above any state constitution or treaty.
VII	Ratification of the Constitution	States how the Constitution would become effective when 9 of the 13 states give approval.

Article I
The Legislative Branch

The Legislative Branch

Article 1 is one of the longest with ten sections, and its purpose was to establish a Congress which, in turn, would propose laws. It divided the Congress into two separate bodies, the Senate and the House of Representatives. An established purpose was to give guidelines for the electing of its members as well as defining and limiting some of the powers of the Congress.

Section 1. All legislative Powers herein granted shall be vested in a Congress of the United States, which shall consist of a Senate and House of Representatives.

Section 1 establishes the bicameral legislative body of the Congress of the United States. It is comprised of the higher house, the Senate, and the lower house, the House of Representatives.

The House of Representatives

Section 2. The House of Representatives shall be composed of Members chosen every second Year by the People of the several States, and the Electors in each State shall have the Qualifications requisite for Electors of the most numerous Branch of the State Legislature.

No Person shall be a Representative who shall not have attained to the Age of twenty-five Years and been seven Years a Citizen of the United States, and who shall not, when elected, be an Inhabitant of that State in which he shall be chosen.

(Representatives and direct Taxes shall be apportioned among the several States which may be included within this Union, according to their respective Numbers, which shall be determined by adding to the whole Number of free Persons, including those bound to Service for a Term of Years, and excluding Indians not taxed, three fifths of all other Persons.)* The actual Enumeration shall be made within three Years after the first Meeting of the Congress of the United States, and within every subsequent Term of ten Years in such Manner as they shall by Law direct. The Number of Representatives shall not exceed one for every thirty Thousand, but each State shall have at Least one Representative; and until such enumeration shall be made, the State of New Hampshire shall be entitled to chuse three, Massachusetts eight, Rhode Island and Providence Plantations one, Connecticut five, New York six, New Jersey four, Pennsylvania eight, Delaware one, Maryland six, Virginia ten, North Carolina five, South Carolina five and Georgia three.

*This sentence in parentheses was altered by the 14th Amendment, section 2.

When vacancies happen in the Representation from any State, the Executive Authority thereof shall issue Writs of Election to fill such Vacancies. The House of Representatives all chuse their Speaker and other Officers; and shall have the sole Power of Impeachment.

Section 2 defines the House of Representatives, which was known as the *lower house* of Congress. It establishes the following requirements:

- Representatives must be at least 25 years old.

- A representative must be a citizen for a minimum of 7 years.

- A representative must live in the state they represent.

- The people will vote for their representatives for terms of two years.

- The representatives are divided among the states proportionally, which means the more heavily populated states will have more representatives in the House. This section also reflects the "Great Compromise," an agreement that each state will be represented according to its population.

- The leader of the House is the Speaker of the House and is chosen by his/her fellow representatives. The Speaker of the House presides over all meetings of the House. It is the right of the House of Representatives alone, to accuse a high government official of a significant crime, such as "treason, bribery, or other high crimes and misdemeanors."

The Senate

Section 3. The Senate of the United States shall be composed of two Senators from each State, chosen by the Legislature thereof, for six Years; and each Senator shall have one Vote.

Immediately after they shall be assembled in Consequence of the first Election, they shall be divided as equally as may be into three Classes. The Seats of the Senators of the first Class shall be vacated at the Expiration of the second Year, of the second Class at the Expiration of the fourth Year, and of the third Class at the expiration of the sixth Year, so that one third may be chosen every second Year; and if Vacancies happen by Resignation, or otherwise, during the Recess of the Legislature of any State, the Executive thereof may make temporary Appointments until the next Meeting of the Legislature, which shall then fill such Vacancies.

No Person shall be a Senator who shall not have attained to the Age of thirty Years, and been nine Years a Citizen of the United States, and who shall not, when elected, be an Inhabitant of that State for which he shall be chosen.

The Vice President of the United States shall be President of the Senate, but shall have no Vote, unless they be equally divided.

The Senate shall chuse [sic] their other Officers, and also a President pro tempore, in the Absence of the Vice President, or when he shall exercise the Office of President of the United States.

The Senate shall have the sole Power to try all Impeachments. When sitting for that Purpose, they shall be on Oath or Affirmation. When the President of the United States is tried, the Chief Justice shall preside: And no Person shall be convicted without the Concurrence of two thirds of the Members present.

Judgment in Cases of Impeachment shall not extend further than to removal from Office, and disqualification to hold and enjoy any Office of honor, Trust or Profit under the United States: but the Party convicted shall nevertheless be liable and subject to Indictment, Trial, Judgment and Punishment, according to Law.

Section 3 defines the Senate, which was known as the upper house of Congress. It establishes the following requirements:

- A senator must be 30 years of age and a citizen for a minimum of 9 years.

- Senators must be voted on every six years, depending on their rotation into office.

- There are two senators for each state.

The Vice President's role is described in the Constitution. He serves as the President of the Senate, but has no vote unless there is a tie. If the Vice President is unable to officiate, the Senate shall have a President pro tempore who serves when the official President of the Senate is unable to serve. The Senate has the sole power to try all impeachments and may make a determination if the accused has betrayed the trust of his office.

Election of Congressional Members and Meeting Requirements

Section 4. The Times, Places and Manner of holding Elections for Senators and Representatives, shall be prescribed in each State by the Legislature thereof; but the Congress may at any time by Law make or alter such Regulations, except as to the Places of chusing [sic] Senators.

The Congress shall assemble at least once in every Year, and such Meeting shall be on the first Monday in December, unless they shall by Law appoint a different Day.

Section 4 states that each state will develop its own means for electing its Senators and Representatives. Amendment 20 provides that a new Congress shall meet at least once in every year on January 3. The President has the power to call Congress into a special session, if necessary.

How Congress Conducts Business

Section 5. Each House shall be the Judge of the Elections, Returns and Qualifications of its own Members, and a Majority of each shall constitute a Quorum to do Business; but a smaller Number may adjourn from day to day, and may be authorized to compel the Attendance of absent Members, in such Manner, and under such Penalties as each House may provide.

Each House may determine the Rules of its Proceedings, punish its Members for disorderly Behaviour, and, with the Concurrence of two thirds, expel a Member.

Each House shall keep a Journal of its Proceedings, and from time to time publish the same, excepting such Parts as may in their Judgment require Secrecy; and the Yeas and Nays of the Members of either House on any question shall, at the Desire of one fifth of those Present, be entered on the Journal.

Neither House, during the Session of Congress, shall, without the Consent of the other, adjourn for more than three days, nor to any other Place than that in which the two Houses shall be sitting.

Section 5 lists the following guidelines:

- Congress is responsible for electing its own officers and setting up the qualifications for each potential officer. It does not give a number for a quorum, but it does state that a majority of each shall constitute a quorum to do business. Absent members may be penalized by provisions established by each house.

- Members who do not meet their obligations or are guilty of unseemly behavior may be punished and even expelled from office by a two-thirds vote.

- All proceedings must be recorded in a journal and published from time to time, excepting those parts requiring secrecy. Also, the votes of individual members must be recorded if one-fifth of those present desire it.

- Neither house can be adjourned for a period of more than three days unless the other house is informed and has given consent.

How the Congress is Compensated

Section 6. The Senators and Representatives shall receive a Compensation for their Services, to be ascertained by Law, and paid out of the Treasury of the

United States. They shall in all Cases, except Treason, Felony and Breach of the Peace, be privileged from Arrest during their Attendance at the Session of their respective Houses, and in going to and returning from the same; and for any Speech or Debate in either House, they shall not be questioned in any other Place.

No Senator or Representative shall, during the Time for which he was elected, be appointed to any civil Office under the Authority of the United States, which shall have been created, or the Emoluments whereof shall have been encreased during such time; and no Person holding any Office under the United States, shall be a Member of either House during his Continuance in Office.

Section 6 establishes how members of Congress will be paid. They will be compensated with salaries, expenses, free postage, and other compensations. Also, they must not be detained while traveling to and from Congress. They have freedom from arrest for any speech or debate they may have made while in a session of Congress. Their first responsibility as a member of Congress is to be present in the legislature. They cannot hold any other public office in the government while serving as a member of Congress.

Revenue Bills, Legislative Process, Presidential Veto

Section 7. All bills for raising Revenue shall originate in the House of Repre-sentatives; but the Senate may propose or concur with Amendments as on other Bills.

Every Bill which shall have passed the House of Representatives and the Sen-ate, shall, before it become a Law, be presented to the President of the United States; If he approve he shall sign it, but if not he shall return it, with his Objections to that House in which it shall have originated, who shall enter the Objections at large on their Journal, and proceed to reconsider it. If after such Reconsideration two thirds of that House shall agree to pass the Bill, it shall be sent, together with the Objections, to the other House, by which it shall likewise be reconsidered, and if approved by two thirds of that House, it shall become a Law. But in all such Cases the Votes of both Houses shall be determined by yeas and Nays, and the Names of the Persons voting for and against the Bill shall be entered on the Jour-nal of each House respectively. If any Bill shall not be returned by the President within ten Days (Sundays excepted) after it shall have been presented to him, the Same shall be a Law, in like Manner as if he had signed it, unless the Congress by their Adjournment prevent its Return, in which Case it shall not be a Law.

Every Order, Resolution, or Vote to which the Concurrence of the Senate and House of Representatives may be necessary (except on a question of Adjourn-ment) shall be presented to the President of the United States; and before the Same shall take Effect, shall be approved by him, or being disapproved by him, shall be repassed by two- thirds of the Senate and House of Representatives, according to the Rules and Limitations prescribed in the Case of a Bill.

Section 7 details one of the basic responsibilities of the legislature; making bills into laws. The following shows how a bill becomes a law:

- Any bill may be brought up in either house, but a bill involving raising money (such as by taxes or fees) must originate in the House.

- The proposed bill must be passed by both houses of Congress. The bill must be in the exact same form as when it is passed by both houses.

- Bills that are voted on by both houses are sent to the President where he, in turn, can either sign the bill (it then becomes law), or he can reject the bill and veto it.

- If the bill is vetoed, the bill is sent back to Congress. The veto can be overturned if both houses vote again and pass it by a two-thirds majority vote. At this point, the bill becomes law and overrides the President's veto.

Powers of Congress

Section 8. *The Congress shall have Power To lay and collect Taxes, Duties, Imposts and Excises, to pay the Debts and provide for the common Defence and general Welfare of the United States; but all Duties, Imposts and Excises shall be uniform throughout the United States;*

To borrow Money on the credit of the United States;

To regulate Commerce with foreign Nations, and among the several States, and with the Indian Tribes;

To establish an uniform Rule of Naturalization, and uniform Laws on the subject of Bankruptcies throughout the United States;

To coin Money, regulate the Value thereof, and of foreign Coin, and fix the Standard of Weights and Measures;

To provide for the Punishment of counterfeiting the Securities and current Coin of the United States;

To establish Post Offices and post Roads;

To promote the Progress of Science and useful Arts, by securing for limited Times to Authors and Inventors the exclusive Right to their respective Writings and Discoveries;

To constitute Tribunals inferior to the supreme Court;

To define and punish Piracies and Felonies committed on the high Seas, and Offences against the Law of Nations;

To declare War, grant Letters of Marque and Reprisal, and make Rules concerning Captures on Land and Water;

To raise and support Armies, but no Appropriation of Money to that Use shall be for a longer Term than two Years;

To provide and maintain a Navy;

To make Rules for the Government and Regulation of the land and naval Forces;

To provide for calling forth the Militia to execute the Laws of the Union, suppress Insurrections and repel Invasions;

To provide for organizing, arming, and disciplining, the Militia, and for governing such Part of them as may be employed in the Service of the United States, reserving to the States respectively, the Appointment of the Officers, and the Authority of training the Militia according to the discipline prescribed by Congress;

To exercise exclusive Legislation in all Cases whatsoever, over such District (not exceeding ten Miles square) as may, by Cession of particular States, and the Acceptance of Congress, become the Seat of the Government of the United States, and to exercise like Authority over all Places purchased by the Consent of the Legislature of the State in which the Same shall be, for the Erection of Forts, Magazines, Arsenals, dock-Yards, and other needful Buildings.

…And To make all Laws which shall be necessary and proper for carrying into Execution the foregoing Powers, and all other Powers vested by this Constitution in the Government of the United States, or in any Department or Officer thereof.

Section 8 is one of the longest sections in Article 1, primarily because it lists and defines the powers and responsibilities of Congress. In this section, the Framers also included a final clause known as the "Elastic Clause." This clause enables Congress to pass any law they deem necessary for the carrying out of any of the previously listed powers.

Limits on Congress

Section 9. The Migration or Importation of such Persons as any of the States now existing shall think proper to admit, shall not be prohibited by the Congress prior to the Year one thousand eight hundred and eight, but a Tax or duty may be imposed on such Importation, not exceeding ten dollars for each Person.

The Privilege of the Writ of Habeas Corpus shall not be suspended, unless when in Cases of Rebellion or Invasion the public Safety may require it.

No Bill of Attainder or ex post facto Law shall be passed.

No Capitation, or other direct, Tax shall be laid, (unless in Proportion to the Census or Enumeration herein before directed to be taken.)[60] No Tax or Duty shall be laid on Articles exported from any State.

---

[60] Section in parentheses was further clarified by the 16th Amendment.

No Preference shall be given by any Regulation of Commerce or Revenue to the Ports of one State over those of another: nor shall Vessels bound to, or from, one State, be obliged to enter, clear, or pay Duties in another.

No Money shall be drawn from the Treasury, but in Consequence of Appropriations made by Law; and a regular Statement and Account of the Receipts and Expenditures of all public Money shall be published from time to time.

No Title of Nobility shall be granted by the United States: And no Person holding any Office of Profit or Trust under them, shall, without the Consent of the Congress, accept of any present, Emolument, Office, or Title, of any kind whatever, from any King, Prince or foreign State.

Section 9 places specific limits on Congress. These limits are valid today. They include the following:

- Protection from being jailed and held without explanation or reason, except in times of extreme emergency.

- Direct taxes shall be apportioned among the states according to their population.

- Congress may not pass laws to give shipping advantages to one state over another. No tax may be levied on goods being shipped out of the country.

- Legal matters, suspension of *habeas corpus*, bills of attainder, and ex-post facto laws are prohibited.

- No law may give preferential treatment to one state over another.

- No money can be exacted from the treasury unless Congress duly passes a law for that purpose.

- No title of nobility, such as King, Prince or Marquis, may be given to anyone holding a government office in the United States.

(In 1913, Amendment 16 was added to the Constitution to establish the right of Congress to tax incomes.)

Limits on States

Section 10. No State shall enter into any Treaty, Alliance, or Confederation; grant Letters of Marque and Reprisal; coin Money; emit Bills of Credit; make any Thing but gold and silver Coin a Tender in Payment of Debts; pass any Bill of Attainder, ex post facto Law, or Law impairing the Obligation of Contracts, or grant any Title of Nobility.

No State shall, without the Consent of the Congress, lay any Imposts or Duties on Imports or Exports, except what may be absolutely necessary for executing it's inspection Laws: and the net Produce of all Duties and Imposts, laid by any State on Imports or Exports, shall be for the Use of the Treasury of the United States; and all such Laws shall be subject to the Revision and Controul of the Congress.

No State shall, without the Consent of Congress, lay any duty of Tonnage, keep Troops, or Ships of War in time of Peace, enter into any Agreement or Compact with another State, or with a foreign Power, or engage in War, unless actually invaded, or in such imminent Danger as will not admit of delay.

Section 10 limits the power of the states and prohibits the following:

- States may not tax goods moving across its borders except as needed to pay normal costs of inspection.

- States cannot mint their own money.

- States cannot declare war against another state or country.

- States have the same restrictions as Congress in Section 9.

Article II
The Executive Branch

Article II describes and establishes the second of the three branches of government, the Executive branch. The role of the President and Vice President is to execute and enforce laws. Other purposes of Article II are rules for elections and the powers of the President. The Framers also included how to impeach a President, if there is evidence of corruption while in office.

There is a significant difference in Article I (the Legislative branch) and Article II (the Executive branch). In Article I the powers of Congress are clearly stated in what they are allowed to do. The same is not done with the Presidency (Article II). Some historians believe this was because the Framers were not sure what type of power the Executive branch should have, so they were careful not to overstate the Presidential powers. This provided more flexibility for the President to meet specific situations.

There is a significant difference in Article I (the Legislative branch) and Article II (the Executive branch). In Article I the powers

*of Congress are clearly stated in
what they are allowed to do.*

The President

Section 1. The executive Power shall be vested in a President of the United States of America. He shall hold his Office during the Term of four Years, and, together with the Vice President chosen for the same Term, be elected, as follows:

Each State shall appoint, in such Manner as the Legislature thereof may direct, a Number of Electors, equal to the whole Number of Senators and Representatives to which the State may be entitled in the Congress: but no Senator or Representative, or Person holding an Office of Trust or Profit under the United States, shall be appointed an Elector.

The [Electors shall meet in their respective States, and vote by Ballot for two Persons, of whom one at least shall not be an Inhabitant of the same State with themselves. And they shall make a List of all the Persons voted for, and of the Number of Votes for each; which List they shall sign and certify, and transmit sealed to the Seat of the Government of the United States, directed to the President of the Senate. The President of the Senate shall, in the Presence of the Senate and House of Representatives, open all the Certificates, and the Votes shall then be counted. The Person having the greatest Number of Votes shall be the President, if such Number be a Majority of the whole Number of Electors appointed; and if there be more than one who have such Majority, and have an equal Number of Votes, then the House of Representatives shall immediately chuse [sic] by Ballot one of them for President; and if no Person have a Majority, then from the five highest on the List the said House shall in like Manner chuse [sic] the President. But in chusing [sic] the President, the Votes shall be taken by States, the Representation from each State having one Vote; a quorum for this Purpose shall consist of a Member or Members from two-thirds of the States, and a Majority of all the States shall be necessary to a Choice. In every Case, after the Choice of the President, the Person having the greatest Number of Votes of the Electors shall be the Vice President. But if there should remain two or more who have equal Votes, the Senate shall chuse [sic] from them by Ballot the Vice President.][61]

The Congress may determine the Time of chusing the Electors, and the Day on which they shall give their Votes; which Day shall be the same throughout the United States.

---

[61]   This clause in parentheses was superseded by the *12th Amendment.*

No person except a natural born Citizen, or a Citizen of the United States, at the time of the Adoption of this Constitution, shall be eligible to the Office of President; neither shall any Person be eligible to that Office who shall not have attained to the Age of thirty-five Years, and been fourteen Years a Resident within the United States.

[In Case of the Removal of the President from Office, or of his Death, Resignation, or Inability to discharge the Powers and Duties of the said Office, the Same shall devolve on the Vice President, and the Congress may by Law provide for the Case of Removal, Death, Resignation or Inability, both of the President and Vice President, declaring what Officer shall then act as President, and such Officer shall act accordingly, until the Disability be removed, or a President shall be elected.][62]

The President shall, at stated Times, receive for his Services, a Compensation, which shall neither be increased nor diminished during the Period for which he shall have been elected, and he shall not receive within that Period any other Emolument from the United States, or any of them.

Before he enters on the Execution of his Office, he shall take the following Oath or Affirmation:

"I do solemnly swear (or affirm) that I will faithfully execute the Office of President of the United States, and will to the best of my Ability, preserve, protect and defend the Constitution of the United States."

Section 1 describes the offices of the President and the Vice President. Their terms were established as four years. Another key piece of information in this section is how the President is elected using the Electoral College. The Electoral College was set up by the Framers to add another system of checks and balances in electing a President. The system gave each state one vote for each member it has in Congress.

Initially, Presidents did not choose their running mates. The person with the most electoral votes was chosen as President. The Vice President would be the person with the second most electoral votes. This was later changed and presidents could select their own running mates to be Vice President. Other requirements of the President were defined and included the following:

- Must be at least 35 years old.

- Must be a natural-born citizen of the United States.

- Must have been a resident of the United States for at least 14 years.

---

[62]   This clause in parentheses has been modified by the 20th and 25th Amendments.

- The President is to be paid a salary, but it cannot change, either up or down, for the term of his Presidency.

A very important feature in Section 1 is the Oath of Office for the President. It is a pledge of loyalty to the country as well as an Oath to defend and protect the Constitution. In the event a President is removed from office, unable to execute his duties while in office, dies or resigns, the Vice President will succeed the President. Originally, the Framers did not clearly specify whether the Vice President permanently took over once the President was no longer in office. However, at the death of William Henry Harrison, John Tyler set the precedent that the Vice President be firmly established as President when the sitting President is no longer in office. Later, the 25th Amendment clearly stated the Vice President would become the President when the sitting President is no longer able to fulfill his duties.

Civilian Power over Military, Cabinet, Pardon Power, Appointments

Section 2. The President shall be Commander in Chief of the Army and Navy of the United States, and of the Militia of the several States, when called into the actual Service of the United States; he may require the Opinion, in writing, of the principal Officer in each of the executive Departments, upon any subject relating to the Duties of their respective Offices, and he shall have Power to Grant Reprieves and Pardons for Offenses against the United States, except in Cases of Impeachment.

He shall have Power, by and with the Advice and Consent of the Senate, to make Treaties, provided two thirds of the Senators present concur; and he shall nominate, and by and with the Advice and Consent of the Senate, shall appoint Ambassadors, other public Ministers and Consuls, Judges of the supreme Court, and all other Officers of the United States, whose Appointments are not herein otherwise provided for, and which shall be established by Law: but the Congress may by Law vest the Appointment of such inferior Officers, as they think proper, in the President alone, in the Courts of Law, or in the Heads of Departments.

The President shall have Power to fill up all Vacancies that may happen during the Recess of the Senate, by granting Commissions which shall expire at the End of their next Session.

Section 2 lists important responsibilities of the President.

- Serves as Commander-in-Chief of the armed forces and of the militia (National Guard) for all the states.

- Appoints a set of advisors to aid him (the Cabinet).

- Pardons criminals he deems worthy.

- Sets up treaties with other nations and the President must submit the treaty to the Senate for approval with a two-thirds vote.

- May select judges for the Supreme Court as well as other governmental posts. (These all must be approved by the Senate).

State of the Union, Convening Congress

Section 3. He shall from time to time give to the Congress Information of the State of the Union, and recommend to their Consideration such Measures as he shall judge necessary and expedient; he may, on extraordinary Occasions, convene both Houses, or either of them, and in Case of Disagreement between them, with Respect to the Time of Adjournment, he may adjourn them to such Time as he shall think proper; he shall receive Ambassadors and other public Ministers; he shall take Care that the Laws be faithfully executed, and shall Commission all the Officers of the United States.

Section 3 describes the duties of the President.

- Must inform Congress on the nation's affairs.

- Has the right to call special sessions of Congress.

- Must enforce federal laws.

- The President will give Congress information of the State of the Union. It does not stipulate how often this is to occur.

- The President may make suggestions to Congress and intervene only when deemed by the President to be necessary.

- The President will act as Head of State by receiving Ambassadors from other countries and other Heads of State.

Disqualification

Section 4. The President, Vice President and all civil Officers of the United States, shall be removed from Office on Impeachment for, and Conviction of, Treason, Bribery, or other high Crimes and Misdemeanors.

Section 4 briefly discusses and provides for the removal or impeachment of the President, Vice President and or other governmental officials.

Article III
The Judicial Branch

Article III. The Judicial Branch establishes the Supreme Court and lists the duties and powers of the Supreme Court and other federal courts. It also defines the power of judicial review and clearly defines treason.

Judicial Powers

Section 1. The Judicial Power of the United States, shall be vested in one supreme Court, and in such inferior Courts as the Congress may from time to time ordain and establish. The Judges, both of the supreme and inferior Courts, shall hold their Offices during good Behaviour, and shall, at stated Times, receive for their Services a Compensation which shall not be diminished during their Continuance in Office.

Section 1 discusses the establishment of the Supreme Court, the highest court in the United States. It also establishes the terms of judges, of both the Supreme Court and lower courts. Judges may serve for life with "good behavior." Judges can and have been impeached. This section states that judges will be compensated. Also, Congress, using discretion, may create lower courts, the orders and judgments of which may be reviewed by the Supreme Court.

Trial by Jury, Original Jurisdiction, Jury Trials

Section 2. The judicial Power shall extend to all Cases, in Law and Equity, arising under this Constitution, the Laws of the United States, and Treaties made, or which shall be made, under their Authority;--to all Cases affecting Ambassadors, other public Ministers and Consuls;--to all Cases of admiralty and maritime Jurisdiction; to Controversies to which the United States shall be a Party;-- to Controversies between two or more States;--[between a State and Citizens of another State;--][63]* between Citizens of different States;--between Citizens of the same State claiming Lands under Grants of different States, [and between a State, or the Citizens thereof, and foreign States, Citizens or Subjects.]*[64]

In all Cases affecting Ambassadors, other public Ministers and Consuls, and those in which a State shall be Party, the supreme Court shall have original Jurisdiction. In all the other Cases before mentioned, the supreme Court shall have appellate Jurisdiction, both as to Law and Fact, with such Exceptions, and under such Regulations as the Congress shall make.

The Trial of all Crimes, except in Cases of Impeachment, shall be by Jury; and such Trial shall be held in the State where the said Crimes shall have been committed; but when not committed within any State, the Trial shall be at such Place or Places as the Congress may by Law have directed.

---

[63]   This section in parentheses is modified by the 11th Amendment.
[64]   This section in parentheses is modified by the 11th Amendment.

Section 2 lists the types of cases that may be heard by the Federal Judiciary and also gives the order of cases that the Supreme Court may hear first (this is known as "original jurisdiction.") All other cases heard by the Supreme Court are done by appeal. This section also ensures a trial by jury in a criminal court. Guilt is determined by twelve fellow citizens and the trial must be in the state where the crime is said to have been committed. All jurors must agree on the verdict.

Treason

Section 3. Treason against the United States, shall consist only in levying War against them, or in adhering to their Enemies, giving them Aid and Comfort. No Person shall be convicted of Treason unless on the Testimony of two Witnesses to the same overt Act, or on Confession in open Court.

The Congress shall have power to declare the Punishment of Treason, but no Attainder of Treason shall work Corruption of Blood, or Forfeiture except during the Life of the Person attainted.

Section 3 clearly states what the "crime of treason" is and how Congress may declare punishment.

Article IV
The States

Article IV covers the responsibilities and limits of the states. It also deals with the state's relationship to the Federal Government and with other states. It gives certain guarantees for the states, and establishes how new states are admitted into the Union.

Each State to Honor all Others

Section 1. Full Faith and Credit shall be given in each State to the public Acts, Records, and judicial Proceedings of every other State. And the Congress may by general Laws prescribe the Manner in which such Acts, Records and Proceedings shall be proved, and the Effect thereof.

Section 1 directs the states to honor the laws, public acts, records and court proceedings of other states. For example, if a couple marries in California they would be considered married by Maryland. Another example would be someone who commits a crime and is found guilty in Virginia would also be guilty in Wyoming. Congress may regulate the required proof each state must have for these acts, (records and court proceedings).

State Citizens, Extradition

Section 2. *The Citizens of each State shall be entitled to all Privileges and Immunities of Citizens in the several States.*

A Person charged in any State with Treason, Felony, or other Crime, who shall flee from Justice, and be found in another State, shall on demand of the executive Authority of the State from which he fled, be delivered up, to be removed to the State having Jurisdiction of the Crime.

[No Person held to Service or Labour in one State, under the Laws thereof, escaping into another, shall, in Consequence of any Law or Regulation therein, be discharged from such Service or Labour, But shall be delivered up on Claim of the Party to whom such Service or Labour may be due.][65]

Section 2 insures that citizens of one state will be treated equally and fairly like citizens of another state. If a person accused of a crime in one state escapes and is caught in another state, that accused person will be extradited and sent back to the state of the crime to stand trial.

New States

Section 3. *New States may be admitted by the Congress into this Union; but no new States shall be formed or erected within the Jurisdiction of any other State; nor any State be formed by the Junction of two or more States, or parts of States, without the Consent of the Legislatures of the States concerned as well as of the Congress.*

The Congress shall have Power to dispose of and make all needful Rules and Regulations respecting the Territory or other Property belonging to the United States; and nothing in this Constitution shall be so construed as to Prejudice any Claims of the United States, or of any particular State.

Section 3 addresses the creation and admittance of new states, the control of federal lands and how they are to be controlled. The "Territorial Clause" gives Congress the power to make rules for the organization of federal property and of governing territories of the United States, like Guam and Puerto Rico.

Republican government

Section 4. *The United States shall guarantee to every State in this Union a Republican Form of Government, and shall protect each of them against Invasion; and on Application of the Legislature, or of the Executive (when the Legislature cannot be convened) against domestic Violence.*

Section 4 guarantees that the country will be a republic where the state derives powers from the people. It also insures that the federal government will protect the states against the invasion of foreign powers (from outside the

---

[65]   This clause in parentheses is superseded by the 13th Amendment.

country) and/or the insurrection of states within the country. It gives the assurance that a state will not be turned into a dictatorship. Help is to be available if a state is not able to handle riots or other local crises.

Article V- Adding Amendments

The Congress, whenever two-thirds of both Houses shall deem it necessary, shall propose Amendments to this Constitution, or, on the Application of the Legislatures of two thirds of the several States, shall call a Convention for proposing Amendments, which, in either Case, shall be valid to all Intents and Purposes, as Part of this Constitution, when ratified by the Legislatures of three fourths of the several States, or by Conventions in three fourths thereof, as the one or the other Mode of Ratification may be proposed by the Congress; Provided that no Amendment which may be made prior to the Year One thousand eight hundred and eight shall in any Manner affect the first and fourth Clauses in the Ninth Section of the first Article; and that no State, without its Consent, shall be deprived of its equal Suffrage in the Senate.

Article V details the method of adding amendments (making changes) to the Constitution. Two-thirds of both Houses must agree to a proposal of adding an amendment. The proposed amendment must then be submitted to the states by Congress and must be ratified by three-fourths of the states before it can take effect. Article V also gives Congress an option of a special convention which requires two-thirds of the state legislators to call for a convention for proposing amendments. However, with the convention method for ratification, to date, only one amendment has been approved — the 21st Amendment. Article V currently states only one limitation on the amending power — that no amendment can negate states of their equal representation in the Senate unless that state has given their consent.

Article VI - Debts, Supremacy, Oaths

All Debts contracted and Engagements entered into, before the Adoption of this Constitution, shall be as valid against the United States under this Constitution, as under the Confederation.

This Constitution, and the Laws of the United States which shall be made in Pursuance thereof; and all Treaties made, or which shall be made, under the Authority of the United States, shall be the supreme Law of the Land; and the Judges in every State shall be bound thereby, any Thing in the Constitution or Laws of any State to the Contrary notwithstanding.

The Senators and Representatives before mentioned, and the Members of the several State Legislatures, and all executive and judicial Officers, both of the

United States and of the several States, shall be bound by Oath or Affirmation, to support this Constitution; but no religious Test shall ever be required as a Qualification to any Office or public Trust under the United States.

Article VI establishes the Constitution, as well as the laws and treaties of the United States made in accordance with it, to be the supreme law of the land. No state constitution or legislation will supersede it. The judges of the Supreme Court are duty bound to use the Constitution to interpret all laws, court rulings and other legal documents. It also validates national debt, which was first created under the *Articles of Confederation.* All federal and state legislators, officers, and judges must take an oath and pledge to uphold and support the Constitution. No religious test will be required for service in public office.

At the beginning of this new government the national debt exceeded over $50,000,000. Alexander Hamilton, as first Secretary of the Treasury, convinced Congress to pay off the national debt at face value and also pay the debts incurred by the states.

Article VII - Ratification of the Constitution

The Ratification of the Conventions of nine States, shall be sufficient for the Establishment of this Constitution between the States so ratifying the Same.

Done in Convention by the Unanimous Consent of the States present the Seventeenth Day of September in the Year of our Lord one thousand seven hundred and Eighty seven and of the Independence of the United States of America the Twelfth in Witness whereof We have hereunto subscribed our Names.

G. Washington—	
Presid. and deputy from Virginia	
Delaware	Geo Read
	Gunning Bedford jun
	John Dickinson
	Richard Bassett
	Jaco: Broom
Maryland	James McHenry
	Dan of St. Thos. Jenifer
	Danl. Carroll
Virginia	John Blair
	James Madison, Jr.
North Carolina	Wm. Blount
	Richd. Dobbs Spaight
	Hu Williamson

South Carolina	J. Rutledge
	Charles Cotesworth Pinckney
	Charles Pinckney
	Pierce Butler
Georgia	William Few
	Abr Baldwin
New Hampshire	John Langdon
	Nicholas Gilman
Massachusetts	Nathaniel Gorham
	Rufus King
Connecticut	Wm. Saml. Johnson
	Roger Sherman
New York	Alexander Hamilton
New Jersey	Wil: Livingston
	David Brearley
	Wm. Paterson
	Jona: Dayton
Pennsylvania	B Franklin
	Thomas Mifflin
	Robt. Morris
	Geo. Clymer
	Thos. FitzSimons
	Jared Ingersoll
	James Wilson
	Gouv Morris
	Attest William Jackson Secretary

Article VII details the requirements for ratification of the Constitution. The Framers at the time of the creation of the Constitution felt it should not take effect until at least nine states had ratified it in state conventions that had met especially for that purpose. However, at the time of the state conventions, the Framers decided to ask for a unanimous vote of confidence for the Constitution. They felt it would be ineffective and destructive to have some of the states ratify the document, live by its principles, while other states would be separated from them because they would not ratify the document. The Framers did allow for an exception in the event this did happen – only nine of the original thirteen states in the United States had to ratify the Constitution before it would officially go into effect.

After the Convention, John Adams said, "*Our people must be consulted, invited to erect the whole building with their own hands, upon the broadest foundations.*" [66]

Because some feared the new government might abuse its powers, they insisted the Constitution contain more specific protection for the rights of the people. The First Congress in 1791 submitted 12 amendments to the states for ratification, ten were ratified. These became known as "The Bill of Rights."

Because some feared the new government might abuse its powers, they insisted the Constitution contain more specific protection for the rights of the people. The First Congress in 1791 submitted 12 amendments to the states for ratification, ten were ratified. These became known as "The Bill of Rights."

---

[66]   Massachusetts Historical Society – http://1ref.us/de

The Bill of Rights and Other Amendments

The first ten amendments to the Constitution, "The Bill of Rights," were ratified effective December 15, 1791. Adding amendments to the Constitution has never been an easy process. To date, over our 240-year history, over 11,000 new amendments have been introduced and discussed in Congressional committees. Most never made it out of committee. Two-thirds of both houses of Congress must agree to a proposed amendment before it is sent to the states for ratification, or a Constitutional Convention may be called and a new amendment proposed. This requires a two-thirds vote from the state legislatures.

The President plays no role in this process. He does not need to give his approval. Once the amendment has passed Congress with a two-thirds vote, the proposed amendment is sent to the states for a vote. If the document is ratified by three-fourths of the states, a formal proclamation is drafted showing that the amendment is valid and is now part of the Constitution.

Amendment 1 – Freedom of Religion, Press, Expression. Passed in Congress 9/25/1789. Ratified 12/15/1791.

Congress shall make no law respecting an establishment of religion, or prohibiting the free exercise thereof; or abridging the freedom of speech, or of the press; or the right of the people peaceably to assemble, and to petition the Government for a redress of grievances.

The **1st Amendment** protects the people's right to worship as they wish, to speak freely without fear of retribution, to meet with others without fear of arrest, to report and publish items of interest without government censorship, and the right to address and petition the government when they disagree with issues. The government may not prevent the gathering together of people to discuss anything they choose, including issues with the government.

Amendment 2 – Right to Bear Arms.
Passed in Congress 9/25/1789. Ratified 12/15/1791.

A well-regulated Militia, being necessary to the security of a free State, the right of the people to keep and bear Arms, shall not be infringed.

The **2nd Amendment** allows for citizens not only to own guns, but to use them for lawful purposes as well. Much debate still persists as to whether this is a viable right for today. The controversy stems from the question, "Does this right protect the state or the individual?"

Amendment 3 – Quartering of Soldiers.
Passed in Congress 9/25/1789. Ratified 12/15/1791.

No Soldier shall, in time of peace be quartered in any house, without the consent of the Owner, nor in time of war, but in a manner to be prescribed by law.

The **3rd Amendment** clearly states that homeowners may not be forced to provide soldiers room and board even in a time of war without the consent of the homeowner.

Amendment 4 – Search and Seizure.
Passed in Congress 9/25/1789. Ratified 12/15/1791.

The right of the people to be secure in their persons, houses, papers, and effects, against unreasonable searches and seizures, shall not be violated, and no Warrants shall issue, but upon probable cause, supported by Oath or affirmation, and particularly describing the place to be searched, and the persons or things to be seized.

The **4th Amendment** prevents the government from arresting citizens or taking property or papers from the citizens without a proper and valid warrant based on probable cause (good reason).

Amendment 5 – Trial and Punishment, Compensation for Takings. Passed in Congress 9/25/1789. Ratified 12/15/1791.

No person shall be held to answer for a capital, or otherwise infamous crime, unless on a presentment or indictment of a Grand Jury, except in cases arising in the land or naval forces, or in the Militia, when in actual service in time of War or public danger; nor shall any person be subject for the same offense to be twice put in jeopardy of life or limb; nor shall be compelled in any criminal case to be a witness against himself, nor be deprived of life, liberty, or property, without due process of law; nor shall private property be taken for public use, without just compensation.

The **5th Amendment** protects citizens from being held for a crime unless properly indicted. It protects the accused from being tried twice for the same crime, a circumstance known as "double jeopardy." It gives citizens certain rights that protect them from being forced to testify against themselves. The prosecution must establish the defendant's guilt through independent evidence and not by forcibly extracting a confession from the suspect. The suspect may voluntarily confess, but the government cannot coerce a confession without due process of law.

The **5ᵗʰ Amendment** also prevents the government from seizing and searching a citizen's property without due process. "Due process" means that a citizen cannot be deprived of his rights by the government. If the government seizes property that is to be used for public interest, the owner must be fairly compensated for the full value of that property.

Amendment 6 – Right to Speedy Trial, Confrontation of Witnesses. Passed in Congress 9/25/1789. Ratified 12 /15/1791.

In all criminal prosecutions, the accused shall enjoy the right to a speedy and public trial, by an impartial jury of the State and district wherein the crime shall have been committed, which district shall have been previously ascertained by law, and to be informed of the nature and cause of the accusation; to be confronted with the witnesses against him; to have compulsory process for obtaining witnesses in his favor, and to have the Assistance of Counsel for his defence .

The **6th Amendment** ensures those who have been arrested that they will not be held by the state for an unspecified time, they will have a speedy trial, an impartial jury, and a defense lawyer. The accused will stand trial in the state where the crime was committed. It also insures that the accused may face and confront witnesses in court.

Amendment 7 – Trial by Jury in Civil Cases. Passed in Congress 9/25/1789. Ratified 12/15/1791.

In Suits at common law, where the value in controversy shall exceed twenty dollars, the right of trial by jury shall be preserved, and no fact tried by a jury, shall be otherwise re-examined in any Court of the United States, than according to the rules of the common law.

The **7th Amendment** ensures a jury trial for federal civil court cases. A verdict may be changed if the law is not correctly interpreted, or if the evidence presented is not adequate to support the establishment of fact.

Amendment 8 – Cruel and Unusual Punishment. Passed in Congress 9/25/1789. Ratified 12/15/1791.

Excessive bail shall not be required, nor excessive fines imposed, nor cruel and unusual punishments inflicted.

The **8th Amendment** states that those who have been convicted of a crime are guaranteed that punishment will be fair and excessively large fines or bail will be prohibited.

Amendment 9 – Construction of Constitution. Passed in Congress 9/25/1789. Ratified 12/15/1791.

The enumeration in the Constitution, of certain rights, shall not be construed to deny or disparage others retained by the people.

The **9th Amendment** is a statement indicating there may be other citizen rights aside from those listed in the Constitution. Even if they are not listed, they cannot be ignored or violated. It provides protection against interference with any other rights that were not thought of at the time of the writing of this amendment in 1791. It also gives assurance that a citizen's rights will not be seized by a dictator.

Amendment 10 – Powers of the States and People. Passed in Congress 9/25/1789. Ratified 12/15/1791.

The powers not delegated to the United States by the Constitution, nor prohibited by it to the States, are reserved to the States respectively, or to the people.

The **10th Amendment** has been the subject of debate for some time. The essence of what it says is that any power not clearly given to the federal government belongs to the states or to the people. It was designed to prevent the government from gaining excessive power. Controversy has arisen between those who believe the government should not take any control that is not expressly mentioned in the Constitution, while others believe the Constitution gives Congress the power to do anything that has not been clearly prohibited by the first eight amendments.

This amendment is important because it gives orders to the federal government that it may not assume powers that have not been specifically assigned to it. Power in the nation will be wielded only by those who have been given authority to it by the people.

Adding Amendments – An Overview

Sadly, although there are actually twenty-seven amendments, most Americans are aware of only the First and Fifth Amendments. The First Amendment gives freedom of speech, but many Americans fail to realize that this amendment actually prevents Congress from making and passing laws that would prevent free speech. The First Amendment is the keystone of the individual rights for which many Americans sought and fought. Their desire was for Americans to be able to speak freely and to use "print" not mandated by the government. This permitted speaking or writing on issues contrary to the position of the government.

The **Fifth Amendment** includes the right for the accused (criminal) not to incriminate himself. It also includes the famous "double jeopardy" provision which prevents the accused from being tried repeatedly for the same crime, thus preventing the accused from being "put in jeopardy of life or limb." Other amendments mark significant milestones in American history. They are:

- The Thirteenth Amendment abolished slavery.

- The Fifteenth Amendment gave minorities the right to vote.

- The Eighteenth Amendment prevented the making, selling, and the transporting of liquor.

- The Nineteenth Amendment allowed women the right to vote.

These were indicative of changing times. At one time in our country's history, the Supreme Court passed a controversial decision that did not consider black people completely human (the Dred Scott decision). However, Congress later brought legislation to overcome these injustices and discrepancies in the law.

Originally, twelve amendments were proposed, two of which were not ratified. The remaining ten we now call the "Bill of Rights." The first two of the twelve were not ratified. What we now consider the First Amendment was originally the Third Amendment when it was proposed. Of the two failed amendments, the second received little support and the first was one state shy of ratification. Finally, after 200 years from the time it was first proposed, it was ratified in 1992, becoming the twenty-seventh and final amendment to the United States Constitution.

Amendments (11–27)

The first ten amendments (The Bill of Rights) outlined in the Constitution are usually easier to name or recognize, but the last seventeen also show the rich legacy of our nation's history. These amendments give us a history lesson in the changing attitudes and viewpoints of Americans through the years.

A good example of this is how the views toward African Americans have changed. In 1857 the Dred Scott vs. Sanford case went to the Supreme Court and the Court ruled that people of African descent were not citizens of this country and could not be protected under the Constitution. This viewpoint changed in two ways. First, in 1866 Congress abolished slavery with the 13th Amendment. In 1870 the 15th Amendment allowed African American men the right to vote.

On January 16, 1919, the 18th Amendment became a part of the Constitution. It dealt with prohibition, which outlawed the making, selling or transporting of liquor. The advocates of this amendment hoped there would be a reduction in the abuse of liquor, and similarly this would eradicate poverty and other crimes associated with it. It was costly both with funds and manpower to police the country and rid it of "moonshine" operations. Polls showed that most Americans were against prohibition. Finally, on February 20, 1933, Congress proposed the 21st Amendment to repeal prohibition. It was voted on and ratified by the states shortly before Christmas of 1933. Prohibition was officially over on December 5, 1933.

Congress and the states approved other amendments to the Constitution, which became part of the law of the land. Often there was a significant amount of time between the date an amendment was proposed in Congress and the date it was ratified by the states. Even now it may take years between when a proposed amendment is voted on, ratified and integrated into the Constitution.

Amendment 11 – Judicial Limits.
Passed in Congress 3/4/1794. Ratified 2/7/1795.

The Judicial power of the United States shall not be construed to extend to any suit in law or equity, commenced or prosecuted against one of the United States by Citizens of another State, or by Citizens or Subjects of any Foreign State.

Amendment 11 was a direct result of the United States Supreme Court case ruling of Chisholm v Georgia (2 U.S. 419) in 1793. In this case, the Supreme Court ruled that the federal courts had the authority to hear and rule on cases where the state was pitted against a private citizen. A state did not have sovereign immunity and could be sued by its citizens. Congress felt that the Supreme

Court was overstepping its boundaries in this case and felt it should be prohibited from doing so again. This amendment limited the jurisdiction of the federal courts to automatically hear cases where a state is pitted against the citizens of another state.

Amendment 12 – Choosing the President, Vice President. Passed in Congress 12/9/1803. Ratified 6/15/1804.

The Electors shall meet in their respective states, and vote by ballot for President and Vice President, one of whom, at least, shall not be an inhabitant of the same state with themselves; they shall name in their ballots the person voted for as President, and in distinct ballots the person voted for as Vice President, and they shall make distinct lists of all persons voted for as President, and of all persons voted for as Vice President and of the number of votes for each, which lists they shall sign and certify, and transmit sealed to the seat of the government of the United States, directed to the President of the Senate;--the President of the Senate shall, in the presence of the Senate and House of Representatives, open all the certificates and the votes shall then be counted;--The person having the greatest number of votes for President, shall be the President, if such number be a majority of the whole number of Electors appointed; and if no person have such majority, then from the persons having the highest numbers not exceeding three on the list of those voted for as President, the House of Representatives shall choose immediately, by ballot, the President. But in choosing the President, the votes shall be taken by states, the representation from each state having one vote; a quorum for this purpose shall consist of a member or members from two-thirds of the states, and a majority of all the states shall be necessary to a choice [And if the House of Representatives shall not choose a President whenever the right of choice shall devolve upon them, before the fourth day of March next following, then the Vice President shall act as President, as in the case of the death or other constitutional disability of the President.][67] The person having the greatest number of votes as Vice President, shall be the Vice President, if such number be a majority of the whole number of Electors appointed, and if no person have a majority, then from the two highest numbers on the list, the Senate shall choose the Vice President; a quorum for the purpose shall consist of two-thirds of the whole number of Senators, and a majority of the whole number shall be necessary to a choice. But no person constitutionally ineligible to the office of President shall be eligible to that of Vice President of the United States.

The **12th Amendment** came about because of a flaw in the 1800 Presidential election process. Prior to this amendment, the President was chosen by

---

[67] This clause was superseded by Section Three of the Twentieth Amendment

garnering the most votes from the electors. In the event this proved to be more than one candidate, the House of Representatives would choose the President. The one with the second largest number of votes would be the Vice President. This became a problem when the electoral college voted along party lines. Serious issues of contention arose because the Vice President had been a defeated electoral opponent in the Presidential election, and this kept both leaders from effectively working together. The Twelfth Amendment allowed for the President and Vice President to be elected as a ticket, eliminating this contention. A majority of electoral votes is still required for the election of the President and Vice President. However, if no candidate has a majority, the House of Representatives (which is under the strict quorum requirements of Article II), will choose a President. The difference in the Twelfth Amendment is that the Senate chooses the Vice President if there is no candidate receiving a majority of electoral votes. Their choice is limited by those with the two highest numbers of electoral votes. The Senate is bound by a quorum requirement of a two-thirds vote. Another stipulation was entered to prevent the House from being deadlocked and the nation from being without a leader. The House must make this choice by March 4.

Amendment 13 – Slavery Abolished.
Passed in Congress 1/31/1865. Ratified 12/6/1865.

Section 1. Neither slavery nor involuntary servitude, except as a punishment for crime whereof the party shall have been duly convicted, shall exist within the United States, or any place subject to their jurisdiction.

Section 2. Congress shall have power to enforce this article by appropriate legislation.

The **13th Amendment** had its roots in President Lincoln's Emancipation Proclamation. It was proposed in 1849 that slaves be freed gradually. This proposal did not receive support. In 1862 President Lincoln issued a decree that unless rebellious states returned to the Union by January 1, freedom would be granted to all slaves in those states. No confederate state accepted the offer.

The Emancipation Proclamation did not free all the slaves, only those residing in confederate states. This proclamation allowed black soldiers to fight for the Union. This Amendment was introduced several times, but was finally passed toward the end of the Civil War before the Confederate States returned to the Union. It passed in the Senate in 1864, but not by the House. Lincoln pushed for this passage. When this was added to the Republican Party's platform, the House finally passed the bill in January of 1865, almost a year after the Senate had passed the bill.

Amendment 14 – Citizenship Rights.
Passed in Congress 6/13/1866. Ratified 7/9/1868.

Section 1. *All persons born or naturalized in the United States, and subject to the jurisdiction thereof, are citizens of the United States and of the State wherein they reside. No State shall make or enforce any law which shall abridge the privileges or immunities of citizens of the United States; nor shall any State deprive any person of life, liberty, or property, without due process of law; nor deny to any person within its jurisdiction the equal protection of the laws.*

Section 1 of the **14th Amendment** defines citizenship, and offers protection of citizens' civil rights from encroachment and violation by any person, organization or any state. The primary intention of this section was to make former slaves citizens and to protect them from any illegal action by the states. It also prohibits states from interfering with the immunities of citizens of the United States.

Section 2. *Representatives shall be apportioned among the several States according to their respective numbers, counting the whole number of persons in each State, excluding Indians not taxed. But when the right to vote at any election for the choice of electors for President and Vice President of the United States, Representatives in Congress, the Executive and Judicial officers of a State, or the members of the Legislature thereof, is denied to any of the male inhabitants of such State, being twenty-one years of age, and citizens of the United States, or in any way abridged, except for participation in rebellion, or other crime, the basis of representation therein shall be reduced in the proportion which the number of such male citizens shall bear to the whole number of male citizens twenty-one years of age in such State.*

Section 2 outlines the rules for allocating the correct proportion of Representatives to the Congress for each state. Primarily, this is done through a census of all the residents for a given state. Adding representatives to those states allowed an increase in size and a reduction in apportionments for those with a decrease. Also, one of the stipulations included in this amendment would cause the number of representatives to be reduced if the state wrongfully denied a person's right to vote. This caused an overriding of the provisions found in Article I, Section 2, Clause 3 of the Constitution, which did not count slaves as a whole person, but as three-fifths of a person. This was done primarily because of the allotment of seats in the House of Representatives and the Electoral College. The age of 21 was changed to 18 by the 26th Amendment.

Section 3. *No person shall be a Senator or Representative in Congress, or elector of President and Vice President, or hold any office, civil or military, under* *the United States, or under any State, who, having previously taken an oath, as a member of Congress, or as an officer of the United States, or as a member of any State legislature, or as an executive or judicial officer of any State, to support the Constitution of the United States, shall have engaged in insurrection or rebellion against the same, or given aid or comfort to the enemies thereof. But Congress may by a vote of two-thirds of each House, remove such disability.*

Section 3 was written after the Civil War. The main objective was to prevent the election or appointment of anyone to a federal or state office who had held any office in public service and then engaged in any type of insurrection, rebellion or treason. Those proposing this amendment allowed an "out" for the former members of the Confederacy who took part in the Civil War. They required a two-thirds vote by each House of the Congress to override this limitation. This did not exact punishment, because many of the Southerners had committed this infraction before it became a law. In fact, Article I, Section 9, of the U.S. Constitution states that all ex-post-facto (after the fact) laws are forbidden. As an example; in 1975 both houses in Congress fully restored Robert E. Lee's citizenship and it was done retroactively back to June 13, 1865. In 1978, both houses of Congress by a two-thirds majority vote, posthumously removed the service ban from Jefferson Davis.

Section 4. *The validity of the public debt of the United States, authorized by law, including debts incurred for payment of pensions and bounties for services in suppressing insurrection or rebellion, shall not be questioned. But neither the United States nor any State shall assume or pay any debt or obligation incurred in aid of insurrection or rebellion against the United States, or any claim for the loss or emancipation of any slave; but all such debts, obligations and claims shall be held illegal and void.*

Section 4 reveals the state of mind of those proposing this amendment. It states clearly that neither the United States nor any state of the Union may pay damages to slaveholders for their loss of slaves or any debts that occurred during the Civil War. As an example; several English and French banks loaned money to the South during the war, and wanted to be paid back by the Union. Under this section, the United States could not be sued for the debts of the South.

Section 5. *The Congress shall have power to enforce, by appropriate legislation, the provisions of this article.*

Section 5, the final section of this amendment, gave Congress the power to reinforce this newest section of the Constitution. The most important provisions of this amendment were to give all people equal protection under the law. Congress was to insure that the laws of a state must treat each individual equally the same as anyone else in similar conditions or in similar circumstances.

Amendment 15 – Race No Bar to Vote, Passed in Congress 2/26/1869. Ratified 2/3/1870.

Section 1. *The right of citizens of the United States to vote shall not be denied or abridged by the United States or by any State on account of race, color, or previous condition of servitude.*

Section 2. *The Congress shall have power to enforce this article by appropriate legislation.*

Sections 1 and 2. The 15th **Amendment** stated that no male could be denied the right to vote regardless of race, national origin, or former position as a slave. Congress was to oversee and enforce this legislation.

Amendment 16 – Status of Income Tax Clarified. Passed in Congress 7/12/1909. Ratified 2/3/1913.

The Congress shall have power to lay and collect taxes on incomes, from whatever source derived, without apportionment among the several States, and without regard to any census or enumeration.

There has been much controversy over this amendment. Many felt (and still do) that this was unconstitutional. This amendment gives Congress the power to collect income taxes. However, it is interesting that when this was written, the leaders of this country were certain that income taxes would never rise above 17%.

Amendment 17 – Senators Elected by Popular Vote. Passed in Congress 5/13/1912. Ratified 4/8/1913.

The Senate of the United States shall be composed of two Senators from each State, elected by the people thereof, for six years; and each Senator shall have one vote. The electors in each State shall have the qualifications requisite for electors of the most numerous branch of the State legislatures.

When vacancies happen in the representation of any State in the Senate, the executive authority of such State shall issue writs of election to fill such vacancies: Provided, That the legislature of any State may empower the executive thereof to make temporary appointments until the people fill the vacancies by election as the legislature may direct.

This amendment shall not be so construed as to affect the election or term of any Senator chosen before it becomes valid as part of the Constitution.

The **17th Amendment** was passed by the Senate on June 12, 1911, and by the House of Representatives on May 13, 1912. It was ratified by the states on April 8, 1913. The purpose of this amendment was to change the way senators were elected. Passing this amendment changed Article I, section 3, Clauses 1 and 2 of the Constitution because it transferred Senator selection from each state's legislature to the people themselves. This allowed a vote for the candidate of their choice in an election. A contingency provision allowed the state's governor (with the authorization of that state's legislature) to appoint a senator in the event that there was a vacancy in the Senate. This appointment to the Senate seat would continue until a special "called" election, or a regular scheduled election could take place.

Amendment 18 – Liquor Abolished.
Passed in Congress 12/18/1917. Ratified 1/16/1919.
Repealed by Amendment 21, 12/5/1933.

[*Section 1. After one year from the ratification of this article the manufacture, sale, or transportation of intoxicating liquors within, the importation thereof into, or the exportation thereof from the United States and all territory subject to the jurisdiction thereof for beverage purposes is hereby prohibited.*

Section 2. The Congress and the several States shall have concurrent power to enforce this article by appropriate legislation.

Section 3. This article shall be inoperative unless it shall have been ratified as an amendment to the Constitution by the legislatures of the several States, as provided in the Constitution, within seven years from the date of the submission hereof to the States by the Congress.]

Sections 1, 2 and 3, The **18th Amendment,** disallowed the "manufacture, sale and transportation" of any type of alcoholic product. Due to pressure from the public, it was repealed by the 21st Amendment on December 5, 1933.

Amendment 19 – Women's Suffrage.
Passed in Congress 6/14/1919. Ratified 8/18/1920

The right of citizens of the United States to vote shall not be denied or abridged by the United States or by any State on account of sex.

Congress shall have power to enforce this article by appropriate legislation.

The **19th Amendment** gave women the right to vote. It clearly states that nothing can restrict the voting rights of women, and also gives Congress the power to enforce this amendment.

Amendment 20 – Presidential, Congressional Terms. Passed in Congress 3/2/1932. Ratified 1/23/1933.

Section 1. *The terms of the President and Vice President shall end at noon on the 20th day of January, and the terms of Senators and Representatives at noon on the 3d day of January, of the years in which such terms would have ended if this article had not been ratified; and the terms of their successors shall then begin.*

Section 1 sets the terms of the President and Vice President. The term of a former President would end at noon on the 20th day of January, while the terms of Senators and Representatives would end at noon on the 3rd day of January. The purpose of this amendment was to establish the beginning and the end of the terms of the President, Vice President, and Congress. It also dealt with different scenarios in which there was no President-elect.

Section 2. *The Congress shall assemble at least once in every year, and such meeting shall begin at noon on the 3rd day of January, unless they shall by law appoint a different day.*

Section 2 states that Congress must meet at least once each year, and the meeting would begin at noon on the 3rd day of January, unless another day was appointed by law.

Section 3. *If, at the time fixed for the beginning of the term of the President, the President-elect shall have died, the Vice President-elect shall become President. If a President shall not have been chosen before the time fixed for the beginning of his term, or if the President-elect shall have failed to qualify, then the Vice President-elect shall act as President until a President shall have qualified; and the Congress may by law provide for the case wherein neither a President-elect nor a Vice President-elect shall have qualified, declaring who shall then act as President, or the manner in which one who is to act shall be selected, and such person shall act accordingly until a President or Vice President shall have qualified.*

Section 3 described several different scenarios. Who would be President if a President died? The first scenario stated that if the President-elect died at the beginning of his term, the Vice President-elect would become President. The second scenario determined what would happen if the President had not been chosen before the time fixed for the beginning of his term, or what would happen if the President-elect failed to qualify for office? The Vice President-elect would act as President until a President would qualify. In the event that neither a President-elect nor a Vice President-elect would have qualified, Congress would then determine who would act as President, until a President or Vice President became qualified for office.

Section 4. The Congress may by law provide for the case of the death of any of the persons from whom the House of Representatives may choose a President whenever the right of choice shall have devolved upon them, and for the case of the death of any of the persons from whom the Senate may choose a Vice President whenever the right of choice shall have devolved upon them.

Section 4 establishes that if a President or Vice President were to die in office, the House of Representatives would choose a President when the right of choice was transferred to them. The Senate also would choose a Vice President when the "right of choice" was transferred to them.

Section 5. Sections 1 and 2 shall take effect on the 15th day of October following the ratification of this article.

Section 5 states that Sections 1 and 2 would take effect on the 15th day of October following this ratification of this amendment.

Section 6. This article shall be inoperative unless it shall have been ratified as an amendment to the Constitution by the legislatures of three-fourths of the several States within seven years from the date of its submission.

Section 6 declares this amendment inoperative unless it is ratified as an amendment to the Constitution by the legislatures of three-fourths of the several States within seven years from the date of its proposal.

Amendment 21 – Amendment 18 Prohibition Repealed Passed in Congress 2/20/33. Ratified 12/5/1933

Section 1. The eighteenth article of amendment to the Constitution of the United States is hereby repealed.

Section 2. The transportation or importation into any State, Territory, or possession of the United States for delivery or use therein of intoxicating liquors, in violation of the laws thereof, is hereby prohibited.

Section 3. The article shall be inoperative unless it shall have been ratified as an amendment to the Constitution by conventions in the several States, as provided in the Constitution, within seven years from the date of the submission hereof to the States by the Congress.

Sections 1, 2 and 3. The 18th Amendment brought a decrease in consumption of intoxicating liquors dropping from two and one-half gallons in 1915 to less than one gallon per person per year. However, because the consumption of intoxicating liquors was not totally eliminated by this amendment, some felt it revealed a flaw in the amendment. As organized crime became more involved in the manufacture and distribution of alcohol, people became disenchanted with the 18th Amendment and called for a repeal. By the time of the Great Depression, a movement had gathered strength and actively sought to repeal the 18th Amendment. Many supporters of the movement felt that this amendment challenged Americans' personal liberty. Finally, 20 years after it became an amendment, the 21st Amendment was passed by Congress on February 20,1933, and ratified by the states' conventions on December 5,1933. This marked the first time in the history of America that an amendment had ever been repealed by another amendment.

Amendment 22 – Presidential Term Limits. Passed in Congress 3/21/47. Ratified 2/27/1951.

Section 1. No person shall be elected to the office of the President more than twice, and no person who has held the office of President, or acted as President, for more than two years of a term to which some other person was elected President shall be elected to the office of the President more than once. But this Article shall not apply to any person holding the office of President, when this Article was proposed by the Congress, and shall not prevent any person who may be holding the office of President, or acting as President, during the term within which this Article becomes operative from holding the office of President or acting as President during the remainder of such term.

Section 2. This article shall be inoperative unless it shall have been ratified as an amendment to the Constitution by the legislatures of three-fourths of the several States within seven years from the date of its submission to the States by the Congress.

Sections 1 and 2. Amendment 22 sought to limit the terms of the Presidency. There had been no limit to the number of times a President could be elected to office. President George Washington might have been in office longer, but he said that two terms were sufficient for him. Franklin D. Roosevelt was elected to office four times, and he died in office during his fourth term. This amendment sought to limit the number of times a President can be elected to office to two terms.

Amendment 23 – Presidential Vote for District of Columbia. Passed in Congress 6/17/60. Ratified 3/29/1961.

Section 1. The District constituting the seat of Government of the United States shall appoint in such manner as the Congress may direct: A number of electors of President and Vice President equal to the whole number of Senators and Representatives in Congress to which the District would be entitled if it were a State, but in no event more than the least populous State; they shall be in addition to those appointed by the States, but they shall be considered, for the purposes of the election of President and Vice President, to be electors appointed by a State; and they shall meet in the District and perform such duties as provided by the twelfth article of amendment.

Section 2. The Congress shall have power to enforce this article by appropriate legislation.

Sections 1 and 2. Amendment 23 gives representational rights to Washington D.C. and also grants Congress the power to enforce this amendment. The District of Columbia would be the seat of government for the United States. It allows for an equal number of electors of President and Vice President equal to the whole number of Senators and Representatives in Congress to which the District would be granted if it were a State. The one restriction would be that the District would not have any more electors than the least populous state. These electors would serve primarily for the election of President and Vice President. They would meet in Washington D.C. and carry out the duties contained in the 12th article of amendment.

Amendment 24 – Poll Tax Barred.
Passed in Congress 8/27/1962. Ratified 1/23/1964.

Section 1. The right of citizens of the United States to vote in any primary or other election for President or Vice President, for electors for President or Vice President, or for Senator or Representative in Congress, shall not be denied or abridged by the United States or any State by reason of failure to pay any poll tax or other tax.

Section 2. The Congress shall have power to enforce this article by appropriate legislation.

Sections 1 and 2, Amendment 24 prohibits poll taxes and also gives Congress the power to enforce this amendment. Citizens of the United States are given the right to vote in any primary, or any election for the President or Vice President, or for the election of a Senator or Representative in Congress. This right would not be denied or altered by the United States or any State of the Union because a voting citizen failed to pay a poll tax or any other type of tax.

Amendment 25 – Presidential Disability and Succession.
Passed in Congress 7/6/1965. Ratified 2/10/1967.

Section 1. In case of the removal of the President from office or of his death or resignation, the Vice President shall become President.

Section 1 states that in the event a President is removed from office because of death or resignation, the Vice President would become the new President.

Section 2. Whenever there is a vacancy in the office of the Vice President, the President shall nominate a Vice President who shall take office upon confirmation by a majority vote of both Houses of Congress.

Section 2 states that if a vacancy occurs in the office of the Vice President, the President will nominate a Vice President. The nominated person must be approved by a majority vote of Congress. Once the vote has been secured, the nominee would assume the office of Vice President.

Section 3. Whenever the President transmits to the President pro tempore of the Senate and the Speaker of the House of Representatives his written declaration that he is unable to discharge the powers and duties of his office, and until he transmits to them a written declaration to the contrary, such powers and duties shall be discharged by the Vice President as Acting President.

Section 3 states that should the President declare he is unable to fulfill the responsibilities of the Presidency, he is to inform the President pro tempore of the Senate and the Speaker of the House of Representatives by a written resignation declaring that he is unable to fulfill the responsibilities of his office. The powers and duties shall then be transferred to the Vice President who then becomes the Acting President.

Section 4. Whenever the Vice President and a majority of either the principal officers of the executive departments or of such other body as Congress may by law provide, transmit to the President pro tempore of the Senate and the Speaker of the House of Representatives their written declaration that the President is unable to discharge the powers and duties of his office, the Vice President shall immediately assume the powers and duties of the office as Acting President.

Thereafter, when the President transmits to the President pro tempore of the Senate and the Speaker of the House of Representatives his written declaration that no inability exists, he shall resume the powers and duties of his office unless the Vice President and a majority of either the principal officers of the executive department or of such other body as Congress may by law provide, transmit within four days to the President pro tempore of the Senate and the Speaker of the House of Representatives their written declaration that the President is unable to discharge the powers and duties of his office. Thereupon Congress shall decide the issue, assembling within forty-eight hours for that purpose if not in session. If the Congress, within twenty-one days after receipt of the latter written declaration, or, if Congress is not in session, within twenty-one days after Congress is required to assemble, determines by two-thirds vote of both Houses that the President is unable to discharge the powers and duties of his office, the Vice President shall continue to discharge the same as Acting President; otherwise, the President shall resume the powers and duties of his office.

Section 4 states that when the Vice President and a majority of either the principal officers of the executive departments (or any other body that Congress may by law provide) transfer in writing to the President pro tempore of the Senate and the Speaker of the House of Representatives their own written declaration that the President is unable to fulfill his responsibilities and run his office, the Vice President will immediately assume the role and duties of the office as Acting President.

If the President declares in writing to the President pro tempore of the Senate and the Speaker of the House of Representatives that this inability no longer exists, he will resume the responsibilities of the office. However, if the Vice President and a majority of either the principal officers of the executive departments (or any other body that Congress may by law provide) state in writing within four days to the President pro tempore of the Senate and the Speaker of the House of Representatives with a written declaration that the President is unable to discharge the powers and duties of his office, then the Congress will make the final decision regarding this issue. Congress must meet within forty-eight hours to make that decision. If the Congress has not met within 21 days and the issue has not been resolved, a two-thirds vote will relieve the Vice President of his duties as Acting President and the President will resume his duties as the President of the United States.

Amendment 26 – Voting Age Set to 18 Years.
Passed in Congress 3/23/1971. Ratified 7/1/1971.

Section 1. The right of citizens of the United States, who are eighteen years of age or older, to vote shall not be denied or abridged by the United States or by any State on account of age.

Section 2. The Congress shall have power to enforce this article by appropriate legislation.

Sections 1 and 2, Amendment 26 grants American citizens who are at least 18 years of age the right to vote. This right is never to be altered or denied by any state. Congress is given the power to enforce this right.

Amendment 27 – Limiting Congressional Pay Increases.
Passed in Congress 9/25/1789. Ratified 5/7/1992.

No law, varying the compensation for the services of the Senators and Representatives, shall take effect, until an election of Representatives shall have intervened.

Amendment 27 states there will be no law changing the compensation of members of the Congress until the election of the Representatives has taken place.

In conclusion, The Constitution has changed, somewhat, through the amendments requiring agreement by different segments of society and the government. Changes in interpretation are common as time progresses, but only by having actual text added can a change be called a part of the Constitution. The majority of new amendments have granted new powers to Congress. Instead of restricting the rights of government, they have increased them. Nine of the last fourteen amendments have given new powers to the Congress. Another change is in the language of the amendments. The language may seem to indicate that the government will guarantee our rights, instead of allowing the Constitution to do it.

It is interesting to see the proposals our legislators bring forward to change the Constitution. Often these amendments reflect the interests of our nation and culture at a certain period in history. A proposed amendment may be mentioned in several sessions of Congress. Here are only a few of the amendments Congress recently proposed:

- Women to maintain their reproductive rights.

- The President and Congress must agree to a balanced budget, and over-spending is allowed only when there is a three-fifths vote of Congress.

- Prayer allowed at public meetings and ceremonies.

- The "Every Vote Counts" amendment allowing a direct election of the President and Vice President, abolishing the Electoral College.

- Allow the continued use of the word "God" in the Pledge of Allegiance and in the national motto.

As history continues to change the shape of our country, so will the Constitution continue to change. Our hope is that it will always be for the better, and our legislators will hold fast to the original intent of the Framers and that we trust a Sovereign God for guidance. May we continue to remember the price they paid for the freedom we enjoy.

"Blessed are those who keep my ways. Hear instruction and be wise, and do not disdain it." (Proverbs 8: 32-33)

Part III, Chapter VIII

INTERPRETATIONS AND POSITIONS

Many issues come before the Congress and Supreme Court each year, and each issue appears to be approached from a "left" or "right" position of Constitutional interpretation. Many of the issues are often decided on the "original intent" or "living document" approach to interpretation. In simple terms, this means the Courts interpret the law based on their view of the Constitution, whether it is a moral, rigid standard or a document that is evolving and subject to the standards of society.

Each time a new Supreme Court Justice appointee is considered, the issue of "original intent" versus a "living constitution" sparks lively debate. The issue of "original intent" and "living constitution" will not cease because most Americans view the Constitution as an extension of their worldview—one that upholds a strong moral compass by which they live and seek to be governed, while others who see truth as relative and subject to change based on the situation.

Some feel that the Constitution does not rest on fixed principles but must be changed according to the changing winds of time. This chapter addresses both viewpoints, examines the tenants of their beliefs, and attempts to determine what will happen if one position takes precedence over the other.

*The issue of "original intent"
and "living constitution" will not
cease because most Americans
view the Constitution as an
extension of their worldview —
one that upholds a strong moral
compass by which they live and
seek to be governed, while others
who see truth as relative
and subject to change based
on the situation.*

The "Living Constitution" View

During the 1940's nearly all jurists of the time were strong "originalists" and used the U.S. Constitution as the sole reference to interpret the law. Slowly through time it began to change. Soon more and more Justices were placed on the bench who did not hold to the Constitution as the final authority. The "living constitution" view became increasingly prevalent in the rulings of court cases.

The "living constitution" view was first mentioned in the 1927 book, *The Living Constitution* by Professor Harold McBain; but its origins have been credited to Oliver Wendell Holmes, Louis D. Brandeis and Woodrow Wilson. Holmes exhibited this view when he ruled on the 1920 *Missouri v. Holland* case. This is one of the first times the Justices considered some other source outside the Constitution to make a ruling. Holmes's explanation in his summary sentence was that the Framers could not have foreseen every conceivable situation, and that they expected jurists to rely on experience and not solely on the Constitution.

There are several points used by those in support of the "living constitution." view. The first deals with the pragmatic view that a document over two hundred years old is not a viable means to develop policy to legislate people today. They contend that the Framers of the Constitution indicated that they did not want their specific intentions to control interpretation and that no constitution could anticipate all the means the government might in the future use to govern the people. Thus, it becomes necessary for judges to consider changing cultural influences and fill in the gaps where appropriate.

The second point used is that the Constitution was written in such a broad way that it makes it viable for the changes our society faces. Regardless of which view is held, the view of a "living document" has continued to build until it has become a significant interpretation today. Some arguments hold that there are many ways to test the validity of a law, and the Constitution is just one of many sources and not the final standard for interpreting the law.

A third point used in support of the "living constitution" view is that there was not one official position held by the Framers, as they discussed and debated many issues. Even if there was one overriding issue that most of the Framers supported, how valid would it be two hundred years later? Along with this, others say the Framers did not want their writings and views of the Constitution to be the only means of interpreting the law. "Good intentions will always be pleaded for every assumption of authority. It is hardly too strong to say that the Constitution was made to guard the people against the dangers of good intentions. There are men of all ages who mean to govern well, but they mean to govern. They promise to be good masters, but they mean to be masters."[68]

A final point used in support of the "living constitution" view is that we cannot know the Framer's moral intent because of their conflicting views on slavery and the role of women. This last and most serious of the arguments states that most court cases are not determined solely by the Constitution.

For example, many scholars from the position of the "living constitution" view consider the Second Amendment to be outdated and no longer needed since we do not have a need for citizens to form a militia. They argue there is no reason for the average citizen to have a gun. Supporters of the "original intent" view believe this would strip Americans of their constitutional right to have a gun. Surprisingly, this is one case where the Supreme Court Justices voted in favor of the Second Amendment and supported the private citizen's right to own a gun in the *District of Columbia v. Heller* case.

Supporters of a "living constitution" view often quote from the Framers the statement, *Supporters of a living constitution strongly believe that the Framers felt their intentions were not to be the final authority.* Yet, they fail to recognize Edmund Randolph's statement in the Preamble of the Committee of Detail at

---

[68]   Daniel Webster; Raymond, Eric S. Quotes on Liberty – http://1ref.us/df

the Constitutional Convention, which says: *"In the draught of a fundamental constitution, two things deserve attention: to insert essential principles only lest the operations of government should be clogged by rendering those provisions permanent and unalterable which ought to be accommodated to times and events, and to use simple and precise language and general propositions according to the example of the constitutions of the several states."*[69]

A significant argument is that the Constitution must be considered a contract between the government and the people. If the terms of the contract were not correctly amended, how then is any of the contract valid and meaningful? What parts would be valid and meaningful and seen as worthwhile?

Judges who purport a "living constitution" view often search outside the Constitution into other countries' court cases to decide what the Constitution ought to mean, hereby, establishing a precedent. An example of this was the *Lawrence v. Texas* case that reached the Supreme Court in 2003. The jurists of the Supreme Court cited the European Court of Human Rights that gave certain rights to homosexuals. This was noted in Justice Anthony Kennedy's majority opinion.

Many believe that those who support the "living constitution" view are more apt to have political bias in their interpretation of the law that can cause more misuses of power yielded by the Jurists.

The "Original Intent" View

Up until the 1930's and 40's, there would have been little difference in the viewpoint of jurists since they looked upon the Constitution as the final standard for arbitrating law. As mentioned in the previous section, soon after the 1940's, many jurists started to question the validity of looking at the Constitution in its original intent.

The "original intent" view states that the Constitution is a document that defines the roles and responsibilities of the various branches of government as well as its limitations and restrictions. Since it is a "fixed" document, the roles of government cannot be changed or modified. Many believe if the "original intent" view were put back into place, there would be proper checks and balances between branches of government. Only through checks and balances can political issues be properly scrutinized and evaluated. They contend that "original intent" reduces the likelihood that unelected judges would seize the reins of power from elected representatives, and that the "original intent" view in the

---

[69]   The Founder's Constitution Preamble, Records of the Federal Convention. – http://1ref.us/dg. 1987 by The University of Chicago

long run better preserves the Court. Also, it is believed that if left to the people to amend the Constitution, it would promote serious debate about government and its limitations.

Some supporters of "original intent" view believe that if personal rights were violated or severely limited according to the Declaration of Independence, it would be the citizens' right to end that government. As the Declaration states, *"...all men are endowed by their Creator with certain unalienable rights, that among these are Life, Liberty, and the Pursuit of Happiness; that to secure these rights, governments are instituted among men, deriving their just powers from the consent of the governed; that whenever any form of government becomes destructive to these ends, it is the right of the people to alter it or abolish it and to institute a new government."*

One of the chief supporters of the "original intent" position was the late Supreme Court Justice Antonin Scalia. He believed there are laws with set meanings that transcend the changes in society. When one becomes a judge he has a tremendous responsibility to protect human rights and to determine what legally fits this country. Scalia spoke of the danger of a "living constitution" when he said, *"The philosophy of a living constitution – which means it doesn't mean what the people agreed to when they adopted it – is a very seductive theory. It is seductive because it empowers judges. It is seductive for law professors because it allows room for their imagination to run wild."*[70]

The "original intent" position surfaced during the hearings of Supreme Court nominee, Robert Bork. Bork held to the view that the Constitution should be interpreted to mean what the Framers held it to mean. He believed Justices were to deliver judgment on the court proceedings, not to legislate from the bench. He was outspoken on his views that judges should hold to neutral principles in interpreting the Constitution. Jurists should not make judgments based on personal feelings and leanings. Rather, decisions should be made by looking at the Constitution and interpreting it according to "original intent."

One of the key components in the arsenal of the "originalist" is research, books, pamphlets and essays of the time period to get a sense of what the Framers meant and how they interpreted the various sections of the Constitution. The "originalist" will research the law to determine the original intent of the document and to determine the thinking of both positions at the time the document was drafted. He will carefully scrutinize and attempt to understand each side of an argument. He might search the following:

---

[70]   Original Intent is Making a Comeback in U.S." November 25 – http://1ref.us/dh, Mooney, Kevin.

- English and Latin dictionaries and encyclopedias;

- Readings found in the schools of that day (could include Greco-Roman classics);

- Popular writings of the day which could include: pamphlets, historical works, and legal documents;

- Historical documents of the time which could include: public speeches, The Federalist Papers, and transcripts of state ratifying conventions; and,

- Legal resources from that period which could include: court case transcripts, legal dictionaries, legal digests, and English statutes.

Middle Ground Position

The "middle ground" approach seeks to blend the best parts of each of these opposing viewpoints to make precedents for the law. Some values are a constant in our society such as *Freedom of Speech* and the other freedoms afforded in the Bill of Rights. Yet, there are others who contend the Framers probably never intended that the burning of the American flag would be protected as free speech.

A compromise of both sides is not easy to achieve. Many of the "original intent" position feel that the courts often become judicial activists and override the will of the people. Protection is provided through Article V that clearly allows for an amendment process that would allow a public forum to address an issue and then vote to ratify the amendment.

Sources of Interpretation

Both sides seem to agree that there are five sources that have guided interpretation of the Constitution. They include:

1. The text and structure of the Constitution;

2. Intentions of those who drafted or voted to ratify the provision in question;

3. Prior precedents (usually judicial);

4. The social, political, and economic consequences of alternative interpretations; and,

5. Natural law.

There is general agreement that the first three sources are appropriate guides to interpretation, but there is considerable disagreement as to the relative weight that should be given to them when they point in different directions. The final two sources cause contention between the two views.

Many interpreters of the Constitution have suggested that the consequences of alternative interpretations are never relevant, even when all other considerations are evenly balanced. Natural law (higher law, God's law) is now only infrequently suggested as an interpretative guide, even though many of the Framers of the Constitution recognized it as a viable means for interpreting law.

Persons who favor heavy reliance on "originalist" sources (text and intentions) are commonly called "originalists." Persons who favor giving more substantial weighting to precedent, consequences, or natural law are called "non-originalists." In practice, disagreement between "originalists" and "non-originalists" often concerns whether to apply heightened judicial scrutiny to certain "fundamental rights" that are not explicitly protected in the text of the Constitution.

Terms Used in Reference to the Interpretations of the Constitution

- Textualist: An "originalist" gives primary weight to the text and structure of the Constitution. Textualists are often skeptical of the ability of judges to determine collective "intent."

- Intentionalist: An 'originalist" gives primary weight to the intention of the *Framers*, members of proposing bodies, and ratifiers.

- Pragmatist: A "non-originalist" gives substantial weight to judicial precedent or the consequences of alternative interpretations, so as to sometimes favor a decision "wrong" on "originalist" terms because it promotes stability or in some other way promotes public good.

- Natural Law Theorist: Believes that a higher moral law ought to triumph in consistent positive law.

Significant Concerns

Many proponents of the "living constitution" view argue that judges are given leeway to interpret law differently than they did one hundred or even fifty years ago. They further espouse that our justices' hands have been tied and that judicial restraint is imposed upon them by defining the Constitution literally and using the Constitution solely to interpret legal matters.

Whereas supporters of the "original intent" view see the danger of judicial activism, which is when Justices interpret legal matters using broad interpretations of the Constitution based on the societal norms or by using other documents aside from the Constitution. Many fear that such judicial activism provides opportunities for jurists to make new laws through their rulings. This is in direct opposition to the checks and balances set up in the Constitution. When this occurs, Americans have no voice in legislative matters.

Some historians believe that both viewpoints allow for changes necessary to make the Constitution relevant in our times. The major difference is not whether the document should change and develop through time, but rather who decides what change is made and how that change will happen. The Constitution itself allows for these changes under Article V, which states, "*The Congress, whenever two-thirds of both Houses shall deem it necessary, shall propose amendments to this Constitution, or, on the Application of the Legislatures of two-thirds of several States, shall call a Convention for proposing Amendments…*"

The polarization of the "living constitution" (the Left) v. "original intent" (the Right) was observed in the 2000 Presidential debates between nominees George W. Bush and Al Gore. Bush viewed the Supreme Court Justices as those *"who should hold the Constitution sacred"* because of their lifetime commitment on the bench. He also said, *"I believe judges ought not to take the part of the legislative branch of Government."*[71] Gore, on the other hand, endorsed the "living constitution" view and stated, *"And in my view, the Constitution ought to be interpreted as a document that grows with our country and our history."*[72] What he did not say is how it should grow or change.

Numerous examples of both judicial activism and restraint occur. It behooves the American public to be discerning in electing officials who will stand true to the Constitution. Although every elected official must take the Oath of Office and agree to support the Constitution, some have ignored the responsibility, and in some cases violated the Oath.

---

[71] Unofficial Debate Transcript of the First Gore-Bush Presidential debate, October 3, 2000. – http://1ref.us/di

[72] Commission on Presidential Debates – http://1ref.us/di

Although every elected official must take the Oath of Office and agree to support the Constitution, some have ignored the responsibility, and in some cases violated the Oath.

What's Right, What's Left?

The terms "right" and "left" first came into use during the 1789 French Revolution. It referred to the seating arrangement of the French National Assembly with those who sat on the left in favor of radical changes of the Revolution.[73] These were the commoners who were known to be more in favor of change. On the right in the seating arrangement were those who were considered "upper class" and the Church. They were more inclined to maintain the status quo. The word "left" came into more common usage after the restoration of the French Monarchy and was used to describe revolutionary movements that included socialism, anarchism and communism.[74] Although the terms "right" and "left" were in usage in other nations around the world in definition of political positions, in the United States it was not until after the Reconstruction Period that the term "left" was used to describe those who supported labor unions, the civil rights movements and anti-war demonstrations.

Today, "right" and "left" are terms generally used to classify political positions and ideologies with Republicans on the right and Democrats on the left. They are often presented as polar opposites, but an individual may take a "left" position on one issue and a "right" position on another. The idea that the "right" is aligned with conservatism and "left" with liberalism has been with us for many years. One should be aware that the political beliefs of many people are a continuum of "right" and "left." The following chart shows how the two positions differ.

---

[73]　Left-right Politics – http://1ref.us/dj
[74]　Left-right Politics – http://1ref.us/dj

Left	Right
Government should be working towards a society that produces equal results for everyone.	Less government control. Less interference in the lives of individuals. Provide equal opportunity for everyone.
Government should provide free healthcare, education and social welfare.	Lower taxes. Healthcare, education and social welfare should be the responsibility of the individual.
Taxation should be high and certain businesses should be under government ownership for profits to pay for benefits.	No government ownership of businesses. Support a free market with profits giving business owners incentive to produce.
Support gay marriage, abortion, and have strong views on conservation and the environment.	Conservative on social issues. Oppose gay marriage, abortion, and businesses be allowed to perform oil exploration or mining, subject to proper controls.
Believe in equal outcomes. Includes affirmative action and cultural rights.	Believe in equal opportunity. Equal treatment for all by law and government, equal pay for equal work and civil and political rights.
Big government	Small government
Associated with more liberal values. Believe government is more important than the individual.	Associated with more conservative values. Believe individual is more important than government.
Support "Living Constitution" interpretation.	Support "Original Intent" interpretation.

Political Correctness, What Does it Mean?

Political correctness is a term used today to refer to language, ideas, and policies that are believed to be discriminatory against politically, socially or economically disadvantaged groups. These groups include those defined by race, religion, sexual orientation or ethnicity. The term was first known to be used in the early 20th century by Communists and Socialists to refer to the "party line" which provided for "correct" positions on many matters of politics. Later in the 20th century it was used to condemn sexist or racist conduct. In the1990's, the term was applied to all attempts to promote multiculturalism and to identify political positions. This became an attempt to change social reality by changing language and making language more gender-neutral. In many instances the term is used as a label for policies supporting multiculturalism and revising curricula to influence thinking and encourage support for current liberal policies.

Progressivism, Socialism, Communism, Liberals

Progressivism

The word or label "progressive" has come into more common use and causes confusion of the meanings of both "socialism" and "progressivism." Although there are many similarities, there are basic differences. Although, through time new concepts may have developed but progressivism is actually a political philosophy that has its roots as a political movement that began in the late 19th century. President Theodore Roosevelt is said to have advanced the progressive concept. Wisconsin's Robert La Follette is said to have been a great champion of the concept as well.[75]

Progressivism seeks to raise the standard of living of the majority in order to achieve social change. They seek both economic and political equality for all members of society as do socialists but their approaches differ. A significant approach of progressives is to convince the poor of their plight, creating a resentment or jealousy of the rich, thus influencing a vote bringing progressives into power for societal change. Progressives accept capitalism but want capitalism to grow under a government regulated business environment. As compared to the role and intent of the Founders, the Founders believed in a limited role of government in the lives of the citizens, whereas the "progressive" concept favors a much more active role for the government in all areas of society.

Socialism

Socialism, by some, is considered to be the mother of progressivism. It is generally understood to be an economic system that seeks to achieve equality among members of society and that all resources should be owned by the people and like communism, controlled by a central organization. Individuals have access to basic articles of consumption, and industry is regulated to benefit society as a whole. The state meets human needs and economic demands through secular means with products that are socially owned.

The people have a role in deciding how the economy should work through communes or elected councils. Socialism would abolish capitalism, as in their

---

[75]   The Progressive Presidents-AP US. History Topic Outlines – http://1ref.us/dk

view, it exploits the working class. The abolishment of capitalism could come through either a popular vote, strikes, uprisings, or revolution.

Communism

Communism, very much like Socialism, is also an economic system that not only seeks equality among members of society but holds a political ideology that advocates a classless society that rejects religion. It holds that the resources of society should be collectively owned by the people but controlled by a central organization. It is strictly a one party system striving for equality allowing no ownership of private property. Capitalism is distrusted and free markets are rejected. The government owns all means of production and is responsible for the distribution of resources.

Liberalism

Liberals appear to be more concerned over a wide range of issues involving civil rights, sexual equality, public education, health reform, international peace, and the environment; unlike progressives who tend to be more oriented towards economic issues, and see financial inequality as the greatest threat to our nation. Not all liberals are progressives nor are all progressives liberal. It can be said, for the most part, that in the political arena, they both imply opposition to conservatism. Liberalism appears to have grown out of progressivism, embracing a stronger role of government in the lives of its citizens.

Author's note: The above brief descriptions are intended only to highlight the basic concepts of their philosophies, their likenesses and their differences.

LANDMARK COURT CASES THAT AFFECTED THE CONSTITUTION

"The Constitution, on this hypothesis, is a mere thing of wax in the hands of the Judiciary, which they may twist and shape into any form as they please."
Thomas Jefferson

The Framers established the U.S. Supreme Court as the highest court in the land. It arbitrates court cases involving individuals, states and even the federal government. Over the years, there has been a shift in the way the Constitution has been interpreted from a moral standard to a document that changes to meet the morays of a society. However, in a stirring message given by Dr. Robert Jeffress, pastor of the First Baptist Church of Dallas, Texas, he states that over the last fifty years our Supreme Court has made four explosive decisions that have so weakened the moral and spiritual structure and foundation of our country that our inevitable collapse is certain.

Over the last fifty years our Supreme Court has made four explosive decisions that have so weakened the moral and spiritual structure and foundation of our country that our inevitable collapse is certain.

These four decisions have changed the direction of our country more than any congressional mandate and more than any executive order from the President of the United States. They are: *Engle v. Itale (1962), Stone v. Graham (1980), Roe v. Wade (1973), and Lawrence v. Garner (2003).*

A Landmark case is a court case that is given special review because it has historical and legal significance. Landmark cases have a lasting effect on the application of a certain previously held law. The following cases have affected society and will continue to influence America's future for better or for worse. Many of the cases dealt with civil rights; but several cases have been challenges to the amendments, especially the First Amendment.

Marbury v. Madison (1803)

One of the earliest cases that tested the Constitution was Marbury v. Madison. This was a Landmark case because it tested the role and duties of the Supreme Court. James Madison, a Democratic Republican, strongly stressed states' rights because he did not trust a strong federal Government. John Adams had been the previous President and before he left office, he made several midnight appointments. One was to William Marbury as Justice of the Peace in the District of Columbia. However, before Marbury was given his governmental commission, Madison took over as President. He feared there were too many Federalists in government positions, and he refused to deliver Adam's commission to Marbury.

Marbury was incensed and took Madison to court so the court would issue the Writ of Mandamus. The Writ of Mandamus allows the judiciary to step in and, in a sense, force the reluctant official to carry out the duty entrusted to him. Marbury and his lawyers argued that the Court had the power to do this under the Judiciary Act. The lawyers of Marbury v. Madison presented their respective cases to a weak court that was headed by Chief Justice John Marshall. President John Adams had appointed Marshall, who was known as a Federalist.

After a few weeks of struggling to come to a decision, Chief Justice Marshall of the Supreme Court delivered this decision: First, he stated that Marbury had been denied his right to his commission and that Madison should have delivered the commission. Then came the big bombshell of surprise - the Supreme Court ruled the Judiciary Act was in conflict with the Constitution.

The Constitution in Article III gives the Supreme Court the power to issue writs, but only under special circumstances in cases involving ambassadors and foreign consuls, meaning that all other citizens would have to go to a lower court for a Writ of Mandamus. This made Marbury's case invalid because

Marshall said that this writ could only be issued in special cases involving ambassadors and foreign consuls. Ordinary citizens had to take their cases to a lower court; this meant that Marbury lost because, as an ordinary citizen, he was in the wrong court.

This also made the Judiciary Act of 1789 unworkable because then any citizen could appeal to the Supreme Court for a writ, and this was a power the Constitution did not give the Supreme Court. Marshall instituted the belief that when the acts of Congress conflict with the Constitution, the Constitution outranked them and must be followed. This made the Judiciary Act of 1789 invalid, which caused Marbury's case to be thrown out.

This court case still affects us today because it gives the Supreme Court power to declare a law passed by Congress as unconstitutional. In other words, the Supreme Court has the final word on any act of Congress. Any act of Congress that is being studied by the Supreme Court is said to be under "judicial review." Judicial review had been used to keep the government out of areas where it has no authority, such as citizens' rights.

McCulloch v. Maryland (1819)

On April 8, 1816, Congress passed an act entitled "Incorporate Subscribers to the Banks of the United States."[76] This allowed the incorporation of the Second Bank of America that had been established in Philadelphia, Pennsylvania. When the Second Bank of America decided to open a branch in Baltimore, the state of Maryland decided since the bank had not been chartered by the state of Maryland, they were subject to taxation.

James McCulloch, head of the Baltimore branch of the Second Bank of America, decided to ignore Maryland's mandate and refused to pay the tax. Maryland argued their case before the Maryland State of Appeals on the grounds that the Constitution does not expressly say that Congress has the power to incorporate the Bank. Thus, the incorporation would be invalid and the State would have a right to impose the tax. The Maryland Court of Appeals voted in favor of Maryland. The lawyers for McCulloch appealed their case to the Supreme Court. After some deliberation, the Supreme Court voted in favor of James McCulloch and the Second Bank of America. Chief Justice Marshall gave these three reasons for the Court's decision.

- First, Marshall stated that since the Constitution was a social agreement between the people of the United States and the Federal Govern-

[76] Williams, Tavi and Nonica Castillo. McCulloch v. Maryland Judicidal Case. – http://1ref.us/dl

ment, the Federal Government was above the State Government by the consent of the people. Thus, the Federal Government could override anything that the State would do.

- Secondly, even though the Constitution gave Congress certain explicit powers, it also implied certain rules that Congress must follow. Although the word "bank" does not occur in the Constitution, it does imply certain powers of Congress expressed under the Taxing and Spending clause. Thus, this implied power to charter a bank was perfectly permissible to Congress.

- Thirdly, the Supreme Court's decision to invoke the "Necessary and Proper" clause gave Congress the freedom to act as long as they were not in violation of the Constitution.

The Supreme Court rejected Maryland's argument that "necessary" involved doing only what was necessary in carrying out the explicitly stated duties of the Constitution. The Court held that for these reasons, the word necessary in the Necessary and Proper clause does not refer to the only way of doing something, but rather applies to various procedures for implementing all constitutionally established powers. Chief Justice John Marshall said in his ruling, *"Let the end be legitimate, let it be within the scope of the Constitution, and all means which are appropriate, which are plainly adapted to that end, which are not prohibited, but consist with the letter and spirit of the Constitution...."*[77] Inasmuch as Congress had the power to charter a bank, Maryland did not have the right to impose a tax on a nationally chartered bank. Thus, this case established the supremacy of the federal Government over the rights of the States. Finally, it firmly established that Congress has implied powers for carrying out what the Constitution explicitly says for creating and maintaining a strong central government.

Scott v. Sanford (1857)

This was one of the most controversial Supreme Court decisions to date and involved the freedom of a slave. Dred Scott was a slave to a United States surgeon, John Emerson. Due to his various military assignments, the surgeon took his family and Scott to Illinois and later to what is now Minnesota. Both Illinois and the Minnesota territories were considered "free" states because they had laws against slavery.

---

[77]   McCulloch v. Maryland – http://1ref.us/dm

While Scott was in Illinois he was encouraged by both black and white abolitionists to sue for his freedom on the grounds that his residence in Illinois (a free state) made him a free man. Scott did not take his master to court at this time. Soon after this the army gave John Emerson orders to return to Missouri, a slave state. He later left the army and took his family and slaves to Iowa territory in 1843. At the death of John Emerson, his wife Irene, inherited the entire estate including the slaves. She and her family moved back to Missouri (a slave state) taking the slaves with them.

Dred Scott and his wife Harriet filed suit against Irene Emerson, their owner. At this time Missouri had a law stipulating that if a slave was taken out of the state to a free state or territory, the slave would be emancipated. Scott sued for his freedom since he had lived on free soil.

It took eleven years for the case to work through the court. In March of 1857, the Supreme Court denied his freedom. The vote was not even close (7 to 2) voting against Dred Scott. Chief Justice Roger B. Taney wrote the majority opinion. Chief Justice Taney was a former slave owner in Maryland and also a staunch supporter of slavery and believed he was protecting the South from Northern aggression. What he did not know was that this decision would be a turning point in American history and would lead to the bloodiest war of its time.

Chief Justice Taney declared that black people had never been and were not citizens of the United States. The Supreme Court decision stated that black people were the property of their slave owners and thus were not entitled to the same rights as their masters. With this ruling, it made the Missouri Compromise of 1820 illegal and slavery was allowed in all American states and territories. This ruling galvanized the two forces that were at odds with each other.

President Abraham Lincoln gave his *House Divided* speech in the Republican Convention on June 16, 1858. Lincoln believed that the Dred Scott decision was a part of a Democratic conspiracy that would make slavery legal in all states. He wanted to rally the people and remind them of the importance of unity in times of adversity. Lincoln was at the forefront of this battle and would ultimately be the President who emancipated the slaves.

Lincoln believed that the Dred Scott decision was a part of a Democratic conspiracy that would make slavery legal in all states. He wanted to rally the people and remind them of the importance of unity in times of adversity.

This decision brought major changes to this country. The period between 1857 and the outbreak of the war in 1861 was a time of desperation among the northern black leadership. Those in the northern black movement were struggling to know how to respond to this decision. They were unsure how to define who they were and what their future would be. They were divided in whether they should join the Republican Party, organize their own party or even remain in America. The Dred Scott case was the battle cry for freedom of the black people and was one of the major events leading to the Civil War. It did not just affect that period of time in America's history, but affected future relations between white and black America.

Plessy v. Ferguson (1896)

A severe period of reconstruction followed the years of the Civil War and split America into factions again over the way African American citizens were treated. After the Civil War, great strides were made in the way African Americans lived. Literacy rates among black people soared from three percent to fifty percent in thirty years, even though education facilities were hardly adequate. Family life was being restored since they were no longer separated by the specter of slavery. People like Booker T. Washington showed African Americans how education should be a necessity and priority for the children of these former slaves.

Despite these advances, there was still much ground to gain. This was in part because of the segregation of races in certain places in the South. After the Compromise of 1877, the Southern states passed Jim Crow laws. Jim Crow laws made it possible for the South to further segregate blacks from whites. In 1890, Louisiana passed Act 111 that stated blacks could not be in the same railcars as whites.

The Committee of Citizens decided to test those laws of segregation when they had Homer Plessy get on a railcar that was for whites only. Plessy was actually seven-eighths white and one-eighth black. However, according to Louisiana law, this meant that Plessy was black, despite the fact that he was very light-skinned. Plessy bought a first class ticket for a railcar for whites. When the authorities discovered Plessy on the railcar, they asked him to leave and go to the segregated car for blacks. Plessy refused, and the authorities forcefully took Plessy off the railcar. When Plessy was expelled, the police were waiting to arrest him.

This was a test case against segregation. The Committee of Citizens sought the assistance of Albion W. Tourgée, a radical Republican jurist who agreed to be lead counsel for Plessy and work on the case pro bono. This case was based on the grounds that Plessy's constitutional rights, which were based primarily on the Thirteenth and Fourteenth Amendments, had been violated.

Plessy's lawyers took the case to the Louisiana Supreme Court where Judge John Howard Ferguson ruled that Louisiana was allowed to regulate the railroad companies as long as they operated within State boundaries. Frustrated by what they considered a lack of justice in Louisiana, Plessy's lawyers appealed their case to the United States' Supreme Court. The Supreme Court passed down a vote of seven to one against Plessy. (Justice David Brewer refused to vote on this issue). The Court rejected the arguments of Plessy since Louisiana's Act 111 did not violate the Fourteenth Amendment. The Supreme Court rejected the idea that the separate railcars implied any inferiority to any black person, so there was no violation of the Fourteenth Amendment.

Justice Henry Brown declared in his majority opinion that *The Separate Car Act* does not conflict with the Thirteenth Amendment, which abolished slavery and is *"too clear for argument."*[78] Justice Marshall Harlan voted against the ruling. It was surprising that he would be the one who wrote the dissent because he came from a slave-holding family. In his dissent, he wrote, *"In the eye of the law, there is in this country no superior, dominant, ruling class of citizens. There is no caste here. Our Constitution is colorblind, and neither knows*

---

[78]   After the Civil War: Plessy v. Ferguson – http://1ref.us/dn Last modified: Fri Sep 17, 1999

nor tolerates classes among citizens. In respect of civil rights, all citizens are equal before the law." [79]

A positive result was seen one hundred years later when Keith Plessy and Phoebe Ferguson, both descendants from the sides of the Plessy v. Ferguson case, came together and created the Plessy and Ferguson Foundation for Education, Preservation and Outreach. The mission of this foundation was for developing new and exciting ways to teach the history of the civil rights movement using art, film or public programs. The objective of this foundation was to sponsor programs that developed understanding of this historic case and how it affected America.

In February 2009, the families of Plessy and Ferguson gathered to see a historical marker on the spot where Homer Plessy was expelled from the train and then arrested. So now, the descendants no longer live in the heritage of past racism and segregation, but live for the present education of today's students about the civil rights struggle and the restoration between white and black people.

Schenck v. the United States (1919)

Does a person's right to free speech include words of insubordination against the federal government? When does free speech stop and a threat to national security begin? As the Secretary of the Socialist Party, Schenck was responsible for the printing and distributing of notices that encouraged men not to sign up for the draft. He had distributed fifteen thousand notices and encouraged men to fulfill their duty by taking a stand against the draft. His chief reason for this was that the draft was illegal and was a part of a wicked plan of an evil capitalistic society. The police charged Schenck with conspiracy under the *Espionage Act* which stated that the draft was not to be obstructed, and more importantly, no one should keep soldiers from their duty of being loyal and obedient to their military leaders and to the government. The police based their charges on the flyers that Schenck distributed.

Schenck's lawyers argued that the *Espionage Act* was not constitutional because it violated Schenck's first amendment rights, which was that he had a right to speak against the Government and express his opinions. Schenck's case worked its way through the federal courts until it reached the Supreme Court. It was determined that Schenck could not speak his mind when it posed a threat to national security. Justice Oliver Wendell Holmes, Jr. wrote that during times

---

[79]   Charles Thompson, "Plessy v. Fergusson: Harlan's Great Dissent," Louis D. Brandeis School of Law Library, accessed September 20, 2010 – http://1ref.us/do.

of war there was a different standard because what might be said in wartime could threaten national security. What may have been permitted and tolerated in peacetime would not be allowed in wartime and was subject to punishment. Holmes coined the phrase *"clear and present danger"* when it came to testing whether or not free speech crossed the line into treason. The Supreme Court unanimously voted against Schenck.

Still today there is no clear answer to the question – when does an action or speech cross the line into what is a *clear and present danger?* Each court decision is based on what appears to be a danger at that time. Often the line between free speech and national security is blurred. This again reminds us of the need for wise and discerning Justices who will leave their personal agendas at the door and rule in the nation's best interest.

Brown v. Board of Education of Topeka, Kansas (1954)

Plessy v. Fergusson was the precursor to this case and left African-Americans wanting more from their government in general and from the court system in particular. *Brown v. Board of Education* was specifically about a man who wanted more for his child. To Oliver Brown "separate but equal" was a cruel hoax that did not exist except in legal documents. He wanted more for his third daughter when she enrolled in his neighborhood school.

The National Association for the Advancement of Colored People (NAACP) began in 1908 with the stated mission of bringing equal rights to African American people. The legal team of the NAACP sought to challenge the "separate but equal" standard as set forth in *Plessy v. Ferguson.* The NAACP recruited over two hundred plaintiffs in five states to sue and challenge various school systems and even boards of education. The plaintiffs worked their way through the court system but failed to win favorable verdicts from the District Courts. They appealed to the U.S. Supreme Court. The NAACP then decided that the plaintiffs from Delaware, Kansas, Virginia, South Carolina and Washington, D.C. would have a better chance for a favorable verdict if they combined their cases. Thus after joining forces, these plaintiffs were better known as *the Oliver L. Brown et al v. Board of Education of Topeka, Kansas.* The objective of this lawsuit was simple – to provide the same educational opportunities for African American children as for the white children of America.

After three years of seemingly endless debate and controversy, the Supreme Court ruled in favor of Oliver Brown and his co-plaintiffs that segregation was unconstitutional. Chief Justice Warren wrote the deciding argument for the Court and stated that *"Segregated schools are not equal and cannot be made equal, and hence they are deprived of the equal protection of the laws.*"[80] The results were quickly seen throughout the South. Southern activists and politicians did as much as they could to work around the new system of desegregation. Though the positive effects of this court case were not as quick in coming as civil rights leaders had hoped, Brown v. Board of Education would be the forerunner of affirmative action in America.

Engle v. Vitale (1962)

The wall of separation of Church and State had its foundation in the Engle v. Vitale case. This case started when parents of five students in New Hyde Park, a suburb of Long Island, New York filed a suit to stop the use of the following prayer: *"Almighty God, we acknowledge our dependence upon Thee, and beg Thy blessings upon us, our parents, our teachers, and our country."*

The New York Board of Regents had adopted the use of this prayer, but only ten percent of public schools in New York had elected to use it in the 1950's. The Board of Regents thought it would promote good character and citizenship. In New Hyde Park, New York, the Union Free School District #9 had a policy that this prayer was to be said aloud at the beginning of the school day in the presence of the teacher.

Five parents felt the prayer violated the religious beliefs of their children and filed suit to prevent it from being used. The five parents were of different religious beliefs – two were Jewish, one Unitarian, one a self-proclaimed atheist, and one held membership in the Ethical Culture Society. The parents strongly believed that their children were being coerced into saying this prayer, even though the school allowed the students to opt out of the exercise or be excused from participating in the prayer. This was, in part, true because the teachers did not give the students permission to leave the room during the prayer, and this appeared to make participation mandatory. The real issue in this case was: "Does the Government have the right to use this establishment of religion?"

The American Civil Liberties Union (ACLU) took the case. The plaintiffs appealed to the New York State Supreme Court and sought to force schools to abstain from using this prayer. Again, the court refused. Justice Bernard S. Meyer stated that although the prayer was clearly religious, it was not a violation of the First Amendment. Also, it was the responsibility of the school district to guard the dignity of the students if they chose not to participate in this prayer.

---

[80]   Brown v. Board of Education, 1954 – http://1ref.us/dp. Accessed January 23, 2016

The ACLU appealed the case to the New York Appellate Division that upheld the decision by a vote of five to two. Their view on this ruling was to look at the *Establishment Clause* that prohibited the adopting of an official religion or favoring a particular religion over another. Their thought was that the prayer did not establish a religion. Also, they believed that the Framers did not mean to prohibit public professions of faith in God, so they would not violate this by prohibiting the prayer in the public schools because they themselves would have violated this amendment in the way they spoke of their faith publicly.

The ACLU and the group of parents who initiated the case took it to the U.S Supreme Court. Their arguments dealt with the separation of Church and State and how the two should not get involved with each other. Simply put, the Regent's prayer was in violation of the First Amendment and could not be used in public schools.

Since the prayer was offered for those who wanted to say it, those who chose not to say it were not forced to do so. Also, since there were many religious elements in society, this prayer was simply a reflection of America's religious heritage. Because of that, this prayer did not establish a religion, and it would be interference and intrusion into the State's affairs to have the Supreme Court vote against the Board of Regents.

---

*The Justices stated that it was
a daily invocation for God's blessing,
so it was a religious exercise.
Since it was a religious exercise
in a government school, it violated the
First Amendment. Ramifications of this
decision are still felt today.
One year after this decision, Bible
reading in the public school was
also considered unconstitutional.*

Finally, after many years of debate, the case came before the Supreme Court which ruled with a seven-to-one vote that the Regents' prayer was inconsistent with the *Establishment Clause*, and therefore, it was unconstitutional. The Justices stated that it was a daily invocation for God's blessing, so it was a religious exercise. Since it was a religious exercise in a government school, it violated the First Amendment.

Ramifications of this decision are still felt today. One year after this decision, Bible reading in the public school was also considered unconstitutional. Public school teachers may use the Bible as a teaching tool but may not read the Bible in the classroom, even on their own time. Because of this restriction, Bible Clubs in public schools are questionable and many times have been banned based on the ruling of separation of church and state.

While Congress recognized the constitutional prohibition against governmental promotion of religion, it believed that non-school-sponsored student speech, including religious speech, should not be eliminated from the school environment. The law applies only to public secondary schools that receive federal financial assistance and that have "a limited open forum" (at least one student-led, non-curriculum club that meets outside of class time.)

Removing prayer and Bible reading from America's public schools has had a "trickle" down effect in the town square as well. Sadly, we hear of countless court battles to remove any religious symbol off public property. Public school officials have prohibited the use of the term "Christmas" or any vestige of it to be used on public school property including the use of Christmas greetings, nativity scenes, or (as seen in one school district) banning of red and green, the Christmas colors. This extreme view of removing religion from the public view is even seen in the military when chaplains are restricted to use the Bible to counsel service military or ordered not to pray in Jesus' name. Again and again, we see legal attacks on churches, Christian schools and ministries and even on God-fearing people who take a stand for their faith.

Miranda v. Arizona (1966)

Just as the Engle-Vitale case changed the relationship between Church and State, so the Miranda case forever changed the relationship between American police officers and arrested suspects. Before Miranda ever reached the Supreme Court, three court cases – *Mapp v. Ohio 1961, Gideon v. Wainwright, 1963 and Escobedo v. Illinois, 1964* – had influenced the Court to hand down its *"fundamentals of fairness."* This was a clear signal from the Court to law officials and the judiciary that convictions that did not follow *"fundamentals of fairness"* would be overturned when they went to appeal. This was especially true when the law on a local or even State level did not follow the due process of the suspect.

Emesto Miranda, age 23, was arrested and charged with kidnapping and sexual assault in Phoenix, Arizona in 1963. The police had arrested Mr. Miranda at his home and charged him with rape, kidnapping, and robbery and taken him to the police station. He was identified in a police line-up and placed in an interrogation room for questioning. This was done without Miranda having a lawyer present during the interrogation process.

Prior to the interrogation, the police did not inform Miranda of his rights. After two hours of intense questioning, the officers walked out considering him mentally unstable. He had no counsel present when he made his confession. Along with the confession was a waiver that stated he understood his rights and had waived them.

Miranda's lawyers felt his rights had been violated and sought an appeal. It worked its way through the courts until it reached the Supreme Court. The Supreme Court accepted Miranda's case. The Justices had to decide whether Miranda's confession was an admissible document since he was not given notice about his right to counsel and his right to remain silent. The other issue involved whether or not Miranda truly waived his rights to counsel or whether he was ignorant of them. Another issue on the agenda was whether voluntary confessions could be accepted in court if the suspect's lawyer was not present. The final issue was whether a suspect could be granted access to an attorney if he could not afford one.

Based on these police violations, Miranda's lawyers argued that the confession was not legally acceptable; and, therefore, Miranda's case must be thrown out. The Supreme Court voted in favor of Miranda by 5 to 4 votes. It was controversial at the time, but it soon changed the history of the accused and made "Miranda Warnings" a staple of police proceedings.

Soon after this decision, Miranda was released from prison. The police found new evidence against Miranda and arrested him on the same charges. Based on the new evidence, Miranda was again found guilty of rape, kidnapping and assault. After the Justices handed down this decision, there was widespread criticism because many felt it was unfair that accused criminals be informed of their rights in the way the court dictated. Richard M. Nixon and other conservatives felt that this hindered the police in doing their job, and they argued using the rising crime rate as proof of this. Despite controversy, the "Miranda Warning" was soon to become the norm in police proceedings.

Roe v. Wade (1973)

No other case has polarized Americans as *Roe v. Wade*. This was a Landmark case in that it caused the Court to rule that the constitutional right to privacy included a woman's right to abort her baby, but it had to be balanced with the state's provisions in regulating abortions. This included the protection of prenatal life and the mother's health. The results of this case have become long reaching and have taken many twists and turns from its original intent.

No other case has polarized Americans as Roe v. Wade. This was a Landmark case in that it caused the Court to rule that the constitutional right to privacy included a woman's right to abort her baby, but it had to be balanced with the state's provisions in regulating abortions.

To understand this case, one must go back to the beginning, back to September of 1969 when Norma L. McCorvey discovered she was pregnant. Her friends advised her to lie, saying it was rape, and return to Dallas where she could obtain an abortion legally. However, because there was no police report that documented this claim, the plan failed.

In 1970, McCorvey hired lawyers, Linda Coffee and Sarah Weddington to get an injunction which would allow her to get an abortion.[81] McCorvey wanted an abortion from an experienced and qualified doctor in a clean, safe clinic. Coffee and Weddington filed suit in a U.S. District Court in Texas for McCorvey who used the alias, Jane Roe, in the suit. At this time, McCorvey was no longer using the word *rape* and admitted that she had lied about that earlier.

---

[81]   Norma McCorvey The Woman Who Was Jane Roe – http://1ref.us/dq and http://1ref.us/dr

Dallas County District Attorney Henry Wade was named as the defendant in the case and represented Texas.

Although the District Court ruled in McCorvey's favor, they did not grant the injunction because of the laws that barred abortion. The basis of the Court's decision was the Ninth Amendment that states, *"The enumeration in the Constitution, of certain rights, shall not be construed to deny or disparage others retained by the people."*[82] Simply stated, this means the Government does not have the right to abridge certain individual freedoms. *Roe v. Wade* appealed the District Court's ruling and worked its way to the Supreme Court. Weddington continued on Roe's behalf, but Texas Attorney General Robert C. Flowers stepped in to replace Wade. Flowers and his team found Texas law that made those seeking an abortion guilty of a crime (except in rape and incest) as unconstitutional. Weddington and her team developed a new judicial theory – that a woman has a right to privacy based on their interpretation of the Ninth and Fourteenth Amendments. In a 6 to 3 vote, the Supreme Court Justices legalized abortion in the first trimester of pregnancy based on these two amendments. The Constitution does not make any mention of this right, but the Justices felt the Constitution did mention that the state could not interfere with an individual's rights regarding life, liberty and property.

Many felt this decision was achieved through deceit and through the Justices' private interpretation of the Constitution, the reason being Roe (who is Norma McCorvey) tried to convince a lower court that she had been raped, and when that fell apart, she retracted her story. Also, deceit was evidenced when Roe perjured herself in her testimony. McCorvey (who is now a Christian and pro-life advocate) admits this.[83] Also, the Justices ignored scientific evidence showing how a fetus is a living, breathing human.

The ramifications of this ruling in 1973 have been clearly seen. Abortion became legal in all states, and what became a right for a mother to terminate her pregnancy in the first trimester has allowed abortion to become prevalent in all trimesters, even minutes before the baby is born (partial birth abortion).[84] There are even arguments for destroying the life of the child at birth if there are

---

82   Roe v. Wade decided January 22, 1973 – http://1ref.us/ds. Accessed August 9, 2010

83   Napikoski, Linda. Norma McCorvey The Woman Who Was Jane Roe – http://1ref.us/dq. Nov. 29,2014. Accessed January 22, 2016

84   Facts About Abortion: U.S. Abortion Law – http://1ref.us/dt Accessed March 2, 2015

physical deformities or illnesses.[85] Abortions have left a legacy of death in this country with over fifty million unborn babies killed since 1973.[86]

Our Nation has been divided on this issue of a right to abortion in a culture war where there are no winners. Both sides are firmly entrenched in their views. However, with the rise of advanced medical technology such as the ultrasound machine, many are realizing that life does begin at conception. Today's opinion polls are showing that more people are against abortion than approve it. But this path of legal killing appears to have opened the door to euthanasia and prenatal stem cell use.

Regents of University of California v. Bakke (1978)

After many years of discrimination and racism, America's schools decided to become more equitable. However, by giving one group of students special treatment, it created more inequity for others.

Such was the case when Allan Bakke, a 34-year-old white male, applied to the University of California, Davis School of Medicine, in 1973 and in 1974. Bakke was passed over and he learned that other "special applicants" were admitted even though their academic scores were significantly lower than his. When Bakke discovered that his application had been rejected to admit members of minority groups or "the economically or educationally disadvantaged,"[87] he was incensed. Although many economically disadvantaged white students sought admission under this provision, none had been successful in obtaining admission.

The school had reserved sixteen places out of one hundred for qualified minorities. This was part of the school's policy on affirmative action that included his college GPA and test scores. Even though his scores exceeded those of other minorities who applied, he was still rejected. Bakke soon discovered he had been rejected based on his skin color.

After his second rejection, Bakke filed suit to compel the University to admit him. He alleged that the University had rejected him based on his race and had violated the *Equal Protection Clause* of the Fourteenth Amendment. The school counter- claimed stating that their special admission program was lawful. If ever there was a split decision on any of the cases, this was the one. Four of the Justices felt that any quota system violated the Civil Rights Act of

---

[85]   Doctors 'should have the right to kill unwanted or disabled babies at birth as they are not a real person' claims Oxford academic – http://1ref.us/du

[86]   By the Numbers: U.S. Abortion Statistics | Focus on the Family – http://1ref.us/dv

[87]   This term was used on the application for medical school. See http://1ref.us/dw

1964. The other four Justices felt that affirmative action, which allowed the use of race as part of the criteria for college admission, was constitutionally permitted. Justice Lewis F. Powell cast the deciding vote that ordered the medical school to admit Bakke. However, the school was not prohibited from using racial quotas in the future.

Powell wrote, *"The guarantee of Equal Protection cannot mean one thing when applied to one individual and something else when applied to a person of another color."*[88] Powell did not feel that affirmative action in the schools should be kept out of the admissions' policy. Justice Thurgood Marshall, the Supreme Court's first African American Justice, felt that this was a way to make up for past discriminations.

Nearly twenty years later, there was a reversal of this decision in the *Texas v. Hopwood,* 1996 case. The Fifth Circuit Court of Appeals found that the University of Texas' affirmative action policy violated the rights of Caucasian applicants. In an effort to increase its minority enrollment of African Americans and Mexican Americans, the school had disregarded the applications of Caucasian students.

Interestingly enough, the Court ruled that the Bakke decision was no longer valid or legally sound. The Court ordered that a school could no longer make race a deciding factor in the admission process. The Court further stipulated that a school may make allowances for a special situation (whether a person's parents had attended the school or whether there are certain economic or social circumstances), but they could not make race the sole factor as to whether or not a person is accepted.

The decision was appealed to the Supreme Court, but the Justices refused to review the lower court's decision. Thus, the *Hopwood* decision became the final law of the land with respect to the use of race in admissions in Louisiana, Mississippi, and Texas (the three states over which the Fifth Circuit maintained jurisdiction). Affirmative action has continued to be a controversial issue.

Stone v. Graham

On November 17, 1989, a decision was made by the U.S. Supreme Court in the case of Stone v. Graham, where a Kentucky statute that required the posting of the Ten Commandments (although purchased with private funds) on the walls of each public school classroom in the state, was unconstitutional because

---

88   Regents of the University of California v. Bakke 438 U.S. 265, 98 S.Ct. 2733, 57 L.Ed.2d 750 (1978) – http://1ref.us/dx

it lacked a secular legislative purpose, and was in violation of the Establishment Clause of the First Amendment.

Although the state legislature had required that a notation in small print be placed at the bottom of each display which read, "*The secular application of the Ten Commandments is clearly seen in its adoption as the fundamental legal code of Western Civilization and the Common Law of the United States.*"[89] Some believed that an avowed secular purpose could provide opportunity for conflict with the Amendment. Because the purpose of posting the Ten Commandments did not confine itself to arguably secular matters, it was determined that it was plainly religious in nature and served no constitutional educational function.

This court rested on a precedent established by a previous case, Lemon v. Kurtzman,1971). The "Lemon test" established a foundation for the Court's post 1971 Establishment Clause rulings. The test had three parts: First, the statute must have a secular legislative purpose; second, its principal effect must be one that neither advances nor inhibits religion; third, the statute must not foster an excessive government entanglement with religion. If the state broke any of the three guidelines outlined in the "Lemon test," it would be in violation of the Establishment Clause.

Lawrence v. Texas (2003)

The U.S. Supreme Court struck down the "Homosexual Conduct" law with this landmark ruling for lesbian and gay Americans' civil rights by a vote of 7-2 and invalidated sodomy laws in thirteen other states, making same-sex activity legal in every U.S. State and territory.

The case began when the police of Houston, Texas were alerted by a report of a weapons violation at the apartment of John Geddes Lawrence. Upon entering the apartment, they found Geddes engaged in a sexual act with another man, Tyron Garner. Both men were detained and charged with violating the Texas "Homosexual Conduct" law. After the men were convicted and fined, Lawrence appealed arguing that the law was unconstitutional because it discriminated against homosexuals in violation of the Equal Protection Clause of the Constitution.

The Supreme Court decision, written by Justice Anthony Kennedy, ruled that the "Homosexual Conduct" law was unconstitutional and overturned the conviction of Lawrence and Garner. The Court held that consensual sexual conduct was protected by substantive due process under the Fourteenth Amendment. This was a stark departure from the Court's conservative posi-

---

[89]   Stone v. Graham,449 U.S. 39 (1980)-First Amendment Schools – http://1ref.us/dy

tion in the 80's and 90's. This case protected the privacy of the bedroom and renewed the Court's power to identify individual rights above those historically protected by the law. The outcome was celebrated by gay rights activists who saw this as a beginning for future legal advances.

Obergefell v. Hodges (2015)

This case is the culmination of a 20-year battle. It actually began when a handful of states foolishly adopted a state version of the failed Equal Rights Amendment (ERA) into its state constitution. Hawaii's state supreme court ruled that the ERA language requires that marriage licenses be issued without regard to sex.

This radical decision landed like a bombshell on America and Congress overwhelmingly passed the Defense of Marriage Act (DOMA) in 1996. It was signed into law by President Bill Clinton. The main purpose of this act was to protect the marriage laws of the other 49 states. About 40 other states had passed similar laws of their own and 31 states put traditional marriage laws into their state constitutions. At this time homosexuals began litigation assaults in state and federal courts across the nation. Many *amicus briefs* were filed to defend the traditional definition of marriage.

Following a Supreme Court decision in June of 2013 in *United States v. Windsor* holding that the restricting U.S federal interpretation of "marriage" and "spouse" applied only to heterosexual unions was unconstitutional, James Obergefell and John Arthur, a same sex couple, married in Maryland, decided to obtain federal legal recognition of their marriage. Their marriage was not recognized in their home state of Ohio. Because Arthur was terminally ill, they wanted Ohio to identify the partner, Obergefell as the surviving spouse on the death certificate.

On June 26, 2015, the nation received the shocking news that the nation's highest court overturned the votes of millions of Americans, demanding they walk away from human nature and the teachings of Scripture and accept the Court's invention of a "right" to same-sex marriage which no Founding Father intended. Justice Samuel Alito in his dissent, affirmed that this action of the Court signals far more than the death of marriage, "Today's decision will also have a fundamental effect on this Court and its ability to uphold the law. If a bare majority of Justices can invent a new "right" and impose that "right" on the rest of the country, the only real limit on what future majorities will be able to do is their own sense of what those with political power and cultural influence are willing to tolerate."[90]

If a bare majority of Justices can invent a new "right" and impose that "right" on the rest of the country, the only real limit on what future majorities will be able to do is their own sense of what those with political power and cultural influence are willing to tolerate.

In a powerful statement by Congressman Joe Pitts (R-Pa.) he reminded people that marriage was the union of a man and woman at the time of the Fourteenth Amendment, at the founding of our country, and in every time and place until 2004.[91] Even then, no court overturned natural law. And today, no court can do that, not even the Supreme Court of the United States. What God imprinted on the human heart, no judge can change.

Phyliss Schafly also added, "*A Supreme Court decision that strikes down state marriage laws is just not a defeat for marriage. It will also limit our First Amendment right to the free exercise of religion.*"[92] Our Founding Fathers recognized the dangers of religious persecution, so they guaranteed through the Bill of Rights that all Americans can freely exercise their faith. Religious freedom is now at risk.

Although this has been a disheartening turn of events, we must stand firm. We have a myriad of promises from God that remind us that He is in control and "the gates of hell shall not prevail" against us. Matthew 16:18 (KJV).

---

[90]   Justice Alitos Dissent in SSM Case National Review – http://1ref.us/dz
[91]   Congressman Pitts Decries Supreme Court Decision of Same Sex – http://1ref.us/e0
[92]   June 2015 Phyllis Schlafly Report – Eagle Forum – http://1ref.us/e1

Conclusion

These Landmark court cases have, in many instances, changed the original meaning of the Constitution or allowed the Justices to read their own views into its meaning. Americans have begun to understand the importance of Justices who will take their oath of office seriously and not interpret the Constitution based on their own personal views.

The Framers believed in the balance of power among governmental branches. It is clear they never meant for Justices to become activists and make new laws based on their personal opinions. Our system of government (although not perfect) has worked well for many years. As Americans, we have the right to voice our objections. It behooves us to stay informed and to elect leaders wisely.

As Christians, how are we to respond? Jesus said that our first responsibility is to be as salt. Salt was a preservative in Jesus' day. In the Bible, it is stated in Matthew, chapter 5, verse 13: *"Ye are the salt of the earth: but if the salt have lost his savour, wherewith shall it be salted? it is thenceforth good for nothing, but to be cast out, and be trodden under foot of men." (KJV)* Salt did not prevent decay, it only extended the shelf life a little longer. May we accept the challenge to be as salt and perhaps delay the cultural decay of our great nation.

The Framers believed in the balance of power among governmental branches. It is clear they never meant for Justices to become activists and make new laws based on their personal opinions.

Part IV

America's Heritage and Hope

"Be of good courage, and He shall strengthen your heart, all ye who hope in the Lord." Psalm 31:24

Part IV-Chapter X

AMERICA'S HERITAGE AND HOPE

The American Flag

It became increasingly necessary for the rebelling colonies fighting for their independence from Britain to find a way to identify their possessions and ships. Colonel Joseph, the military secretary under George Washington, in a letter dated October 20, 1775 stated, *"Please affix upon some particular Colour for a flag-& a Signal, by which our Vessels may know one another."*[93] Ship captains were then left with the responsibility of agreeing on a signal banner.

In 1777, the Continental Congress adopted an official standard. It is said that it came as a response to a request by an Indian named Thomas Green. Green had asked for a flag to take to the Indian chiefs of the nation to assure safe passage when traveling on missions for the Continental Army. On June 14, 1777, the first flag of the United States was adopted when Congress stated that *"Resolved that the flag of the United States be thirteen stripes, alternate red and white, that the Union be thirteen stars, white in a blue field representing a new constellation."*[94]

Today, June 14 is celebrated as Flag Day when most Americans show their patriotism, reverence, and respect for what our flag represents. The flag of the United States has thirteen horizontal stripes, seven red and six white. These stripes represent the thirteen original states. The flag also has a field of blue,

---

[93] History of the Flag of the United States of America: 1882, James R. Osgood and Company, Boston, p 227

[94] Federal Citizen Information Center: Our Flag – http://1ref.us/e2

which now contains fifty stars; one star for each state. The single point of each star points upward. The colors of the flag are symbolic: the red for courage, the white for purity, and the blue for loyalty. The American flag should always be honored and given a special place in the hearts of all Americans because the freedom and liberties we enjoy today were purchased by great sacrifice.

For more than 200 years, the American flag has been the symbol of our nation's strength and unity. It has been a source of pride and inspiration for all Americans down through the ages. The flag has undergone many changes since the first official flag of 1777, but it remains one of the nation's most widely recognized symbols. It has been changed twenty-six times since the thirteen states adopted it.[95] The version with forty-eight stars remained unchanged for 47 years or until the forty-ninth star version became official on July 4, 1959. On July 4, 1960, at 12:01 P.M. the fifty-star flag was raised as the official flag of the United States at Fort McHenry National Monument, Baltimore, Maryland.

When Alaska and Hawaii were under consideration for statehood in the 1950's, a request went out for proposals for a design to include fifty stars, representing fifty states. More than 1500 designs were eventually submitted to President Dwight D. Eisenhower. Many schools encouraged students to participate. Of these proposals, one was submitted by a high-school student, Robert G. Haft, as part of a classroom project. He had asked his mother to help him make a flag but she refused to do any of the work for him. He received a "B" grade for his efforts. He discussed his project with his teacher who jokingly said, "*If your flag is accepted by Congress, your grade will be reconsidered.*" His flag design was accepted by Congress and adopted by a presidential proclamation. He then got his "A." [96]

Throughout the world the flag is recognized as a symbol of the United States, a nation of liberty. It has, through the years received many nicknames: "The Stars and Stripes," "Old Glory," and "The Star Spangled Banner."

Betsy Ross, a young widow of twenty-four who supported herself by continuing the upholstery business of her late husband, John Ross, (who had died in the service of his country) has been given credit for making the first American flag. The story is told that she made the flag after a visit in June, 1776 by George Washington, Robert Morris, and her husband's uncle, George Ross. It appears that a flag was needed and the story credits her for making a flag from a pencil sketch handed to her by George Washington. She demonstrated to them

---

[95]   Flag of the United States - Wikipedia, the free encyclopedia – http://1ref.us/e3

[96]   The Current Version of the U.S Flag Proposed by a High School Student – http://1ref.us/e4

how to cut a five-pointed star with a single clip of the scissors. Her idea of a five pointed-star, along with the arrangement of the stars and stripes was accepted by a committee. A flag was completed and presented to Congress. She was then informed that her flag would be accepted as the nation's flag.

Throughout the world the flag is recognized as a symbol of the United States, a nation of liberty. It has, through the years received many nicknames: "The Stars and Stripes," "Old Glory," and "The Star Spangled Banner."

However, this story is in reality only a legend. Even if she did not make the first flag—even if the visit by George Washington never happened—Betsy Ross, nevertheless, still represents a national symbol. She also represents what many women of her time found as reality in a time of war such as widowhood, single motherhood, the necessity of managing their household and property, and even providing for their families.

There is a song, *"This is my country to have and to hold…."* We sing it without much thought, but "holding" our country is a battle that is fought every day in many ways. Our flag is precious, a symbol of what we hold dear and deserves great respect and honor.

Special Regulations for Honoring Our Flag:

1. The flag is normally flown outdoors only during daylight hours. It may be flown at night if it is lighted.

2. When the flag is hung against a wall, the union (blue field) of the flag should be upward and at the flag's own right, (the observer's left).

3. When displayed with another flag against the wall, from crossed staffs, the United States flag should be on the flag's own right, with its staff in front of the other staff.

4. The flag should never be allowed to touch the ground, trail in water, or be used in any other way in which it could be easily soiled.

5. When the flag is carried with another flag, the flag of the United States should be on the right. When carried with two other flags, it should be in the middle.

6. The flag at half-staff is a sign of mourning. When flown at half-staff, the flag should be raised to the peak for an instant and then lowered to the half-staff position.

7. The flag flown upside down is a sign of distress.

8. The flag should always be allowed to hang free. It should never be used as a drapery.

9. The law forbids use of the flag in connection with any merchandise for sale.

10. An old, torn, or soiled flag should not be thrown away. It should be destroyed as a whole, by burning.

11. Two persons are required to fold an American flag correctly.

Special Holidays for Flag Display

Americans have many special holidays to celebrate the numerous historical times and events of our history. It is at these times the American flag is always proudly displayed. Some are as follows:

Lincoln's Birthday or President's Day (first Monday in February)
Washington's Birthday (third Monday in February)
Mother's Day (second Sunday in May)
Memorial Day (last Monday in May, at half-staff until noon)
Labor Day (first Monday in September)
Columbus Day (second Monday in October)
Veteran's Day (November 11)
Thanksgiving Day (fourth Thursday in November)
Martin Luther King's Birthday (third Monday in January)

The Meaning of the Thirteen Folds of the American Flag

At many military funerals an honor guard gives close attention to the flag and its handling. For example, meticulous attention is given to the thirteen folds. After the flag has been folded thirteen times, it takes on the appearance of a cocked hat like that worn by soldiers of the Colonial period. It is to remind us of the soldiers, sailors, and marines who served under General Washington and the sacrifices they made for us, as well as those who have served in the military since that time. Each of the flag's thirteen folds has a special meaning.

- The 1st fold of the flag is the symbol of life.

- The 2nd fold is the symbol of our belief in eternal life.

- The 3rd fold is made in remembrance and honor of the veterans departing our ranks who gave a portion of their lives for the defense of our country to attain peace throughout the world.

- The 4th fold represents our weaker nature, for as Americans trusting in God, it is to Him we turn in times of peace as well as in times of war for His divine guidance.

- The 5th fold is a tribute to our country, for in the words of Stephen Decatur, "*Our Country, in dealing with other countries, may she always be right, but it is still our country, right or wrong.*"

- The 6th fold is for where our hearts lie. It is with our heart that we pledge allegiance to the flag of the United States of America, and to the republic for which it stands, one nation, under God, indivisible, with Liberty and Justice for all.

- The 7th fold is a tribute to our Armed Forces. For it is through the Armed Forces that we protect our country and our flag against all enemies, whether they be found within or without the boundaries of our republic.

- The 8th fold is a tribute to the one who entered the valley of the shadow of death that we might see the light of day.

- The 9th fold is a tribute to womanhood, and to mothers. For it has been through their faith, their love, loyalty and devotion that the character of the men and women who have made this country great has been molded.

- The 10th fold is a tribute to the father, for he too has given his sons and daughters for the defense of our country since they were first born.

- The 11th fold represents the lower portion of the seal of King David and King Solomon and glorifies in the Hebrew eyes, the God of Abraham, Isaac, and Jacob.

- The 12th fold represents an emblem of eternity and glorifies, in the Christian's eyes, God the Father, the Son, and the Holy Spirit.

- The 13[97] fold, or when the flag is completely folded, the stars are upper-most reminding us of our nation's motto, "In God We Trust."[97]

(See Appendix: The story behind "Old Glory.")

THE PLEDGE OF ALLEGIANCE

I pledge allegiance to the Flag of the United States of America and to the Republic for which it stands, one Nation under God, indivisible, with liberty and justice for all.

What does it mean to pledge allegiance? A pledge is a promise and allegiance means loyalty. When we recite the Pledge of Allegiance, we stand facing the flag with the right hand over the heart in an expression of honor and respect.

When we pledge allegiance to the flag, we do the following:

- Promise loyalty to the flag itself.

- Promise loyalty to all 50 states.

- Promise loyalty to the Government that unites us all, recognizing that we are one Nation under God, and that we should not be divided.

In September of 1892, a youth magazine, *The Youth's Companion,* published a *Pledge to the Flag* for children to recite during a program commemorating the 400th birthday of Columbus' discovery of America. That was the earliest known version of the Pledge.[98]

From this beginning, two men, Francis Bellamy and James Upham, both educators, planned the celebrations that covered the nation's forty-four states. One month after the "Pledge" was published in The *Youth's Companion*, 12 million school children across the nation recited the words of the "Pledge." That was the beginning of the "Pledge of Allegiance" that we know and recite today.

After that initial Columbus Day celebration, reciting the Pledge became a daily routine in America's public schools. It had not gained much attention until Flag Day, June 14, 1923, where it received major attention from citizens who gathered for the first National Flag Conference in Washington, D.C.

Although the Pledge gained favor among adults, its popularity increased during World War II. On June 22, 1942, the Pledge became official when Congress included the Pledge to the Flag in the United States Flag Code (Title 36).

---

[97]   The Meaning of the Folding of the American Flag – http://1ref.us/e6 /

[98]   Youth Companion & Pledge of Allegiance – http://1ref.us/e5

In 1945, the Pledge to the Flag received the official title of "The Pledge of Allegiance."

Slight changes were made over the years but the last change occurred on June 14, 1954, (Flag Day) when President Dwight D. Eisenhower approved adding the words "under God." This authorized change essentially said:

"In this way we are reaffirming the transcendence of religious faith in America's heritage and future; in this way we shall constantly strengthen those spiritual weapons which forever will be our country's most powerful resource in peace and war."[99]

The story is told that on February 7, 1954, a Presbyterian minister, Rev. Macpherson Docherty, made the difference by preaching a sermon on Lincoln's Gettysburg Address at the New York Avenue Presbyterian church located near the White House when President Eisenhower was in attendance. His message included a comparison of the United States to ancient Sparta. Ancient Sparta had great national might but it was not because of their walls, their shields, or their weapons of war, but their spirit. Likewise, the might of the United States should not be thought of as coming from her nuclear weapons or military strength but rather from our great "American spirit." The minister further appealed to the words in the Gettysburg address where President Lincoln used two words "under God" to describe the uniqueness and strength of America. That week, with the encouragement of President Eisenhower, Rep. Charles Oakman introduced a bill to Congress supporting the addition of "under God," and the bill was signed into law.

The Pledge of Allegiance

I pledge allegiance	I promise to be faithful and true (promise my loyalty)
To the flag	To the emblem that stands for and represents
Of the United States	All 50 states, each of them individual, and individually represented on the flag
Of America	Yet formed into a UNION of one Nation.
And to the Republic	And I also pledge my loyalty to the Government that is itself a Republic, a form of government where the people are sovereign,

---

[99]   Dwight D. Eisenhower's Religion and Political Views – http://1ref.us/e7

For which it stands,	This government also being represented by the Flag to which I promise loyalty.
One Nation under God,	These 50 individual states are united as a single Republic under the Divine Providence of God, "our most powerful resource" (according to the words of President Eisenhower)
Indivisible,	Cannot be separated. (This part of the original version of the pledge was written just 50 years after the beginning of the Civil War and demonstrates the unity sought in the years after that divisive period in our history.)
With Liberty	The people of this Nation being afforded the freedom of "life, liberty, and the pursuit of happiness",
And Justice	And each person entitled to be treated justly, fairly, and according to proper law and principle,
For all.	And these principles afforded to every American, regardless of race, religion, color, creed, or any other criteria. Just as the flag represents 50 individual states that cannot be divided or separated, this Nation represents millions of people who cannot be separated or divided.

AMERICA'S MONUMENTS AND SYMBOLS OF FAITH

Through the years, special symbols have become uniquely American, celebrating not only America's success as a Constitutional Republic but her independence as well. National symbols are an important part of our nation's history, in that they connect our feelings, and our sense of pride to specific events in our history. They serve as a significant reminder of the gratitude and debt we owe to those who have gone before us, and inspiration to those who will follow. The Founding Fathers frequently made reference to their reliance on Divine Providence. For example, the closing words of the Declaration of Independence are "… *with a firm reliance on the protection of divine Providence, we mutually pledge to each other our Lives, our Fortunes, and our sacred Honor.*"

The National Anthem

The war of 1812 is often referred to as the Second War for Independence. It was caused by the British attacking American ships in the Atlantic Ocean and impressing men into their navy. Over a period of time approximately 600 Americans were thus taken. Finally, after many appeals to the British to cease and desist in this pernicious practice, we were forced to go to war to stop it. In 1814 our capitol in Washington, DC was set ablaze and destroyed by the British, and they decided that Baltimore, Maryland, would be their next target. The British plan was to attack Baltimore from the sea, enter the harbor, and send in a large landing force.

In August 1814, the British forces arrested an American civilian, William Beanes of Upper Marlborough, Maryland, and held him prisoner aboard a warship in the Chesapeake Bay. America's General John Mason, who was in charge of prisoner exchanges, asked two Americans, Francis Scott Key, an attorney and amateur poet, and John Skinner to communicate and negotiate with the British for the release of Beanes. It was at this time the British began their bombardment of Fort McHenry, which was situated to protect Baltimore from such an attack.

As a result of negotiations by General John Mason with the British, they agreed to release Beanes but held Key and Skinner as captives until the attack was over, thinking by then they would have captured Baltimore. The bombardment began on September 13, 1814, and continued all day and night. The British were amazed at the willpower, commitment and strength of the American forces at Fort McHenry. They had felt this would be another easy victory like Washington, D.C. The Americans had hoisted at Fort McHenry, a very large American flag that could easily be seen by the British.

To the surprise of the British, at dawn they observed that the flag was still flying, a proud signal to the British that they had not succeeded in their attack on Fort McHenry. Francis Scott Key had watched all night as the cannons shot their large destructive warheads and the rockets blazed overhead. He had expected that by morning Fort McHenry would be no more and the British would have been successful in their attack. However, to his utter amazement, the stars and stripes still waved in the morning breezes. Being moved in spirit, he took a letter from his pocket, and began writing on the backside a poem about what he had just witnessed.

The prisoners, Francis Scott Key and John Skinner were released that day, and Key returned to Baltimore. Key continued to work on his poem, which was published shortly thereafter and eventually became the "Star Spangled Banner." Today it is known as our National Anthem, inspired by the heroic efforts of the men at Fort McHenry. In respect for our National Anthem and what it represents, we stand at attention and face our flag with our right hand over our heart as the anthem is sung. Our flag has been a source of pride and inspiration for all Americans.

(See Appendix: The Star Spangled Banner)

The American Creed

The American Creed was written as a result of a nationwide contest. An idea was conceived that a national creed should be written to express, in brief, a summary of American political faith, founded upon the fundamental things most distinctive to our nation. Mayor James Preston of Baltimore, Maryland, offered a reward of one thousand dollars for the winning creed. The idea was suggested to Mr. William Tyler Page of Friendship Heights, Maryland, that he consider writing the creed and entering the contest.

Coming home from church in May, 1917, Mr. Page decided to compose a creed fashioned along the lines of the Christian or Apostle's Creed. He was a student of history and was familiar with the great documents of our nation and many of those of our Founding Fathers. Over a period of time he made many changes, but he finally completed it and sent it in.

In March 1918, Mr. Page received notice that he had won the competition. His creed had been selected from more than three thousand entries. It was accepted by the Speaker of the House of Representatives, representing Congress and the United States Commissioner of Education on April 3, 1918. It reads as follows:

"I believe in the United States of America as a government of the people, by the people, for the people; whose just powers are derived from the consent of the governed; a democracy in a republic, a sovereign Nation of many sovereign States; a perfect union, one and inseparable; established upon those principles of freedom, equality, justice, and humanity for which American patriots sacrificed their lives and fortunes. I therefore believe it is my duty to my country to love it, to support its Constitution, to obey its laws, to respect its flag, and to defend it against all enemies."

"In God We Trust"

It was during the Civil War that the motto *In God We Trust* first appeared on the United States coins. It was due to the efforts of Secretary of the Treasury, Salmon Chase. Early in Chase's tenure as Secretary of the Treasury, a clergyman had written to him suggesting that American coins ought to bear a motto demonstrating the nation's dependence upon God.

In response to the suggestion, Secretary Chase sent the following memo to the director of the Mint: *"No nation can be strong except in the strength of God, or safe except in His defense. The trust of our people should be declared on our national coins. You will cause a device to be prepared without unnecessary delay with a motto expressing in the fewest words possible this national recognition."*[100]

The director of the Mint composed several mottos, and Secretary Chase chose *In God We Trust*. In April 1864, an act was passed authorizing the issuing of a two-cent piece bearing the motto. Later, all American coins were issued

---

[100]   History of 'In God We Trust' – http://1ref.us/e8

bearing these words. In 1955 Congress passed a bill to have the motto placed on paper currency, and it first appeared on bills two years later. In 1956 Congress passed a resolution declaring *In God We Trust* the national motto. The use of the phrase has had three court challenges including one that led to a 1996 ruling by the 10th U.S. Court of Appeals in Denver, Colorado. The Supreme Court refused to hear the case.

A movement to post the motto in schools began with the American Family Association in Tupelo, Mississippi. Mississippi brought this to public attention and passed a law requiring the motto be placed in every classroom, cafeteria and gym. Tim Wildmon, President of the American Family Association stated: *"America has a rich Christian and deep religious heritage. If the President of the United States can be sworn in by placing his hand on the Holy Bible, certainly kids can know what the national motto is."*[101]

Every coin minted in the United States now bears, along with the bust of a past hero, these words: *IN GOD WE TRUST*. The Founding Fathers believed implicitly that God had been their champion and recognized that Sovereign action had been actively involved in assisting them in winning the war for our independence.

The Founding Fathers believed implicitly that God had been their champion and recognized that Sovereign action had been actively involved in assisting them in winning the war for our independence.

They had witnessed the tremendous cost and sacrifice that had been paid to secure our freedom; and without Providence's interposition, we would never have won. They were grateful for His interposition, and were never ashamed to admit it and constantly acknowledged that fact. They remembered what David had written in Psalm 127:1: *Except the Lord build the house, they labour in vain that build it. . .*

---

[101]   USATODAY.com – 'In God We Trust' movement gains energy – http://1ref.us/e9

The Great Seal of the United States

On July 4, 1776, Thomas Jefferson, John Adams, and Benjamin Franklin were appointed by Congress to take charge of designing an official seal for the new American nation. Over a period of years, several committees worked on a design for the new seal. It was William Barton, a heraldry specialist, who designed most of the reverse side of the seal; and Charles Thompson, Secretary of the Congress, designed the face of the seal.

The Great Seal was officially adopted on June 20, 1782. The face of the seal is used to authenticate important official documents of the Federal Government. Both sides of the seal are pictured on the reverse side of the dollar bill.

The face of the seal is dominated by the American Eagle, which has become a symbol of the United States. The eagle's breast is protected by a shield of red, white, and blue. The blue originally represented the Congress, but since 1789 it represents all three branches of the Federal Government.

The thirteen red and white stripes represent the original colonies. In the crest above the eagle, America is represented as a new constellation of thirteen stars. The radiant glow surrounding the constellation symbolizes God's protection of the Nation. In its right talon the eagle holds an olive branch bearing thirteen leaves and thirteen olives; in its left talon the eagle holds thirteen arrows. The olive branch and arrows symbolize that the Nation prefers peace but is prepared to wage war when necessary. In its beak the eagle holds a scroll written in Latin *E pluribus unum* or out of many, one, meaning America is one nation composed of many states.

The American Eagle

The delegates to the Constitutional Convention argued for six years as to what our national symbol would be. Benjamin Franklin suggested the wild turkey to be our national symbol, but Congress did not agree. They saw the high-flying eagle as a symbol of courage and strength and its habitat was North America.

For many years the eagle has been admired for its grandeur, its grace in flight, its great size and awesome power. The soaring eagle is also a stirring picture of the true meaning of liberty. Assisted by his powerful wings, the eagle glides effortlessly to altitudes of over 2,400 feet and is capable of using its wings to carry other eagles to safety. Turbulent winds only cause them to fly higher and faster. The eagle represents freedom. Living as they do on the tops of lofty mountains amid the solitary grandeur of nature, they have unlimited freedom.

With strong pinions, they sweep into the valleys below or upward into the boundless spaces beyond.

It is said that the eagle may have been used as a national emblem because, at one of the first battles of the Revolution (which occurred early in the morning) the patriots were heard to say that the noise of the struggle awakened the sleeping eagles on the heights. They flew to their nests and then circled about over the heads of the fighting men, *screeching freedom*. Thus the eagle, full of the boundless spirit of freedom, living above the valleys, strong and powerful, has become the national emblem of our country, which offers freedom in word and fact. In 1782 the eagle was officially chosen to be our national symbol. The eagle appears on the seals of many of our states and on most of our gold and silver coins.

The Liberty Bell

In 1751 the Liberty Bell was made in Great Britain at the Whitechapel Bell Foundry for the fiftieth anniversary of the Pennsylvania colony. The metals consisted of copper (70%), and tin (25%) and traces of zinc, arsenic, gold and silver. The cost of the bell, including insurance and shipping in 1752 was $225.50. It weighed 2,080 pounds, was 12 feet in the lip circumference, and measured 3 feet from the lip to the top.[102]

It was taken to Philadelphia in 1752. Unfortunately, at the time of testing, the bell cracked. Bell makers melted it down and recast it with stronger metals. Although the new bell worked, the people were not pleased with the sound. The bell was recast again, restoring the correct balance of metal and was placed in the steeple of the State House in 1753.

According to tradition, the most famous ringing was to summon the citizens of Philadelphia for the reading of the Declaration of Independence. The bell was also rung to announce the opening of the First Continental Congress in 1774 and again in 1775 after the Battle of Lexington and Concord.

In 1776, four days after the signing of the Declaration of Independence and while the delegates were in Philadelphia, the people gathered to hear the

---

[102]   Liberty Bell Facts and Figures – http://1ref.us/ea

reading of the Declaration. It was then the bell was rung and it rang out loud and clear on that very special occasion. At that time few knew the words on the bell, although they had been on the bell for more than twenty years. They are: *"And ye shall hallow the fiftieth year, and Proclaim liberty throughout all the Land unto all the inhabitants thereof…." Leviticus 25:10*

In 1777 British soldiers marched on Philadelphia. Fearing the British soldiers would steal the bell and destroy it, the citizens loaded the bell onto a wagon and hauled it to Allentown, Pennsylvania where it was hidden in the basement of a church. Unfortunately, during the journey, the bell fell from the wagon and was slightly damaged. It was again repaired and in 1778 the bell was taken back to Philadelphia. It rang out again when the Revolutionary War ended, at the signing of the Declaration of Independence, and again when the Constitution of the United States was signed. It also rang for the fiftieth anniversary of the Declaration of Independence.

In 1835 the bell cracked again while tolling on the death of John Marshall, Chief Justice of the United States. In 1830's the bell became famous as the LIBERTY BELL. Its home would remain in Philadelphia and the jagged crack would be symbolic of America's struggle for freedom. The Liberty Bell is known as the bell that proclaimed "liberty and justice for all" across the land. On February 22, 1846, the bell tolled for several hours in the tower of Independence Hall in honor of George Washington's birthday. At that time, when the bell was rung, the crack grew from top to bottom. In 1837, abolitionists, in their efforts to end slavery, adopted it as a symbol of emancipation and liberty.

The Capitol

"In no other place in the United States are there so many, and such varied official evidences of deep and abiding faith in God on the part of Governments as there are in Washington D.C." Senator Robert Byrd.

On June 25, 1962, The Supreme Court had just declared prayer in the schools to be unconstitutional. Senator Robert Byrd of West Virginia, a Bible teacher and respected member of the U.S. Senate, was so moved by the disastrous decision, that two days later he delivered an

address to his colleagues in Congress reminding them of the Christian symbolism throughout our Capitol. He verbally escorted them to the Library of Congress, the Washington Monument, the Lincoln Memorial, the Jefferson Memorial, the Supreme Court, and other landmarks. Then he concluded as follows:

"Inasmuch as our greatest leaders have shown no doubt about God's proper place in the American birthright, can we, in our day, dare do less? In concluding his remarks, Senator Byrd cited the words of Jefferson as a *forceful and explicit warning that to remove God from this country will destroy it."*[103]

Every session of the House and the Senate begins with prayer. Each house has its own chaplain. The Eighty-third Congress set aside a small room in the Capitol, just off the Rotunda, for private prayer and meditation by members of Congress. The room is always open when Congress is in session, but it is not open to the public. The room's focal point is a stained glass window showing George Washington kneeling in prayer. Behind him are etched these words from Psalm 16:1: *Preserve me, O God, for in Thee do I put my trust.*

Inside the Rotunda is a picture of the Pilgrims about to embark from England on the sister ship of the *Mayflower*, the *Speedwell*. The ship's revered chaplain, Brewster, who later joined the *Mayflower*, has an open Bible in his lap. Very clear are the words, *the New Testament according to our Lord and Savior, Jesus Christ.*[104] On the sail is the motto of the Pilgrims; *In God We Trust, God with Us.*[105]

The phrase, *In God We Trust,* appears opposite the President of the Senate, who is the Vice President of the United States. The same phrase, in large words is inscribed in the marble backdrop of the Speaker of the House of Representatives.

The Supreme Court

Above the head of the Chief Justice of the Supreme Court are the Ten Commandments, with the great American eagle protecting them. Moses is included among the great lawgivers in Herman A. MacNeil's marble sculpture group on the east front. The crier who

---

103   William J Federer's American Minute for November 20th – http://1ref.us/eb

104   William J Federer's American Minute for November 20th – http://1ref.us/eb

105   William J Federer's American Minute for November 20th – http://1ref.us/eb

opens each session closes with the words, *God save the United States and the Honorable Court.*[106]

The Library of Congress

Numerous quotations from Scripture can be found within the walls of the Library of Congress. Each one reminds the American of his responsibility to his Maker: *He hath showed thee, O man, what is good; and what doth the Lord require of thee, but to do justly and love mercy and walk humbly with thy God (Micah 6:8).*

In the lawmakers' library preserves of documents is the Psalmist's acknowledgement that all nature reflects the order and beauty of the Creator. *"The heavens declare the glory of God, and the firmament showeth His handiwork" (Psalm 19:1).* And still another reference: *"The light shineth in darkness, and the darkness comprehendeth it not" (John 1:5).*

The Lincoln Memorial

Millions have stood in the Lincoln Memorial and gazed up at the statue of the great Abraham Lincoln. The sculptor who chiseled the

---

[106] In God We Trust: America's Historic Sites Reveal her Christian Foundations | Providence Foundation – http://1ref.us/ec

features of Lincoln in granite almost makes it appear that Lincoln is speaking his own words as they are inscribed into the walls:

"*...that this nation, under God, shall have a new birth of freedom - and that government of the people, by the people, and for the people, shall not perish from the earth.*"

At the opposite end, on the north wall, his Second Inaugural Address refers to "*God,*" the "*Bible,*" "*Providence,*" "*the Almighty,*" *and* "*Divine attributes.*" It also says: "*As was said 3000 years ago, so it still must be said, "The judgments of the Lord are true and righteous altogether.*"

The Jefferson Memorial

On the south banks of Washington's Tidal Basin, stands the memorial to Jefferson. In it are many of his quotes, "*God who gave us life gave us liberty. Can the liberties of a nation be secure when we have removed a conviction that these liberties are the gift of God? Indeed, I tremble for my country when I reflect that God is just, that his justice cannot sleep forever. Commerce between slave and*

master is despotism. Nothing is more certainly written in the book of fate that these people are to be free. Establish the law for educating the common people. This is the business of the state to effect and on a general plan." Attributed to Thomas Jefferson, Jefferson Monument Wall Inscription (1943).

The Washington Monument

The Washington Monument was completed in 1888 as a monument to the city's namesake and America's first President, George Washington. The monument is 555 feet high and on the top are two words "*Laus Deo.*" Invisible to mankind because of their location, they face skyward overlooking the 69 square miles that comprise the District of Columbia. These two, seemingly insignificant unnoticed words, perhaps out of mind, nevertheless, are very meaningfully placed at the highest point over what is the probably the most powerful city in the world. The words, "*Laus Deo*" in Latin, consist of four syllables and seven letters. Translated it means "*Praise be to God.*"

The construction of the giant obelisk began in 1848 during the presidency of James Polk and was not completely finished until 1888 when it was then opened to the public. It took 25 years to finally complete this wonderful tribute to the Father of our Nation. It has been noted that the color of the brick changes about one-third of the way up. This appears to be the result of the halting of construction during the Civil War and identical bricks were not available. The construction did not begin again until the war ended. In 1910 a law was enacted restricting building heights to be no taller than the width of the street it faces. That law is still in effect. No building can be taller than 13 stories. Pennsylvania Avenue is a zoning exception.

From atop this magnificent granite and marble structure, visitors may take in the beautiful panoramic view of the city with its division into four major segments. From that vantage point, one can see the original plan of the designer, Charles L'Enfant imposed upon the landscape, with the White House to the north, the Jefferson Memorial to the south, the Capitol to the east and the Lincoln Memorial to the west.

On the 12th landing of the monument is a prayer offered by the city of Baltimore. On the 20th landing is a memorial presented by Chinese Christians. On the 24th landing is a presentation made by Sunday School children from New York and Philadelphia, quoting Proverbs 10:7, Luke 18:16, and Proverbs 22:6 *Praise be to God!* When the cornerstone was laid on July 4, 1848, deposited within it were items including the Holy Bible presented by the American

Bible Society.[107] This was and continues to be an important symbol indicating our firm belief in God and our profound belief in and respect for our greatest Founder and first President of our Constitutional Republic, George Washington.

A quote of George Washington inside the monument reads: "*I have no lust for power but wish with as much fervency as any Man upon this wide extended Continent, for an opportunity of turning the Sword into a plow share.*" Unfortunately, the public no longer has access to this wonderful quote because the steps to the top of the monument are closed.

---

[107] Religion in Eighteenth Century America – Religion and the Founding of the American Republic – http://1ref.us/fx

Part IV Chapter XII

COLONIAL LIFE AND CUSTOMS

The following "snapshots" into colonial life during the period of 1763-1789 give insight and understanding of the perils and pleasures experienced by our forefathers to whom we owe so much. America's heritage is so rich and bountiful, laced with confidence and hope, that we need to take a journey back to the time of the birth of our Constitution. There we would learn of and appreciate the sacrifices that were made to guarantee the liberty we enjoy today.

Our Constitution is not just a set of rules by which we are governed, but it is the very foundation of our country—the SUPREME LAW OF THE LAND.

Our Constitution is not just a set of rules by which we are governed, but it is the very foundation of our country— the SUPREME LAW OF THE LAND.

The Declaration of Independence of 1776 represents the promise of the Constitution. As we look back and study the life-styles and customs of those who were involved in the birth of the Constitution, it becomes very clear that in spite of hardship and struggle, they were real people just like us. We owe them a great debt of gratitude for the lessons they taught us and the heritage we claim. Most colonists had a strong faith in God and in their government. Of course, changes in life-style and customs occurred as time passed, but the colonists accepted the responsibilities as citizens of a new nation with thanksgiving.

Religion

Religion was a critical part of colonial life. Many immigrants had fled their homes to avoid religious persecution and looked to life in a new land where their faith would be respected and allowed. Even though the Church of England was the legal church of the colonies, early on immigration included Catholics, Lutherans, Presbyterians, Methodists, Jews and Quakers. Religion was a defining characteristic of the community. They lived by the moral codes of their faith; and for most people, the Bible was the basis of their laws and regulations. They remembered with gratitude God's protection and provision during stressful times. This was especially true in New England where the colonists exhibited a high level of religious energy and a commitment to their faith. Church attendance was high, reaching to 75 to 80%.[108] Although a religious faith was important in the lives of the colonists, vices did exist but these violations of faith were dealt with appropriately.

THE OLD SOUTH.

As mentioned earlier, in the 1730's a religious awakening occurred and is often referred to as "The Great Awakening." A key figure was an Anglican clergyman, George Whitefield, one of the founders of Methodism. His message with the concept of a new birth in Jesus Christ, swept the colonies. It was

---

[108]   Faith of Our Forefathers (May 1998) - Library of Congress Information Bulletin – http://1ref.us/ed

reported that over 23,000 in Boston alone came to hear his message of redemption through the blood of Christ.[109]

Churches were built in all shapes and sizes. The churches not only reflected the customs and traditions of the people but the wealth and social standing of the denomination as well. The churches exhibited differences, from the bare essentials needed for worship to others with beautiful wood-carved pulpits.

Education

Education was important to the colonists. Due to a lack of actual textbooks, many parents taught their children to read by reading the Bible. In New England, villages of one hundred families or more set up grammar schools for both boys and girls. Education was considered important for boys, more than for girls. Boys were taught math and Latin in preparation for college or perhaps a career in a counting house. Girls were taught to read, but there was little to no emphasis on preparation for college.

Children learned to read from Hornbooks, which were nothing more than slabs of wood with paper glued to them. The teacher or parent would place what was to be learned on the Hornbook. Later, in 1886, the first edition of the McGuffy Reader, containing a spelling book and key texts for teaching reading was published by William Holmes McGuffy. Selections in the reader were drawn from what was considered the best of English literature and many extracts from the Bible.

Pencils and paper as we know them today were not available. Paper was scarce, and the only writing instrument was a "quill" pen made from goose feathers. Ink was made from crushed walnuts and water or strained berry juice. A few homes had slates for writing and slate pencils, which were probably imported from England. Learning to write a "good hand" was considered very important and boys were even encouraged to attend writing schools. Our original Constitution is a testimony to the beauty and style of writing as taught at that time. (See Appendix, The History of the Quill Pen.)

School buildings were rare, and most of those that did exist consisted of one room. Teachers were usually the local "parson" or clergyman. This was considered appropriate since the clergy were usually the best qualified and trained to teach.

In some of the middle colonies, schools were private or sectarian (church affiliated) and filled the same role as the schools in New England. However, if you were Catholic, if at all possible, you went to a Catholic school. Because the

---

[109] George Whitefield: Did You Know? | Christian History – http://1ref.us/ee

south was more rural, there were fewer schools. Wealthy children were tutored and children from families of lesser means were either taught by parents or older siblings. Not many children in the south received formal education.

Secondary schools were rare. However, there were secondary schools in major towns such as: New York, Philadelphia, and Charlestown. The subjects offered prepared young men for a career in accounting, surveying, language, or the ministry. Among the first colleges were Harvard (1636), The College of William and Mary (1683), St. John's College (1696), Yale (1701), The College of New Jersey (Princeton, 1746), and King's College (Columbia, 1784). Boys typically entered college at the age of 14 or 15.

Manners-Social Graces

Based on their country of origin, there was great diversity among the colonists. This influenced their ideas, manners, customs and social graces. Although the colonists possessed various theological views, it appeared they co-mingled well with those of different theological views. They held to a common love for liberty and the concept of majority rule. Perhaps because of their struggle to come to America or their involvement in conflict, they were united in resistance to any outside aggression.

There was significant emphasis on manners and social graces. The colonists held to the importance of civility that characterized true Englishmen. There were many rules, and for all ages, including the children. Manners were an indication of family background and social class. George Washington's *Rules for Civility* were widely accepted as a standard for civility. They believed that all rules of civility should be observed because they were based on the basic principles of kindness, respect, and courtesy. Children were expected to "behave", especially at the table.

Some of the rules were:

- Stand until the blessing is said and you are told to be seated.
- Don't ask for anything.
- Never speak unless spoken to.
- Break your bread; never bite into a whole slice.
- Never take salt with a greasy knife. (Salt was served in small dishes called "salt cellars.")
- Never speak to your parents without some form of respect such as Madam, Sir.
- Make not a noise with thy tongue, lips or breath.

Much of the attitude and behavioral expectations of colonial Americans were based on the Bible and Christ's teachings of relationship with Him and your fellow man.

Much of the attitude and behavioral expectations of colonial Americans were based on the Bible and Christ's teachings of relationship with Him and your fellow man.

Although some of their rules for living may seem strict to us today, their adherence to Godly principles was important as it helped them through difficult times and the growing pains of becoming a new nation. Even though church affiliation was diverse, most agreed upon the basic principles for living as set forth by their religion.

Colonists both in the north and in the south were aware of the importance of good manners. Although the typical lifestyle was plain and simple, they attempted to regulate society's habits and tastes by formal standards. All persons were respected, one person was considered as good as another, and your station in life was by the direction of Providence. Great respect was shown towards all women, not for the sake of chivalry but from a sense of appreciation. Since many colonists were farmers, manual labor was considered honorable and dignified.

Titles were an indication of distinction and were to be respected. Even the "voice" should be well-trained and pleasant sounding. Colonists from the southern states adhered more to English customs. They were hospitable and given to social refinement that included dress and behavior.

Colonial Dress

Most of the colonists dressed simply. How you dressed was an indication of social standing or position. Those of wealth followed English fashion with imported garments or fabrics. Men of wealth also had an interest in fashion and often wore silk stockings, as did the women. They were so interested in shapely legs that some even had pads sewn into their stockings. Garments made of velvet with ruffles at the neck and sleeves were common. They wore hats, often

pinned to keep the brim from flap-
ping. This was the beginning of the
famous Tricorn hat. Because there
were no shops or department stores
at that time, clothing was either made
at home or ordered from European
dressmakers, depending upon one's
means. Fabric was either imported
from England or spun at home on a
"spinning wheel." Garments had to
be sewn by hand as sewing machines,
such as the popular Singer, did not
come into use until 1851. Needles
were hand- made by local craftsmen.

Children dressed much like their
parents. The little girls wore long loose
dresses, skirts, bonnets, and based on
the weather, long wool stockings. Boys
wore shirts, knee breeches, vests, and
when the weather was cold, a knit cap.
In the northern colonies, clothing was
often made of "linsey-woolsey," which
was woven of linen and wool threads.

MARGUERITE.

Children didn't like "linsey-woolsey"; they said it made them itch too much.

If the colonists desired a special color in their clothing, they resorted to
dying, a rather tedious process. The color red was made from the juice of a
pokeberry, yellow or brown color from sassafras or butternut bark. All colors
tended to fade as the garments were washed. There was no such thing as "col-
orfast" material.

Even the shoes of the colonists were made at home, as only the wealthier
colonists were able to buy them from a shoemaker. The children went barefoot
in summer, but in winter when shoes were needed to keep their feet warm, their
fathers would, most likely, make a pair from whatever materials were available.
They were usually made of animal skins and in the style of a moccasin. Lynn,
Massachusetts, became the shoe capital of the Colonial period for those who
could afford them, and a shoemaker was called a "cordwainer." The term is
derived from the word "cordwain," or "cordovan" a leather produced in Cor-
doba, Spain. "Cobbler" was a name given to one who repaired shoes. Animal
hides were the leathers used, and it was said that the hide of dogs was used for

RECEPTION IN CHEW HOUSE.

ladies' soft, supple dancing shoes. Hence, came the expression "putting on the dog."

After the Revolution, the fashion scene began to change. Although wigs had been popular, some removed their wigs and began to wear their hair long or in what we now call "ponytails." Wigs were still a prominent sign of the era and were in style during the whole century. It had become a basic element in the dress of the wealthy and middle class. Through the years the style of wigs changed, but during the late 1700's it became popular to wear a tied up wig with curls along the sides. Powdering a wig was done, usually white, but some used color as well. Wigs were made of goat or horse hair. It has been said that the word "powder room" originated with the powdering of the hair.

Ladies wigs were usually very neat, upswept with two little side curls on each side. The expression, "a chip off the old block" appears to have originated when a wig-maker knocked a wooden block head to the floor, picked it up and if it was damaged said, "There's a chip off the old block."

Mealtime

Mealtime was a family time for the colonial household. Father sat at the head of the table and mother at the end, closest to where the food was prepared. Children sat at the sides and were expected to exhibit good manners. Father said the "blessing" before the food was passed. In the wealthy home, the same customs were observed but food would be served by the servants.

The diet was simple, and portions were modest as food was expensive and not plentiful. Vegetable gardens were essential and the entire family worked the garden. Even the small houses in the village had gardens. It was hard work to make gardens that produced enough food for the summer and winter and also to sell. Many families had one pig, a cow, and some chickens. Wealthy families had servants who tended the garden, took care of the livestock, and cooked the meals. But most were farmers, and they spread their efforts over a whole range of possible forms of produce. They ate what was available to them at the time. Orchards were a prized possession for both food and drink. They grew special herbs and spices that helped preserve food.

The main crops were corn, beans, squash, pumpkins, turnips and potatoes. Corn was the main crop; and it was used in every possible way including johnnycakes, slapjacks and mush. The German settlers introduced "hoecakes." This was a type of doughnut dipped in molasses and the shape was an elongated oval, similar to an ear of corn. There was no coffee, but cider or a tea substitute was enjoyed.

In New England, colonial families ate baked beans on Sunday. The mother would begin the beans on Saturday night by putting them into a pot called a "bean pot" with a piece of salt pork and molasses. The beans would cook all night in the fireplace and be ready for Sunday. This custom is still observed today in many New England homes.

Because there was no refrigeration, meat had to be smoked, salted or pickled. They used root cellars and a springhouse for refrigeration. Because meat could only be kept a few days, it was generally smoked, heavily salted, and stored in a small "smokehouse." If eggs were served, they were usually boiled. Fruit was seasonal and the growing season in the south was longer than in the north.

Americans have always loved desserts, but in colonial days they were not so varied as those on today's menus. Dessert was served as a status symbol in the houses of the wealthy. It was not an everyday thing, even for them. Flour and sugar were expensive and the middle class families had to "make do" with fruit and food with a natural sweetness.

Breakfast was usually oatmeal or cornmeal mush. Cornmeal mush was made by boiling cornmeal in water, similar to the way today's "grits" are prepared. Meat was considered essential for energy and was usually served as roasted wild game, venison or bear. However, because meat was scarce, small portions were served.

A midday meal was served sometime between 2 and 4 o'clock and was expected to hold them over until late evening. It was usually soup, meat of some kind (if available) or fish. Greens or vegetables from the garden completed the meal. If there was a dessert, it would be some sort of a pudding such as Indian pudding, which was made with cornmeal and molasses. A very simple "supper" was served in the evening. It was very light, perhaps from leftovers from the larger midday meal with some fruit and light dessert. Yes, they did have ice cream but only on rare occasions and in winter, and for obvious reasons. It was made from cream, sugar, and fresh fruit. The mixture was put into a tin container with a small crank, which turned the inside tube of ice and salt.

Christmas was to all colonists, as to us, a very special time and celebrated as their resources provided. For the well-to-do it included: fruitcakes, pudding, ginger-flavored cakes, and a large bowl of a drink (a spiced ale) called "wassail". A typical Christmas dinner for the wealthy might be:

Haunch of Venison Roast Chine of Pork

Onions in Cream Pigeon Pasties Roast Goose

Potatoes Raw celery

Mincemeat Pie Pumpkin Pie Apple Pie

Indian Pudding Plum Pudding

Cyder

Wassail

For beverages, the colonists had given up tea during the War for Independence because of the hated tax. They showed their resourcefulness and made a rather delightful drink from goldenrod, sage, blackberry bush, and the common currant bush. Not many hostesses had china cups; so a lady might carry her own cup, saucer and spoon with her when invited to a tea. She might also tuck a little sugar away. Sugar was expensive and used sparingly.

Because they did not have a way to purify water, they resorted to other beverages such as peach or apple cider. They felt that water made them sick, and perhaps it did. Milk was scarce as there were not many cows. Beer was a common beverage, even for the children.

(See Appendix, Recipes from the Colonial Hearth)

Music

Colonial people enjoyed a variety of music just as we do now. Much of the music was brought to America from other countries by people who immigrated to our shores. The music that was most popular included: hymns of the church, ballads, folk songs, dance tunes, parodies, drum signals, minuets, military marches, comic arias, and sonatas. Music helped to wile away the hours and provided lots of entertainment. Music contributed greatly to the definition of the new country. It expressed their lives, their struggles and their victories.

Ballads centered around the war, and eternal themes of love, death and disappointment. One of the popular ballads was *Barbara Allen*. It dealt with unrequited love and betrayal. It has been said that fourteen year-old Abe Lincoln sang this ballad as he was working in the fields at his home in Indiana.

Despite the hostility to dancing on the part of many of their clergy, most loved to dance, which was usually some type of Celtic or English. Their dances included: reels, jigs, and minuets. Dancing was one of the favorite pastimes, and dances could range from a country band to high society where dancing was done according to many rules and regulations. Dancing was a form of socializing for those who worked hard in the fields and had little opportunity to socialize. Dance teachers traveled from town to town teaching the latest dances that came from England and France. The French Minuet and the English Country dance were favored because they were easy to learn. Their dance forms were modest and respectful.

The most popular instruments were: the violin, the accordion and a version of our piano. Everyone from the slaves to the wealthy played either the violin or the "fiddle." Flutes and fifes of various types were played by men and the harpsicord was generally played by women. The English guitar was also popular. Music theaters provided performances of ballad operas and colonists would often return home with the words and music to play and sing.

Church music was the most varied, and was available to all. It was a very important part of worship, as it expressed God's love, protection and care for them; and it gave them the opportunity to offer praise for His bountiful blessings. The average New England congregation sang Psalms, anthems and fuging tunes. (Fuging tunes were sacred tunes written for a 4- part chorus.) It appears the colonists were keenly aware of God's protection and blessings during their difficult times.

In the early 1700's traveling musicians were paid to teach church members to read music. Church members in the south were influenced by the Church of England and appeared to be less enthusiastic about church music. The organ was the instrument of choice, but there were more organs in private homes than in the churches. A well-known clergyman of the time, Cotton Mather, wrote in his instruction to new clergymen, *"For I would not have a day pass without you singing, but so as at the same time to make a melody in your heart to the Lord."*[110]

The Negro spirituals became a popular choral style after the Civil War, and is attributed to the influence of the music of the colonial period. Amazingly, the Library of Congress has catalogued over six thousand Negro spirituals.

---

[110]   Music history of the United States during the colonial era – Wikipedia, the free encyclopedia – http://1ref.us/ef

The question arises: "Where did the slaves learn about Jesus and a chariot that would *swing low to carry them home?* It is clear they heard the Gospel message at the plantation and sang about it in their everyday life.

Among the favorite hymns of the Colonial Period were:

- *A Charge to Keep I Have* by Methodist Charles Wesley and Lowell Mason in 1780. (Charles Wesley was the author of over 6500 hymns.)

- *All Glory Laud and Honor* by Theodolph of Orleans, A Palm Sunday processional hymn written about 820 A.D.

- *Am I a Soldier of the Cross*? by Isaac Watts, often called the Father of English Hymnody

- *Glorious Things of Thee Are Spoken* by John Newton in 1779. John Newton was one of the evangelical preachers of the 18th century, a slave trader before a conversion to Christ. His most popular hymn was *Amazing Grace*.

A favorite fun tune of the period was *Yankee Doodle*. It is believed to have been written in 1775 by an Army surgeon to mock the Colonial troops. It caught on and additional verses were added to it.

Colonial Games and Toys

Because there were no factories making toys, parents made the children's toys from whatever materials were available to them. Toys tended to be things found in nature or things that could be easily made at home. Dolls were made of rags or cornhusks and stuffed with cotton. Spinning tops were made with leftover wood. Because families were usually large, there were always brothers, sisters, neighbors, and perhaps cousins for playmates.

Children had to learn to work at an early age as there were always many chores and responsibilities to share. Skills were learned through many of the games and toys. Through some games they learned to throw, how to do things with their hands, and how to follow directions. Good manners in games were expected of all children. They were instructed to be fair and to wait for their turn. Boys were taught early to be respectful of girls. Some of their favorite games were: *London Bridge, Hopscotch, Hoops, Pick-up Sticks, Marbles, Leap Frog, and Blind Man's Bluff*. There were board games as well. A particularly popular one was "*Nine Men's Mice.*" This game could be played on a piece of paper or even in the dirt. Moving pieces could be stones, beans or corn kernels. Riddles were fun too, such as:

- What has teeth but cannot eat? (comb)
- What has a tongue but cannot talk? (shoe)
- What has 3 feet but cannot walk? (stool)
- What has a mouth but cannot talk? (river)
- What falls down but never gets hurt? (waterfall)

Travel – Transportation

Travel was limited and was done either by stagecoach or horseback. There were inns along most highways for the weary travelers, but accommodations were simple and rooms often had to be shared. Roads were bad, very muddy at times, and the colonists often carried additional shoes with them to change before going into church.

Mail was carried by post riders. They followed bridle paths and trails. Mail delivery was not regular and only when it was worthwhile for payment of the trip, perhaps once a month. The mail for a whole year in colonial times was less than one day in New York City today. Benjamin Franklin was a postmaster in 1753 and held that post for 20 years.

THE CHEW COACH.

Inns

Inns or taverns were not only an integral part of colonial life in America, but were also considered a necessity. The modes of travel and transportation of the day mandated the location of a tavern every few miles of the main thoroughfares, where tired and hungry travelers could find food and drink and a bed or floor upon which to sleep. Most colonial taverns were the only available public meeting places in early American towns and countryside.

Men from all walks of life met in the taverns to discuss business, discuss politics, and gossip over hearty food and drink. The taverns served as a town hall, a news center, general store and military station.

It has been reported that throughout the colonies everyone drank liquor, from babes to ministers, due to their rigorous lifestyle, scanty diets, bitter cold winters without home heating and lack of medicine. Many families drank homemade wine, brandy and ale made from the apples of the many trees they planted. It could very well be said that much discussion of a new United States took place before crackling fires in these many colonial taverns.

News

There were a few newspapers, but delivery was only by private arrangement. The papers were small and ill-printed. The contents consisted of: poetry, ads, arrangement of cargoes, European news, and essays on politics, morals and religion. One of the first daily newspapers, *The Pennsylvania Packet*, was printed in 1784. Circulation was limited, reaching perhaps three to five thousand, and was available three times a week. Subscribers were often slow to pay, and a tax on paper added to the difficulties of the publishers.

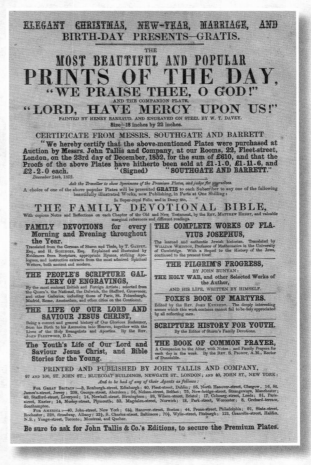

Medicine

Illness was rampant in the colonies, and life expectancy for the early colonists was only thirty-six years.[111] This is understandable when you consider they had little or no knowledge of sanitation or medicine. Doctors were few and there was no running water. Bathing was limited and consisted of applying water to the body with a cloth, commonly called a "wash rag." The early

---

111 Life and Death in The Liberty Era 1750-1800 | Legacy.com – http://1ref.us/eg

colonists believed that a thin layer of dirt on their bodies was a protection, and because of this belief, diseases spread quickly and whole families were sometimes wiped out. Diseases were varied, the most common being: small pox, chilblain (swelling of hands and feet due to exposure to cold), pneumonia, scarlet fever, rickets (caused by a lack of vitamin C), cholera (caused by the consumption of contaminated water) diphtheria, and dropsy. Malaria was common in the south and was carried by mosquitoes.

Some of the remedies of that time were:

- To stop bleeding they roasted salted beef in hot ashes and placed it on the wound.

- To get rid of lice or ticks, they applied cottonwood that had been boiled in lye.

- For a sore throat, diphtheria or fever: a mixture of 2 teaspoons of charcoal and 10 drops of spirits of turpentine into one cup of fresh milk. Gargle frequently.

- For a headache, a mixture of one teaspoon of charcoal and one-third teaspoon of soda in very warm water.

- For a toothache, powdered alum with salt and place on the tooth.

- For a burn, a paste of wheat flour and cold water. Place on burn. Replace when dry.

- For the "itch," an ointment with 60 grains of iodide of potassium, 2 ounces of lard, mixed well and rubbed on the body after bathing. This was to be applied 3 times a week for 7 or 8 days or until "itch" was gone.

Medical knowledge came from England or from a few medical journals. There were limited medical requirements to become a doctor and only a few medical schools. Their ideas about medical care were diverse. Some felt that illness was caused by evil spirits and "blood-letting" was often used to cure medical problems. With time and education, newer and better methods of treating illnesses appeared and life expectancy improved.

Money-Currency

There were limited mines from which to extract metal local; thus currency was limited. They relied upon the British Pound, the Dutch Guilder and the Spanish Eight-Piece. Bartering was often a source of exchange, using wheat, corn, coal and even cattle. Before 1776, paper notes were produced. After the Revolutionary War started, Continental notes were printed, but Britain would not recognize them as legal. Counterfeiting appeared, and because there was no backing for these Continental notes, their value dropped. It is reported that one Philadelphia merchant paid 20,000 notes for a ham.

There was no consistency of exchanging money among the colonies since each had its own monetary system. During the Constitutional Convention, they agreed to a new procedure which was stated in the *Constitution*, *Article I, Section 8*. Precious metals would be the backing for the new monetary system of the United States Because of the huge debts incurred by the states during the Revolutionary War, Congress voted to pay these debts. The Secretary of the Treasury, Alexander Hamilton, proposed that the much-needed revenue be raised through taxes to which Congress agreed.

The first bank of the United States was chartered by Congress in 1789 shortly after the signing of the Constitution and was authorized to issue banknotes. The U.S Federal government did not start printing its own paper money until 1862.

CONTINENTAL MONEY.

APPENDIX

TIMELINE OF EVENTS
Leading to the Ratification of the Constitution of the United States

September 5, 1774-The First Continental Congress; a meeting of a committee to decide what action should be taken against British rule. *A Declaration of Rights* was written.

April, 1775-The events at Lexington and Concord start the American Revolution.

June 19, 1775-George Washington becomes the Commander of the Continental army.

July 4, 1776-The Declaration of Independence is drafted, signed and approved.

November 15, 1777-The *Articles of Confederation* are accepted at the Continental Congress.

March 1, 1781-The 13 states vote their approval for the *Articles of Confederation*.

September 3, 1783-The Treaty of Paris is signed by United States and England. England signs a separate treaty with France and Spain.

January 14, 1784-Congress ratifies the Treaty of Paris which officially ends the Revolutionary War.

August, 1786 – February, 1787-Shays' Rebellion occurs in western Massachusetts. This showed the leaders of the colonies the need for a strong central government.

May 25, 1787-The Constitutional Convention begins meetings in Philadelphia, Pennsylvania. Every state except Rhode Island is represented. (Rhode Island was skeptical but later became the 13th state to ratify the Constitution.)

July 16, 1787-The Constitutional Convention meets to work out different parts of the Constitution. Roger Sherman proposes the Connecticut Compromise which combines the best components of the Virginia and New Jersey Plans.

September 17, 1787-The 12 state delegations vote to approve the Constitution. 39 delegates place their signature on the Constitution. 42 delegates are present. The Constitutional Convention formally closes its meetings.

December 7, 1787-Delaware becomes the first state to vote to accept the Constitution.

June 21, 1788-New Hampshire is the ninth state to ratify the Constitution which puts the plans for America's government into effect.

February 4, 1789-The first presidential election is complete, but the results will not be tallied and shown until April 6

March 4, 1789-Congress meets for the first time as a governing body in New York

April 30, 1789-George Washington is inaugurated as the first president of the United States

June 8, 1789-The Bill of Rights is proposed to be a part of the Constitution by James Madison in the House of Representatives

September 25, 1789-Congress approves 12 amendments to the Bill of Rights They are sent to the states for ratification.

November 20, 1789-New Jersey ratifies the Bill of Rights

May 29, 1790-Rhode Island is the last of the 13 states to approve the Constitution.

December 1791-The Bill of Rights is voted on and 10 of the 12 amendments are accepted as part of the Constitution.

BACKGROUND INFORMATION
on the Framers of the Constitution of the United States

NAME	STATE	POLITICAL EXPERIENCE	OCCUPA-TION	AGE AS DELEGATE
Baldwin, Abraham	Georgia	Served in public office	Minister, Lawyer	38
Bassett, Richard	Delaware	None	Lawyer, Slave Owner	36
Bedford, Gunning Jr.	Delaware	Congressional	Lawyer	40
Blair, John	Virginia	Judge of the Supreme Court in Virginia	Lawyer, Slave Owner	50
Blount, William	N. Carolina	Senator and state legislator	Politician, Merchant, Slave Owner	36
Brearley, David	New Jersey	Judge of the Supreme Court of New Jersey	Lawyer	40
Broom, Jacob	Delaware	None	Merchant, Farmer	35
Butler, Pierce	S. Carolina	Member of the Legislature of South Carolina	Soldier, Politician, Slave Owner	40
Carroll, Daniel	Maryland	Signed the Articles of Confederation	Farmer, Slave Owner	57
Clymer, George	Pennsylvania	Signed the Declaration of Independence	Merchant	40
Davie, William R.	N. Carolina	None	Lawyer	30

NAME	STATE	POLITICAL EXPERIENCE	OCCUPA- TION	AGE AS DELEGATE
Dayton, Jonathan	New Jersey	None	Merchant, Lawyer	26
Dickinson, John	Delaware	Signed the Articles of Confederation, former governor	Lawyer	55
Ellsworth, Oliver	Connecticut	Judge of the Supreme Court in Connecticut	Lawyer	37
Few, William	Georgia	Member of Congress	Lawyer, Farmer	35
FitzSimons, Thomas	Pennsylvania	Member of Legislature in Pennsylvania	Merchant	40
Franklin, Benjamin	Pennsylvania	President of the Supreme Executive Council	Inventor, Slave Owner	82
Gerry, Elbridge	Massachusetts	Signed the Declaration of Independence & the Articles of Confederation	Merchant	37
Gilman, Nicholas	New Hampshire	Member of Congress	Merchant	30
Gorham, Nathaniel	Massachusetts	Served as President of Continental Congress	Merchant	46
Hamilton, Alexander	New York	Member of Congress	Lawyer	33
Houston, William C.	New Jersey	Member of Congress	Teacher	30

NAME	STATE	POLITICAL EXPERIENCE	OCCUPA-TION	AGE AS DELEGATE
Houstoun, William	Georgia	Member of Congress	Lawyer	32
Ingersoll, Jared	Pennsylvania	Member of Congress	Lawyer	36
Jenifer, Daniel of St. Thomas	Maryland	Member of Congress, Aid de Camp to Major General Lee	Lawyer, Slave Owner	55
Johnson, William S.	Connecticut	Agent for the state of Connecticut	Lawyer, College President	60
King, Rufus	Massachusetts	Member of Congress	Lawyer	33
Langdon, John	New Hampshire	Former Governor	Merchant	30
Lansing, John Jr.	New York	Mayor of Albany, NY	Lawyer	32
Livingston, William	New Jersey	Member of Congress	Lawyer	60
Madison, James Jr.	Virginia	Member of Congress	Politician, Slave Owner	37
Martin, Alexander	N. Carolina	Governor of N. Carolina, Colonel in the American Army	Politician	40
Martin, Luther	Maryland	None	Lawyer	34
Mason, George	Virginia	None	Politician, Slave Owner	60
McClurg, James	Virginia	None	Doctor	38

NAME	STATE	POLITICAL EXPERIENCE	OCCUPA-TION	AGE AS DELEGATE
McHenry, James	Maryland	Aid to General Washington & the Marquis de la Fayette	Doctor	32
Mercer, John F.	Maryland	Member of Congress	Lawyer	28
Mifflin, Thomas	Pennsylvania	President of Continental Congress	Merchant	40
Morris, Gouvenour	Pennsylvania	Signed the Declaration of Independence & the Articles of Confederation	Lawyer	38
Morris, Robert	Pennsylvania	Signed the Articles of Confederation, helped write 3 of the basic documents	Merchant	50
Paterson, William	New Jersey	None	Lawyer	34
Pierce, William L.	Georgia	Served in the American Revolution	Merchant	34
Pinckney, Charles Cotesworth	S. Carolina	Officer in the American Army	Lawyer, Slave Owner	40
Pinckney, Charles	S. Carolina	Member of Congress	Lawyer, Slave Owner	29
Randolph, Edmund J.	Virginia	Governor of Virginia	Lawyer	32
Read, George	Delaware	Signed the Declaration of Independence	Lawyer, Judge	50

NAME	STATE	POLITICAL EXPERIENCE	OCCUPATION	AGE AS DELEGATE
Rutledge, John	S. Carolina	Governor of S. Carolina	Lawyer, Slave Owner	48
Sherman, Roger	Connecticut	Member of Congress, Signed the Declaration of Independence & the Articles of Confederation, helped write 3 of the basic documents	Lawyer, Merchant	60
Spaight, Richard D.	N. Carolina	Member of Congress	Politician, Slave Owner	32
Strong, Caleb	Massachusetts	None	Lawyer	35
Washington, George	Virginia	Commander in Chief of the American Army	Soldier, Slave Owner	52
Williamson, Hugh	N. Carolina	Member of Congress	Educator, Scientist, Doctor	48
Wilson, James	Pennsylvania	Signed the Declaration of Independence	Lawyer, Merchant	45
Wythe, George	Virginia	Signed the Declaration of Independence	Lawyer	55
Yates, Robert	New York	None	Lawyer, Judge	55

THE DECLARATION OF INDEPENDENCE

Action of the Second Continental Congress
July 4, 1776

The Unanimous Declaration of the Thirteen United States of America

The Declaration of Independence is a statement adopted by the Continental Congress on July 4, 1776, in which it was made clear that the thirteen colonies were now independent states and no longer a part of the British Empire. It was initially published as a printed broadside and distributed to the public. The Declaration listed colonial grievances against King George III and asserted natural rights which included a right to revolution.

The Declaration of Independence is a statement adopted by the Continental Congress on July 4, 1776, in which it was made clear that the thirteen colonies were now independent states and no longer a part of the British Empire.

"When in the Course of human events, it becomes necessary for one people to dissolve the political bands which have connected them with another, and to assume among the powers of the earth, the separate and equal station to which the Laws of Nature and of Nature's God entitle them, a decent respect to the opinions of mankind requires that they should declare the causes which impel them to the separation.

We hold these truths to be self-evident, that all men are created equal, that they are endowed by their Creator with certain unalienable Rights, that among these are Life, Liberty and the pursuit of Happiness.- That to secure these rights, Governments are instituted among Men, deriving their just powers from the con-

sent of the governed,- That whenever any form of Government becomes destructive of these ends, it is the Right of the People to alter or to abolish it, and to institute new Government, laying its foundation on such principles and organizing its powers in such form, as to them shall seem most likely to effect their Safety and Happiness. Prudence, indeed, will dictate that Governments long established should not be changed for light and transient causes; and accordingly all experience hath shewn, that mankind are more disposed to suffer, while evils are sufferable, than to right themselves by abolishing the forms to which they are accustomed. But when a long train of abuses and usurpations, pursuing invariably the same Object evinces a design to reduce them under absolute Despotism, it is their right, it is their duty, to throw off such Government, and to provide new Guards for their future security- Such has been the patient suffering of these Colonies; and such is now the necessity which constrains them to alter their former Systems of Government. The history of the present King of Great Britain is a history of repeated injuries and usurpations, all having in direct object the establishment of an absolute Tyranny over these States. To prove this, let Facts be submitted to a candid world.

He has refused his Assent to Laws, the most wholesome and necessary for the public good.

He has forbidden his Governors to pass Laws of immediate and pressing importance, unless suspended in their operation till his Assent should be obtained; and when so suspended, he has utterly neglected to attend to them.

He has refused to pass other Laws for the accommodation of large districts of people, unless those people would relinquish the right of Representation in the Legislature, a right inestimable to them and formidable to tyrants only.

He has called together legislative bodies at places unusual, uncomfortable, and distant from the depository of their public Records, for the sole purpose of fatiguing them into compliance with his measures.

He has dissolved Representative Houses repeatedly, for opposing with manly firmness his invasions on the rights of the people.

He has refused for a long time, after such dissolutions, to cause others to be elected; whereby the Legislative powers, incapable of Annihilation, have returned to the People at large for their exercise; the State remaining in the mean time exposed to all the dangers of invasion from without, and convulsions within.

He has endeavoured to prevent the population of these States; for that purpose obstructing the Laws for Naturalization of Foreigners; refusing to pass others to encourage their migrations hither, and raising the conditions of new Appropriations of Lands.

He has obstructed the Administration of Justice, by refusing his Assent to Laws for establishing Judiciary powers.

He has made Judges dependent on his Will alone, for the tenure of their offices, and the amount and payment of their salaries.

He has erected a multitude of New Offices, and sent hither swarms of Officers to harass our people, and eat out their substance.

He has kept among us, in times of peace, Standing Armies without the Consent of our legislatures.

He has affected to render the Military independent of and superior to the Civil power.

He has combined with others to subject us to a jurisdiction foreign to our constitution, and unacknowledged by our laws; giving his Assent to their Acts of pretended Legislation:

For Quartering large bodies of armed troops among us:

For protecting them, by a mock Trial, from punishment for any Murders which they should commit on the Inhabitants of these States:

For cutting off our Trade with all parts of the world:

For imposing Taxes on us without our Consent:

For depriving us in many cases, of the benefits of Trial by Jury:

For transporting us beyond Seas to be tried for pretended offences:

For abolishing the free System of English Laws in a neighboring Province, establishing therein an Arbitrary government, and enlarging its Boundaries so as to render it at once an example and fit instrument for introducing the same absolute rule into these Colonies:

For taking away our Charters, abolishing our most valuable Laws, and altering fundamentally the Forms of our Governments:

For suspending our own Legislatures, and declaring themselves invested with power to legislate for us in all cases whatsoever.

He has abdicated Government here, by declaring us out of his Protection and waging War against us.

He has plundered our seas, ravaged our Coasts, burnt our towns, and destroyed the lives of our people.

He is at this time transporting large Armies of foreign Mercenaries to compleat the works of death, desolation and tyranny, already begun with circumstances of Cruelty & perfidy scarcely paralleled in the most barbarous ages, and totally unworthy the Head of a civilized nation.

He has constrained our fellow Citizens taken Captive on the high Seas to bear Arms against their Country, to become the executioners of their friends and Brethren, or to fall themselves by their Hands.

He has excited domestic insurrections amongst us, and has endeavoured to bring on the inhabitants of our frontiers, the merciless Indian Savages, whose known rule of warfare, is an undistinguished destruction of all ages, sexes and conditions.

In every stage of these Oppressions We have Petitioned for Redress in the most humble terms: Our repeated Petitions have been answered only by repeated injury. A Prince whose character is thus marked by every act which may define a Tyrant, is unfit to be the ruler of a free people.

Nor have We been wanting in attentions to our British brethren. We have warned them from time to time of attempts by their legislature to extend an unwarrantable jurisdiction over us. We have reminded them of the circumstances of our emigration and settlement here. We have appealed to their native justice and magnanimity, and we have conjured them by the ties of our common kindred to disavow these usurpations, which, would inevitably interrupt our connections and correspondence. They too have been deaf to the voice of justice and of consanguinity. We must, therefore, acquiesce in the necessity, which denounces our Separation, and hold them, as we hold the rest of mankind, Enemies in War, in Peace Friends.

We, therefore, the Representatives of the United States of America, in General Congress, Assembled, appealing to the Supreme Judge of the world for the rectitude of our intentions, do, in the Name, and by Authority of the good People of these Colonies, solemnly publish and declare, That these United Colonies are, and of Right ought to be Free and Independent States; that they are Absolved from all Allegiance to the British Crown, and that all political connection between them and the State of Great Britain, is and ought to be totally dissolved; and that as Free and Independent States, they have full Power to levy War, conclude Peace, contract Alliances, establish Commerce, and to do all other Acts and Things which Independent States may of right do. And for the support of this Declaration, with a firm reliance on the protection of divine Providence, we mutually pledge to each other our Lives, our Fortunes and our sacred Honor."

THE ARTICLES OF CONFEDERATION

To all to whom these Presents shall come, we the undersigned Delegates of the States affixed to our Names send greeting.

Articles of Confederation and perpetual Union between the states of New Hampshire, Massachusetts Bay, Rhode Island and Providence Plantations, Connecticut, New York, New Jersey, Pennsylvania, Delaware, Maryland, Virginia, North Carolina, South Carolina and Georgia.

I.

The Stile of this Confederacy shall be
"The United States of America".

II.

Each State retains its sovereignty, freedom, and independence, and every power, jurisdiction, and right, which is not by this Confederation expressly delegated to the United States, in Congress assembled.

III.

The said States hereby severally enter into a firm league of friendship with each other, for their common defense, the security of their liberties, and their mutual and general welfare, binding themselves to assist each other, against all force offered to, or attacks made upon them, or any of them, on account of religion, sovereignty, trade, or any other pretense whatever.

IV.

The better to secure and perpetuate mutual friendship and intercourse among the people of the different States in this Union, the free inhabitants of each of these States, paupers, vagabonds, and fugitives from justice excepted, shall be entitled to all privileges and immunities of free citizens in the several States; and the people of each State shall have free ingress and regress to and from any other State, and shall enjoy therein all the privileges of trade and commerce, subject to the same duties, impositions, and restrictions as the inhabitants thereof respectively, provided that such restrictions shall not extend so far as to prevent the removal of property imported into any State, to any other State, of which the owner is an inhabitant; provided also that no imposition, duties or restriction shall be laid by any State, on the property of the United States, or either of them.

If any person guilty of, or charged with, treason, felony, or other high misdemeanor in any State, shall flee from justice, and be found in any of the United States, he shall, upon demand of the Governor or executive power of the State from which he fled, be delivered up and removed to the State having jurisdiction of his offense.

Full faith and credit shall be given in each of these States to the records, acts, and judicial proceedings of the courts and magistrates of every other State.

V.

For the more convenient management of the general interests of the United States, delegates shall be annually appointed in such manner as the legislatures of each State shall direct, to meet in Congress on the first Monday in November, in every year, with a power reserved to each State to recall its delegates, or any of them, at any time within the year, and to send others in their stead for the remainder of the year.

No State shall be represented in Congress by less than two, nor by more than seven members; and no person shall be capable of being a delegate for more than three years in any term of six years; nor shall any person, being a delegate, be capable of holding any office under the United States, for which he, or another for his benefit receives any salary, fees or emolument of any kind.

Each State shall maintain its own delegates in a meeting of the States, and while they act as members of the committee of the States.

In determining questions in the United States in Congress assembled, each State shall have one vote.

Freedom of speech and debate in Congress shall not be impeached or questioned in any court, or place out of Congress, and the members of Congress shall be protected in their persons from arrests or imprisonments, during the time of their going to and from, and attendance on Congress, except for treason, felony, or breach of the peace.

VI.

No State, without the consent of the United States in Congress assembled, shall send any embassy to, or receive any embassy from, or enter into any conference, agreement, alliance or treaty with any King, Prince or State; nor shall any person holding any office of profit or trust under the United States, or any of them, accept any present, emolument, office or title of any kind whatever from any King, Prince or foreign State; nor shall the United States in Congress assembled, or any of them, grant any title of nobility.

No two or more States shall enter into any treaty, confederation or alliance whatever between them, without the consent of the United States in Congress assembled, specifying accurately the purposes for which the same is to be entered into, and how long it shall continue.

No State shall lay any imposts or duties, which may interfere with any stipulations in treaties, entered into by the United States in Congress assembled, with any King, Prince or State, in pursuance of any treaties already proposed by Congress, to the courts of France and Spain.

No vessel of war shall be kept up in time of peace by any State, except such number only, as shall be deemed necessary by the United States in Congress assembled, for the defense of such State, or its trade; nor shall any body of forces be kept up by any State in time of peace, except such number only, as in the judgment of the United States in Congress assembled, shall be deemed requisite to garrison the forts necessary for the defense of such State; but every State shall always keep up a well-regulated and disciplined militia, sufficiently armed and accoutred, and shall provide and constantly have ready for use, in public stores, a due number of field pieces and tents, and a proper quantity of arms, ammunition and camp equipage.

No State shall engage in any war without the consent of the United States in Congress assembled, unless such State be actually invaded by enemies, or shall have received certain advice of a resolution being formed by some nation of Indians to invade such State, and the danger is so imminent as not to admit of a delay, till the United States in Congress assembled can be consulted: nor shall an State grant commissions to any ships or vessels of war, nor letters of marque or reprisal, except it be after a declaration of war by the United States in Congress assembled, and then only against the Kingdom or State and the subjects thereof, against which war has been so declared, and under such regulations as shall be established by the United States in Congress assembled, unless such State be infested by pirates, in which case vessels of war may be fitted out for that occasion, and kept so long as the danger shall continue or until the United States in Congress assembled shall determine otherwise.

VII.

When land forces are raised by any State for the common defense, all officers of or under the rank of colonel, shall be appointed by the legislature of each State respectively, by whom such forces shall be raised, or in such manner as such State shall direct, and all vacancies shall be filled up by the State which first made the appointment.

VIII.

All charges of war, and all other expenses that shall be incurred for the common defense or general welfare, and allowed by the United States in Congress assembled, shall be defrayed out of a common treasury, which shall be supplied by the several States in proportion to the value of all land within each State, granted to or surveyed for any person, as such land and the buildings and improvements thereon shall be estimated according to such mode as the United States in Congress assembled, shall from time to time direct and appoint.

The taxes for paying that proportion shall be laid and levied by the authority and direction of the legislatures of the several States within the time agreed upon by the United States in Congress assembled.

IX.

The United States in Congress assembled, shall have the sole and exclusive right and power of determining on peace and war, except in the cases mentioned in the sixth article -- of sending and receiving ambassadors -- entering into treaties and alliances, provided that no treaty of commerce shall be made whereby the legislative power of the respective States shall be restrained from imposing such imposts and duties on foreigners, as their own people are subjected to, or from prohibiting the exportation or importation of any species of goods or commodities whatsoever -- of establishing rules for deciding in all cases, what captures on land or water shall be legal, and in what manner prizes taken by land or naval forces in the service of the United States shall be divided or appropriated -- of granting letters of marque and reprisal in times of peace -- appointing courts for the trial of piracies and felonies committed on the high seas and establishing courts for receiving and determining finally appeals in all cases of captures, provided that no member of Congress shall be appointed a judge of any of the said courts.

The United States in Congress assembled shall also be the last resort on appeal in all disputes and differences now subsisting or that hereafter may arise between two or more States concerning boundary, jurisdiction or any other causes whatever; which authority shall always be exercised in the manner following. Whenever the legislative or executive authority or lawful agent of any State in controversy with another shall present a petition to Congress, stating the matter in question and praying for a hearing, notice thereof shall be given by order of Congress to the legislative or executive authority of the other State in controversy, and a day assigned for the appearance of the parties by their lawful agents, who shall then be directed to appoint by joint consent, commissioners or judges to constitute a court for hearing and determining the matter in question: but if they cannot agree, Congress shall name three persons out of each of the United States, and from the list of such persons each party shall alternately strike out one, the petitioners beginning, until the number shall be reduced to thirteen; and from that number not less than seven, nor more than nine names as Congress shall direct, shall in the presence of Congress be drawn out by lot, and the persons whose names shall be so drawn or any five of them, shall be commissioners or judges, to hear and finally determine the controversy, so always as a major part of the judges who shall hear the cause shall agree in the determination: and if either party shall neglect to attend at the day appointed, without showing reasons, which Congress shall judge sufficient, or being present shall refuse to strike, the Congress shall proceed to nominate three persons out of each State, and the secretary of Congress shall strike in behalf of such party absent or refusing; and the judgment and sentence of the court to be appointed, in the manner before prescribed, shall be final and conclusive; and if any of the parties shall refuse to submit to the authority of such court, or to appear or defend their claim or cause, the court shall nevertheless proceed to pronounce sentence, or judgment, which shall in like manner be final and decisive, the judgment or sentence and other proceedings being in either case transmitted to Congress, and lodged among the acts of Congress for the security of the parties concerned: provided that every commissioner, before he sits in judgment, shall take an oath to be administered by one of the judges of the supreme or superior court of the State, where the cause shall be tried, "well and truly to hear and determine the matter in question, according to the best of his judgment, without favor, affection or hope of reward:" provided also, that no State shall be deprived of territory for the benefit of the United States.

All controversies concerning the private right of soil claimed under different grants of two or more States, whose jurisdictions as they may respect such lands, and the States which passed such grants are adjusted, the said grants or either of them being at the same time claimed to have originated antecedent to such settlement of jurisdiction, shall on the petition of either party to the Congress of the United States, be finally determined as near as may be in the same manner as is before prescribed for deciding disputes respecting territorial jurisdiction between different States.

The United States in Congress assembled shall also have the sole and exclusive right and power of regulating the alloy and value of coin struck by their own authority, or by that of the respective States -- fixing the standards of weights and measures throughout the United States -- regulating the trade and managing all affairs with the Indians, not members of any of the States, provided that the legislative right of any State within its own limits be not infringed or violated -- establishing and regulating post offices from one State to another, throughout all the United States, and exacting such postage on the papers passing through the same as may be requisite to defray the expenses of the said office -- appointing all officers of the land forces, in the service of the United States, excepting regimental officers -- appointing all the officers of the naval forces, and commissioning all officers whatever in the service of the United States -- making rules for the government and regulation of the said land and naval forces, and directing their operations.

The United States in Congress assembled shall have authority to appoint a committee, to sit in the recess of Congress, to be denominated 'A Committee of the

States', and to consist of one delegate from each State; and to appoint such other committees and civil officers as may be necessary for managing the general affairs of the United States under their direction -- to appoint one of their members to preside, provided that no person be allowed to serve in the office of president more than one year in any term of three years; to ascertain the necessary sums of money to be raised for the service of the United States, and to appropriate and apply the same for defraying the public expenses -- to borrow money, or emit bills on the credit of the United States, transmitting every half year to the respective States an account of the sums of money so borrowed or emitted, -- to build and equip a navy -- to agree upon the number of land forces, and to make requisitions from each State for its quota, in proportion to the number of white inhabitants in such State; which requisition shall be binding, and thereupon the legislature of each State shall appoint the regimental officers, raise the men and cloath, arm and equip them in a soldier-like manner, at the expense of the United States; and the officers and men so cloathed, armed and equipped shall march to the place appointed, and within the time agreed on by the United States in Congress assembled: but if the United States in Congress assembled shall, on consideration of circumstances judge proper that any State should not raise men, or should raise a smaller number of men than its quota, and that any other State should raise a greater number of men than the quota thereof, such extra number shall be raised, officered, cloathed, armed and equipped in the same manner as the quota of each State, unless the legislature of such State shall judge that such extra number cannot be safely spread out in the same, in which case they shall raise, officer, cloath, arm and equip as many of such extra number as they judge can be safely spared. And the officers and men so cloathed, armed, and equipped, shall march to the place appointed, and within the time agreed on by the United States in Congress assembled.

The United States in Congress assembled shall never engage in a war, nor grant letters of marque or reprisal in time of peace, nor enter into any treaties or alliances, nor coin money, nor regulate the value thereof, nor ascertain the sums and expenses necessary for the defense and welfare of the United States, or any of them, nor emit bills, nor borrow money on the credit of the United States, nor appropriate money, nor agree upon the number of vessels of war, to be built or purchased, or the number of land or sea forces to be raised, nor appoint a commander in chief of the army or navy, unless nine States assent to the same; nor shall a question on any other point, except for adjourning from day to day be determined, unless by the votes of the majority of the United States in Congress assembled.

The Congress of the United States shall have power to adjourn to any time within the year, and to any place within the United States, so that no period of

*adjournment be for a longer duration than the space of six months, and shall pub-
lish the journal of their proceedings monthly, except such parts thereof relating to
treaties, alliances or military operations, as in their judgment require secrecy; and
the yeas and nays of the delegates of each State on any question shall be entered on
the journal, when it is desired by any delegate; of a State, or any of them, at his or
their request shall be furnished with a transcript of the said journal, except such
parts as are above excepted, to lay before the legislatures of the several States.*

X.

*The Committee of the States, or any nine of them, shall be authorized to exe-
cute, in the recess of Congress, such of the powers of Congress as the United States
in Congress assembled, by the consent of the nine States, shall from time to time
think expedient to vest them with; provided that no power be delegated to the said
Committee, for the exercise of which, by the Articles of Confederation, the voice of
nine States in the Congress of the United States assembled be requisite.*

XI.

*Canada acceding to this confederation, and adjoining in the measures of the
United States, shall be admitted into, and entitled to all the advantages of this
Union; but no other colony shall be admitted into the same, unless such admission
be agreed to by nine States.*

XII.

*All bills of credit emitted, monies borrowed, and debts contracted by, or under
the authority of Congress, before the assembling of the United States, in pursuance
of the present confederation, shall be deemed and considered as a charge against the
United States, for payment and satisfaction whereof the said United States, and the
public faith are hereby solemnly pledged.*

XIII.

*Every State shall abide by the determination of the United States in Congress
assembled, on all questions which by this confederation are submitted to them. And
the Articles of this Confederation shall be inviolably observed by every State, and
the Union shall be perpetual; nor shall any alteration at any time hereafter be made
in any of them; unless such alteration be agreed to in a Congress of the United
States, and be afterwards confirmed by the legislatures of every State.*

*And whereas it hath pleased the Great Governor of the World to incline the
hearts of the legislatures we respectively represent in Congress, to approve of, and
to authorize us to ratify the said Articles of Confederation and perpetual Union.
Know Ye that we the undersigned delegates, by virtue of the power and authority*

to us given for that purpose, do by these presents, in the name and in behalf of our respective constituents, fully and entirely ratify and confirm each and every of the said Articles of Confederation and perpetual Union, and all and singular the matters and things therein contained: And we do further solemnly plight and engage the faith of our respective constituents, that they shall abide by the determinations of the United States in Congress assembled, on all questions, which by the said Confederation are submitted to them. And that the Articles thereof shall be inviolably observed by the States we respectively represent, and that the Union shall be perpetual.

In witness whereof we have hereunto set our hands in Congress. Done at Philadelphia in the State of Pennsylvania the ninth day of July in the Year of our Lord One Thousand Seven Hundred and Seventy-Eight, and in the Third Year of the independence of America.

Agreed to by Congress 15 November, 1777. In force after ratification by Maryland, 1 March, 1781.

Source:
Documents Illustrative of the Formation of the Union of the American States. Government Printing Office, 1927.
House Document No. 398.
Selected, Arranged and Indexed by Charles C. Tansill

Article I
Name for the New Nation
The name of the new confederacy shall be "The United States of America".

Article II
Sovereignty of the States
Each state retains its sovereignty, freedom, and independence. And reserves to itself every power not expressly delegated to the United States Congress.

Article III
Confederation for Mutual Welfare
The several states enter into a firm league of friendship and bind themselves to assist each other for their common defense, the security of their liberties, and their mutual welfare.

Article IV
Interstate Rights and Responsibilities

To facilitate relations between the states, the free inhabitants of each state shall be entitled to all of the privileges and immunities enjoyed by citizens of the several states. They shall also enjoy freedom of travel and the privileges of trade and commerce. The property of the Confederacy of the United States shall be immune to taxation or regulation by the states. Criminals fleeing from one state to another shall be subject to extradition and each of the states shall give full faith and credit to official acts of the other states.

Article V
Structure of Continental Congress

The legislature of each state shall have delegates selected annually to meet in Congress the first Monday in November each year. No state shall be represented by less than two or more than seven delegates. Each state shall finance the support of its delegates. Each state shall have one vote. Delegates shall enjoy freedom of speech and shall not be questioned outside of Congress for statements made therein. They shall not be subject to arrest while serving Congress except for treason, felony, or breach of peace.

Article VI
Limitations on States

No state without the consent of Congress shall enter into any treaty with a foreign power or another state. No state shall impose any duties in violation of a treaty. No state shall maintain a standing army or navy in peacetime except that which is required for its defense. Each state shall maintain and equip a disciplined militia. No state shall engage in war without the consent of Congress unless actually invaded; nor shall any state commission ships or issue letters of marque and reprisal until a declaration of war by Congress.

Article VII
Appointment of Militia Officers

When land forces are raised by any state, all officers from colonel on down shall be appointed by the state.

Article VIII
Meeting the Cost of War

The expenses of any war shall be paid for out of the treasury of the confederacy, and shall be funded by the states in proportion to the value of the land within each state.

Article IX

Powers of the Congress

The Congress shall have the following powers: to determine peace and war; receive ambassadors; negotiate treaties; set rules for captures and prizes on land and water; grant letters of marque and reprisal in peacetime; appoint special courts for trial of piracies and crimes on the high seas, and to determine final appeals on captures. It shall also settle disputes between states over boundaries and the private right of soil claimed under different grants. It shall fix the value of coins struck by their own authority or any of the states; fix standards of weights and measures; regulate trade with Indians not members of any state; establish post offices; appoint all officers of the army and navy except regimental officers who shall be appointed by the legislature of each state; and make rules for the regulation of the armed forces. The Congress shall have the authority to appoint a Committee of the States to manage the affairs of the United States while Congress is recessed; to appoint other committees as needed; to appoint a presiding officer of the Congress; to appropriate funds for the payment of debts; to borrow money or emit bills on the credit of the United States; and to make requisition on the states for military manpower and money proportionate to the number of white inhabitants.

The vote of nine states shall be required to declare war; grant letters of marque and reprisal in peacetime; enter into any treaties or alliances; coin money and regulate the value thereof; set up a budget; emit bills of credit; borrow money; appropriate money; determine the strength of the army or navy; and appoint a commander-in-chief of the army or navy.

A minority may vote to adjourn from day to day but a majority of seven of the states must approve any other action besides those enumerated in the above paragraph which requires nine.

Article X

Committee of the States

While Congress is in recess, the "Committee of the States" or any nine of the states shall be vested with powers to act on behalf of the Congress. However, none of the powers enumerated above which require the approval of nine states shall be delegated to the Committee.

Article XI

Invitation to Canada

Canada, on her own volition, may join the United States as an equal member, but no other colony shall be admitted without consent of at least nine states.

Article XII

Past Debts to be Honored

The new confederation pledges that it will honor all bills of credit, debts, and contracts entered into by the Congress before these Articles of Confederation become operative.

Article XIII

Amendments Require Unanimous Approval

No changes shall be made in these Articles without the unanimous approval of all of the states. The delegates further pledge on behalf of the respective states that these articles shall constitute a "perpetual union" (stated four times) and each state pledges to uphold and support the decisions of the Congress.

THE PRICE PAID FOR FREEDOM[1]

For most of the signers of the Declaration of Independence, the cost of freedom required the ultimate sacrifice. Five signers were captured by the British as traitors and tortured before they died. Twelve had their homes ransacked and burned. Two lost their sons in the Revolutionary War and another had two sons captured.

For most of the signers of the Declaration of Independence, the cost of freedom required the ultimate sacrifice.

What kind of men were they? Twenty-four were lawyers and jurists. Eleven were merchants, nine were farmers and large plantation owners; men of means who were well-educated. But they signed the Declaration of Independence knowing full well that the penalty would be death if they were captured.

Carter Braxton of Virginia, a wealthy planter and trader, saw his ships swept from the seas by the British Navy. He sold his home and properties to pay his debts and died in rags.

Thomas McKean was so hounded by the British that he was forced to move his family almost constantly. He served in Congress without pay and his family was kept in hiding. His possessions were taken from him and poverty was his reward.

Vandals or soldiers looted the properties of William Ellery, George Clymer, Lyman Hall, George Walton, Button Gwinnett, Thomas Heyward Jr., Edward Rutledge, and Arthur Middleton.

At the Battle of Yorktown, Thomas Nelson Jr. noted that the British General Cornwallis had taken over the Nelson home for his headquarters. The owner quietly urged General George Washington to open fire. The home was destroyed and Nelson died bankrupt.

Francis Lewis had his home and properties destroyed. The enemy jailed his wife and she died within a few months of imprisonment.

---

[1]   The Price They Paid : snopes.com – http://1ref.us/eh

John Hart was driven from his wife's bedside as she lay dying. Their 13 children fled for their lives. His fields and grist mill were laid waste. For more than a year he lived in forests and caves, returning home to find his wife dead and his children vanished. A few weeks later he died from exhaustion and a broken heart. Robert Morris and Philip Livingston suffered similar fates.

Such were the stories and sacrifices of the American Revolution. These were not wild-eyed, rabble-rousing ruffians. They were soft-spoken men of means and education. They had security, but they valued liberty more. Standing tall, straight, and unwavering, they pledged: *"For the support of this Declaration, with a firm reliance on the protection of Divine Providence, we mutually pledge to each other our lives, our fortunes, and our sacred honor."*

HOW THE BIBLE HELPED SHAPE
THE UNITED STATES CONSTITUTION

"In the pages of the New Testament can be found the concepts of God, man, law and government that gave rise to the growth of constitutionalism-of liberty under law-first in ancient Israel, then in medieval Britain, next in colonial America, and finally, right in the Federal Convention of 1787.

Unlike the pagan nations, such as Mesopotamia and Egypt that surrounded it, ancient Israel rejected the notion that human rulers were virtual gods, entitled to absolute control over their subjects. The Israelites were convinced that God is the ultimate Sovereign, and that He wants men to obey Him, not human tyrants and—be free!

Biblical Christianity came to Britain at the end of the first century, long before Pope Gregory sent the first Roman missionaries to England in 59 A.D. Historian Leslie Hardinge documents that from the first coming of Christianity to Britain, *great stress was laid upon God's Law in all its bearings…*"[2] The Scriptures were considered supreme authority.

About the year 432 A.D, the Celtic Christian missionary, Patrick, began to convert the Irish people and their chieftains, and convinced them to make the Mosaic Law (which Patrick had summarized in a book called *Liber ex Lege Moisi*) the law of Ireland.

Around 565 A.D, The Celtic Christian missionary Columbia converted the King of the Picts, who in turn made the Ten Commandments the civil law of Scotland. Alfred the Great placed the Decalogue at the beginning of England's legal code about the year 900 A.D. The English "common law" was developed case by case, but with the Commandments as a guide. Later, all thirteen colonies made that "common law" the basic law of America, and it undergirded, and was protected by the United States Constitution.

The Magna Carta of 1215 was a specific statement of common law principles, derived from Scripture, and insisted that everyone, even the King, is bound by the law. Scholars recognize that the Magna Carta laid the groundwork for our Constitution.

Pastor Thomas Hooker, preached from Deut. 1:13, "*Take you wise men, and understanding, and known among our tribes, and I will make them rulers over you,*" which inspired America's first constitution, the Fundamental Orders of Connecticut. It limited government's powers, provided for representation

---

[2]   The Celtic Church in Britian, Leslie Hardinge, copyright 2005–TEACH Services, Inc. p. 72

and a pattern of federalism. In American political writing in the Founding Era, from 1760 to 1787, by far the most frequently cited book was the Bible, the chief influence on the Constitution."

Authored by Bill Bright and used by permission of *Campus Crusade International*

SEPARATION OF CHURCH AND STATE

"Separation of church and state" is a phrase invoked by the Supreme Court and used frequently today. The origin was through an exchange of letters between Thomas Jefferson and the Baptist Association of Danbury, Connecticut.

Thomas Jefferson was America's first anti-Federalist president. This pleased the Baptist denomination in that, for the most part, they were anti-Federalists as well. This position of the Baptists was understandable for they had often found themselves suffering from the centralization of power. They suffered fines, personal injury, imprisonments, and land confiscation. Out of circumstances hostile to their very survival, they called for the freedom to worship as they desired and to propagate their faith without reservation. This existed between 1630 and the 1780's.

They sent a letter of congratulations to the President but in the same letter expressed their grave concern over the First Amendment and its guarantee of "the free exercise of religion." They were concerned that the right to "free exercise of religion" was a government-given (thus inalienable) right rather than a God-given right. They were concerned that the government someday would attempt to regulate religious expression.

The President understood this concern as it was also his own. He made numerous declarations about the constitutional inability of the Federal government to regulate, restrict, or interfere with religious expression.

Jefferson had committed himself as President to pursuing the purpose of the First Amendment, thus preventing the "establishment of a particular form of Christianity" by the Episcopalians, Congregationalists, or any other denomination. In a letter to the Danbury Baptists on January 1, 1802 he gave his assurance that the free exercise of religion would never be interfered with by the Federal government. He explained his position and said the Constitution had created "a wall of separation between Church and State." Although this originally applied only to the Federal government, it has forced the states to take a "hands off" position.

The phrase "separation of church and state" so frequently invoked today was rarely mentioned by any of the Founders; and even Jefferson's explanation of his phrase is diametrically opposed to the manner in which the courts apply it today.

It is interesting that Jefferson and Madison joined with the other Founders in expressing hope that all religions be encouraged in order to promote the moral fiber and religious tone of the people.

THE FIRST PRAYER IN CONGRESS

O Lord, our Heavenly Father, high and mighty, King of kings, and Lord of lords, who dost from Thy throne behold all the dwellers on earth and reignest with power supreme and uncontrolled over all the Kingdoms, Empires and Governments; look down in mercy, we beseech Thee, on these our American States, who have fled to Thee from the rod of the oppressor, and thrown themselves on Thy gracious protection, desiring to be henceforth dependent only on Thee. To Thee have they appealed for the righteousness of their cause; to Thee do they now look up for that countenance and support, which Thou alone canst give. Take them, therefore, Heavenly Father, under Thy nurturing care; give them wisdom in Council and valor in the field; defeat the malicious designs of our cruel adversaries; convince them of the unrighteousness of their cause and if they persist in their sanguinary purposes, of own unerring justice, sounding in their hears, constrain them to drop the weapons of war from their unnerved hands in the day of battle!

Be Thou present, O God of wisdom, and direct the councils of this honorable assembly; enable them to settle things on the best and surest foundation. That the scene of blood may be speedily closed; that order, harmony, and peace may be effectually restored, and truth and justice, religion and piety, prevail and flourish amongst the people. Preserve the health of their bodies and vigor of their minds; shower down on them and the millions they here represent, such temporal blessings as Thou seest expedient for them in this world and crown them with everlasting glory in the world to come. All this we ask in the name and through the merits of Jesus Christ, Thy Son and our Savior. Amen.

Offered by the Reverend Jacob Duche, September 7, 1774, 9 0'clock a.m.

GEORGE WASHINGTON'S PRAYER FOR AMERICA

Almighty God; we make our earnest prayer that Thou wilt keep the United States in Thy holy protection, that thou wilt incline the hearts of the citizens to cultivate a spirit of subordination and obedience to government; and entertain a brotherly affection for one another and for their fellow citizens of the United States of America at large. And finally that Thou wilt most graciously be pleased to dispose us all to do justice, to love mercy and to demean ourselves with that charity, humility and pacific temper of mind which were the characteristics of the Divine Author of our blessed religion, and without whose example in these things we can never hope to be a happy nation. Grant our supplication, we beseech Thee, through Jesus Christ our Lord. Amen

This prayer was adapted from his circular Letter to the Governors of the United States.

April 30, 1789

A PROCLAMATION OF THANKSGIVING
By the President of the United States of America

It is the duty of all Nations to acknowledge the providence of Almighty God, to obey his will, to be grateful for his benefits, and humbly to implore his protection and favor—and Whereas both Houses of Congress have, by their joint Committee requested me *"To recommend to the People of the United States, a day of public thanksgiving and prayer, to be observed by acknowledging with grateful hearts the many and signal favors of Almighty God, especially by affording them an opportunity peaceably to establish a form of government for their safety and happiness"*

NOW THEREFORE, I do recommend and assign Thursday the 26th day of November next to be devoted by the People of these States, to the service of that great and glorious Being, who is the beneficent Author of all the good that was, that is, or that will be—That we may then all unite in rendering unto him our sincere and humble thanks—for his kind care and protection of the People of this country previous to their becoming a Nation—for the signal and manifold mercies, and the favorable interpositions of his providence, which we experienced in the course and conclusion of the late war—for the great degree of tranquility, union and plenty, which we have since enjoyed—for the peaceable and rational manner in which we have been enabled to establish constitutions of government for our safety and happiness, and particularly the national One now lately instituted, for the civil and religious liberty with which we are blessed, and the means we have of acquiring and diffusing useful knowledge; and in general, for all the great and various favors which he hath been pleased to confer upon us.

And also that we may then unite in most humbly offering our prayers and supplications to the great Lord and Ruler of Nations, and beseech him to pardon our national and other transgressions—to enable us all, whether in public of private stations, to perform our several and relative duties properly and punctually—to render our national government a blessing to all the People, by constantly being a government of wise, just, and constitutional laws, discreetly and faithfully executed and obeyed—to protect and guide all Sovereigns and Nations (especially such as have shewn kindness unto us) and to bless them with good government, peace, and concord—To promote the knowledge and practice of true religion and virtue, and the increase of science among them and Us—and generally, to grant unto all mankind such a degree of temporal prosperity as he alone knows to be best.

Given under my hand at the City of New York the third day of October in the year of our Lord, 1789.   GO. WASHINGTON

THE ISSUE OF SLAVERY

In the history of the world, nearly every nation has had slaves. The Chinese kept thousands of slaves. Babylon boasted of slaves from a dozen different countries. The dark-skinned Hittites, Phoenicians, and Egyptians had white slaves. The Nazis had white slaves. The problem of slavery still exists today in many parts of the world. Slavery is not a racial problem; it is a human problem.

Originally, all of the colonies had slaves and bond servants. Even many "free" blacks owned slaves, especially in Louisiana, Virginia, South Carolina and Maryland. In our modern culture, we do not "own" the persons who work for us as servants, cleaning persons, landscapers, etc. We hire them and they accept pay in return. In colonial days, slave traders brought boatloads of Africans to America to be sold as workers. They were not prepared for a life of competitive independence. Slavery was a business, yet many Americans were against the transportation and sale of slaves and the Founders desired to move toward the elimination of slavery.

Thomas Jefferson, at age twenty-five, was elected to the Virginia state legislature and his first act was to begin the elimination of slavery. In the original draft of the Declaration of Independence, one of the principle charges made by Jefferson against the King of England and his predecessors was the fact that they would not allow the American colonies to outlaw the importation of slaves. Many religious leaders campaigned against the importation of slaves almost from the arrival of the first boatload in 1619.

The southern states were stubborn on the issue of slavery. The farmers and land owners in the southern states needed help with the production of cotton and tobacco. Not enough labor was available through the citizenry, and for those who could afford to own slaves, it appeared to be an answer to their need for labor. The Founders were willing to allow twenty years for further maturity of a non-slave economy in certain states, but they also wished to loudly declare that slavery was not an acceptable practice. They put a provision in the Northwest Ordinance (1787) that in the new states, there would be no slavery. However, it took the Civil War, the Emancipation Proclamation of President Lincoln, and the Thirteenth Amendment to end slavery.

The instructions by planters (land owners) to the overseers of slave labor almost universally emphasized that slaves were to be treated with firmness without brutality. Cleanliness was insisted upon. The use of alcohol was not permitted. Many slaves were allowed to sell produce from their own patches. Pregnant and nursing mothers were given special attention and were given only as much work as they were able to do. The health of the mother was very important to the family. Slaves were usually sold as family units, possibly for no other reason than keeping families together. Many slave families developed a fondness for their owners and their families, and were treated kindly and with respect. For this reason, many slaves chose not to leave when they were declared "free".

The worst offences of slaves against their owners was rebellion and running away. Running away was an especially heinous offence, not only because of the loss of the slave but even more on the account of the moral effect upon others.

Most Americans have come to love the "Negro Spiritual." The Library of Congress in its music division has catalogued over 6,000 "spirituals." The "spirituals" are songs, most of which were written by slaves, extemporaneously, as an expression of their faith in a loving and just God. In the evenings, by candlelight, or the open fire, the family would gather around and sing. Music and rhythm were natural to them and the songs were passed on, one to another by oral repetition.

Because the slaves coming to America were unchurched and with little or no religious faith, many became Christians, that is, if Christianity was the religion of their masters. One can believe that the influence was strong because of the many "spirituals" we enjoy today. The "spirituals" usually expressed in song the Bible stories or verses they knew. Some of the favorites were *Go Down Moses, Swing Low, Sweet Chariot, and The Gospel Train.*

The Founders were well aware of the nature of man and attempted to move towards the expungement of slavery. From the time of the enactment of the Constitution, America has made great strides in resolving this issue.

GEORGE WASHINGTON AND SLAVERY

WASHINGTON.

At the time of George Washington's birth, slavery was a fact of life. When his father died in 1743, George became a slave owner. At age 11, he owned ten slaves and 500 acres of land. At the age of 22, he owned 36 slaves. When he married Martha Custis, her 20 slaves came to Mount Vernon. The slave population at that time had grown and at the time of his death, there were 316 slaves living at Mount Vernon.

It took much skill to run the estate at Mount Vernon. Many of the slaves were trained in crafts, coopering, carpentry, blacksmithing, shoemaking, and milling. Others were needed to serve in the home as servants, boatmen, or field hands. The female slaves were taught spinning, weaving, and sewing, while others worked in the laundry, the dairy, or the kitchen.

The food grown at Mount Vernon was shared with the slaves and their families. If there was a surplus, it was sold at the market. Many slaves had their own gardens and could sell their food to the local markets for extra income. Once a year the slaves were issued clothing. The slaves worked from sunrise to sunset with two hours off for meals. They received several days off at Christmas, the Monday after Easter, and Pentecost. If they had to work on

MOUNT VERNON

Sunday during harvest, they received a day off later and were compensated with pay.

George Washington's attitude toward slavery changed as he grew older. By the time of his presidency, he seemed to believe that slavery was wrong and against the principles of the new nation. As President, he did not lead a public fight against slavery. He had worked too hard to build the country to risk tearing it apart. However, privately, he led by example. He arranged for all the slaves he owned to be freed at the death of his wife. He left instructions for their care, the training of their children, and for continuing support of the elderly.

Note: This information became available through Washington's extensive record keeping, such as his 1799 slave census. This helped Mount Vernon historians research and interpret slave life on his farms.

THE STAR- SPANGLED BANNER

O say can you see, by the dawn's early light'
What so proudly we hailed at the twilight's last gleaming,
Whose broad stripes and bright stars, through the perilous fight
O're the ramparts we watch'd, were so gallantly streaming?
And the Rockets red glare, the Bombs bursting in air,
Gave proof through the night that our Flag was still there;
O! say does that star-spangled Banner yet wave,
O're the Land of the free, and the home of the brave?

On the shore dimly seen through the mists of the deep,
Where the foe's haughty host in dread silence reposes,
What is that which the breeze, O're the towering steep,
As it fitfully blows, half conceals, half discloses?
Now it catches the gleam of the morning's first beam.
In full glory reflected saw shines in the stream,
'Tis the star-spangled banner - O long may he wave
O'er the land of the free and the home of the brave.

And where is that band who so vauntingly swore
That the havoc of war and the battle's confusion,
A home and a country, shall leave us no more?
Their blood has washed out their footsteps pollution.
No refuge could save the hireling and slave,
From the terror of flight or the gloom of the grave,
And the star-spangled banner in triumph doth wave,
O're the land of the Free and the Home of the Brave.

O! thus be it ever when freemen shall stand,
Between their lov'd home, and the war's desolation,
Blest with vict'ry and peace, May the Heav'n rescued land,
Praise the Power that hath made and preserv'd us a nation!
Then conquer we must, whaen our couse it is just.
And this is our motto—**"In God is our Trust,"**
And the star-spangled Banner in triumph shall wave,
O're the Land of the Free, and the Home of the Brave.

Francis Scott Key, 1779–1814

SELECTED SIGNIFICANT QUOTES

The Constitution of the United States was not made merely for the generation that then existed, but for posterity- unlimited, undefined, endless perpetual posterity.
Henry Clay, American statesman and orator, 1777–1852

Don't interfere with anything in the Constitution. That must be maintained, for it is the only safeguard of our liberties.
Abraham Lincoln, 16th President of the United States, 1809–1865

If we and our posterity reject religious instruction and authority, violate the rules of eternal justice, trifle with the injunctions of morality and recklessly destroy the political constitution which holds us together, no man can tell how sudden a catastrophe may overwhelm us, then shall bury all our glory in profound obscurity.
Daniel Webster, American statesman and senator, 1782–1852

The liberties of our country, the freedoms of our civil Constitution are worth defending at all hazards. It is our duty to defend them against all attacks. We have received them as a fair inheritance from all worthy ancestors. They purchased them for us with toil and danger and expense of treasure and blood. It will bring of everlasting infamy on the present generation-enlightened as it is- if we should suffer them to be wrested from us by violence without a struggle, or by the artifices of designing man.
Samuel Adams, Founding Father, orator and philosopher, 1722–1803

The Constitution is not an instrument for the government to restrain the people. It is an instrument for the people to restrain the government- lest it come to dominate our lives and interests.
Patrick Henry, Statesman and orator, 1736–1799

To live under the American Constitution is the greatest political privilege that was ever accorded to the human race.
Calvin Coolidge, 30th President of the United States, 1872–1933

"GIVE ME LIBERTY, OR GIVE ME DEATH!"

All our work, our whole life is a matter of semantics, because words are the tools with which we work, the material out of which laws are made, out of which the Constitution was written. Everything depends on our understanding of them.
Felix Frankfurter, Associate Judge of the Supreme Court, 1882–1965

But there is a higher law than the Constitution, which regulates our authority over the domain and devotes to the same noble purposes.
William Seward, Senator and Governor, 1801–1872

Do not separate the text from the historical background. If you do, you will have perverted and subverted the Constitution, which can only end in a distorted, bastardized form of illegitimate government.
James Madison, 4th President of the United States and "Father of the Constitution", 1751–1836

The Constitution is not neutral. It was designed to take the government off the backs of the people.
William O. Douglas, Associate Judge of the Supreme Court, 1898–1980

As the British Constitution is the most subtle organism which has proceeded from the womb and the long gestation of progressive history, so the American Constitution is, so far as I can see, the most wonderful work ever struck off at a given time by the brain and purpose of man.
W. E. Gladstone, Prime Minister of the United Kingdom, 1809–1898

The happy union of these States is a wonder; their Constitution a miracle; their example the hope of liberty throughout the world.
James Madison, 4th President of the United States and "Father of the Constitution", 1751–1836

Firearms are second only to the Constitution in importance; they are the peoples' liberty's teeth.
George Washington, 1st President of the United States

A general dissolution of principles and manners will more surely overthrow the liberties of America than the whole force of the common enemy...
Samuel Adams, 1722–1803

This is a religious people...From the discovery of this continent to the present hour, there is a single voice making this affirmation
Supreme Court Justice, David Josiah Brewer, 1837–1910

All must admit that the reception of the teaching of Christ results in the purist patriotism, in the most scrupulous fidelity to public trust, and in the best type of citizenship.

Grover Cleveland, President of the United States, 1837–1908

…The United States are under the peculiar obligations to become a holy people unto the Lord our God.

Ezra Stiles, President of Yale College, 1778–1795

Knowing that intercessory prayer is the mightiest weapon and supreme call for Christians today, I pleadingly urge our people everywhere to pray…

General Robert E. Lee, 1807–1870

Religion is of general and public concern, and on its support depend, in great measure, the peace and good order of government, the safety and happiness of the people….

Samuel Chase, signer of the Declaration of Independence

You have…received a public education, the purpose whereof hath been to qualify you to better serve your Creator and your country… Your first great duties…are those you owe to Heaven, to your creator and Redeemer. Let these be ever present to your minds and exemplified in your lives and conduct.

William Samuel Johnson
(1727–1819) president of
Columbia University

JOHNSON'S HOUSE.

The longer I live, the more convincing proofs I see of this truth, that God governs in the affairs of men. And if a sparrow cannot fall to the ground without His notice, is it possible that an empire can rise without His aid?

Benjamin Franklin, 1787

The patriot who feels himself in the service of God, who acknowledges Him on all his ways, has the promise of the Almighty direction, and will find His word in his greatest darkness, "a lantern to his feet and a lamp unto his paths." ...
        Francis Scott Key (1779–1843) wrote "The Star Spangled Banner."

I believe no man was ever early instructed in the truths of the Bible without having been made wiser or better. If moral precepts alone could have transformed mankind, the mission of God into our world would not have been necessary...
        Benjamin Rush, Founding Father, first to call for public schools.

Resistance to tyranny becomes the Christian and social duty of each individual... Continue steadfast, and with a proper sense of your dependence on God, nobly defend those rights which heaven gave, and no man ought to take from us.
        Resolution of the Massachusetts Provincial Congress, 1774

STATE PREAMBLES

Beginning as early as 1777, states incorporated a preamble to be included in each state constitution, all expressing gratitude and reverence to God.

Alabama, 1901
We the people of the state of Alabama, invoking the favor and guidance of Almighty God, do ordain and establish the following constitution....

Alaska, 1956
We, the people of Alaska, grateful to God and to those who founded our nation and pioneered this great land....

Arizona, 1911
We, the people of Arizona, grateful to Almighty God for our liberties, do ordain this constitution....

Arkansas, 1874
We, the people of Arkansas, grateful to Almighty God for the privilege of choosing our own form of government....

California, 1879
We, the people of California, grateful to Almighty God for our freedom....

Colorado, 1876
We the people of Colorado, with profound reverence for the Supreme Ruler of the Universe....

Connecticut, 1818
The people of Connecticut, acknowledging with gratitude the good providence of God in permitting them to enjoy....

Delaware, 1897
Through Divine Goodness all men have, by nature, the rights of worshipping and serving their Creator according to the dictates of their consciences....

Florida, 1885
We, the people of the state of Florida, grateful to Almighty God for our constitutional liberty, establish this constitution....

Georgia, 1777

We, the people of Georgia, relying upon the protection and guidance of Almighty God to ordain and establish this constitution....

Hawaii, 1959

We, the people of Hawaii, grateful for Divine Guidance... establish this constitution....

Idaho, 1889

We, the people of the state of Idaho, grateful to Almighty God for our freedom, to secure its blessings....

Illinois, 1870

We, the people of the state of Illinois, grateful to Almighty God for the civil, political, and religious liberty which He hath so long permitted us to enjoy and looking to Him for a blessing on our endeavors....

Indiana, 1851

We, the people of Indiana, grateful to Almighty God for the free exercise of the right to choose our form of government....

Iowa, 1857

We, the people of the state of Iowa, grateful to the Supreme Being for the blessings hitherto enjoyed, and feeling our dependence on Him for a continuation of these blessings, establish this constitution....

Kansas, 1859

We, the people of Kansas, grateful to the Almighty God for our civil and religious privileges establish this constitution....

Kentucky, 1891

We, the people of the Commonwealth are grateful to Almighty God for the civil, political, and religious liberties....

Louisiana, 1921

We, the people of the state of Louisiana, grateful to Almighty God for the civil, political and religious enjoy....

Maine, 1820

We, the people of Maine acknowledging with grateful hearts the goodness of the Sovereign Ruler of the Universe in affording us the opportunity...and imploring His aid and direction....

Maryland, 1776

We, the people of the state of Maryland, grateful to Almighty God for our civil and religious liberty....

Massachusetts, 1780

We, the people of Massachusetts acknowledging with grateful hearts, the goodness of the Great Legislator of the Universe in the course of His providence an opportunity, and devoutly imploring His direction....

Michigan, 1908

We, the people of the state of Michigan, grateful to Almighty God for the blessings of freedom, establish this constitution....

Minnesota, 1857

We, the people of the state of Minnesota, grateful to God for our civil and religious liberty, and desiring to perpetuate its blessings....

Mississippi, 1890

We, the people of Mississippi in convention assembles, grateful to Almighty God, and invoking His blessing on our work....

Missouri, 1845

We, the people of Missouri, with profound reverence for the Supreme Ruler of the Universe, and grateful for His goodness, establish this constitution....

Montana, 1889

We, the people of Montana, grateful to Almighty God for the blessings of liberty establish this constitution....

Nebraska, 1875

We, the people, grateful to Almighty God for our freedom establish this constitution....

Nevada, 1864

We, the people of the state of Nevada, grateful to Almighty God for our freedom, establish this constitution....

New Hampshire, 1792, Part I. Art. V

Every individual has a natural and unalienable right to worship God according to the dictates of his own conscience....[3]

New Jersey, 1844

We, the people of the state of New Jersey, grateful to Almighty God for civil and religious liberty which He hath so long permitted us to enjoy, and looking to Him for a blessing on our endeavors....

New Mexico, 1911

We, the people of New Mexico, grateful to Almighty God for the blessings of liberty....

New York, 1846

We, the people of the state of New York, grateful to Almighty God for our freedom, in order to secure its blessings....

North Carolina, 1846

We, the people of North Carolina, grateful to Almighty God, the Sovereign Ruler of Nations, for our civil, political, and religious liberties, and acknowledging our dependence upon Him for the continuance of those....

North Dakota, 1889

We, the people of North Dakota, grateful to Almighty God for the blessings of civil and religious liberty, do ordain....

Ohio, 1852

We, the people of Ohio, grateful to Almighty God for our freedom, to secure its blessings and to promote our common....

Oklahoma, 1907

Invoking the guidance of Almighty God, in order to perpetuate the blessings of liberty, establish this constitution....

Oregon, 1857, Bill of Rights, Article 1, Section II

All men shall be secure in the natural right to worship Almighty God according to the dictates of their consciences....[4]

---

[3]   New Hampshire's constitution does not contain a preamble. The phrase above appears in Part I, Article V of the New Hampshire constitution

[4]   Oregon's state preamble does not mention God: however, this reference to God appears in Article I, Section II

Pennsylvania, 1776

We, the people of Pennsylvania, grateful to Almighty God for the blessings of civil and religious liberty, and humbly invoking His guidance....

Rhode Island, 1842

We, the people of the state of Rhode Island grateful to Almighty God for the civil and religious liberty which He hath so long permitted us to enjoy, and looking to Him for a blessing....

South Carolina, 1778

We, the people of the state of South Carolina, grateful to God for our liberties, so ordain and establish this constitution....

South Dakota, 1889

We, the people of the South Dakota, grateful to Almighty God for our civil and religious liberties...

Tennessee, 1796, Article I, Section III

That all men have a natural and indefeasible right to worship God according to the dictates of their conscience....[5]

Texas, 1845

We, the people of the republic of Texas, acknowledging, with gratitude, the grace and beneficence of God...

Utah, 1896

Grateful to Almighty God for life and liberty we establish this constitution....

Vermont, 1777

Whereas all governments ought to be instituted and supported for the security and protection of the community, as such, and to enable the individual to compose it, to enjoy their natural rights, and other blessings which the Author of existance has bestowed upon man....

Virginia, 1776, Bill of Rights

That religion, or the duty of which we owe our Creator can be directed only by reason and that it is the mutual duty of all to practice Christian forbearance, love, and charity....

---

[5]   Tennessee's preamble does not mention God; however, this reference to God appears in Article I, Section III.

Washington, 1889

We the people of the state of Washington, grateful to the Supreme Ruler of the Universe for our liberties, do ordain this constitution....

West Virginia, 1872

Since through Divine Providence we enjoy the blessing of civil, political, and religious liberty, we, the people of West Virginia reaffirm our faith in the constant reliance upon God....

Wisconsin, 1848

We, the people of Wisconsin, grateful to Almighty God for our freedom, domestic tranquility....

Wyoming, 1890

We, the people of the state of Wyoming, grateful to God for our civil, political, and religious liberty establish this constitution....

A BRIEF HISTORY OF STEEL ENGRAVINGS

The beautiful reproductions of steel engravings used in *A Constitution is Born* were provided by Mr. Ron Mann, former Director of the Bicentennial of the United States Constitution. Many of the reproductions date back to the late 1700's.

Steel engraving in colonial times was the process used for reproduction of images. It was introduced in 1792 by Jacob Perkins, an American inventor and was initially used for printing bank notes.

The process began with itching out the desired image on a flat metal plate and then with a "graver", the artist pushed against the flat plate with his thumb and forefinger making ridges and lines to take the ink. The "graver" was a shaped bar of hardened steel with a sharp point and a wooden handle. Early on the flat surface plate was usually of copper but was later replaced with steel. The copper, being a soft metal, could be heated and made flat again should the artist desire changes. Steel became the metal of choice as it was more durable and could be case hardened to ensure repeated use.

CHARLESTON IN 1776.

THE HISTORY OF THE QUILL PEN

Did you know that the Constitution of the United States was signed with a quill pen? Writing with a quill pen goes back as far as the seventh century. Great manuscripts were written with the quill pen, including the Bible. Scribes decorated their pages with beautiful markings, all done with a quill pen. Americans will remember the beautiful script of "We the People."

The best pens were made from flight feathers of geese. After plucking the feathers the shaft had to be carved, sharpened, and the point split. Each pen was unique and no two quills wrote the same. To make a quill pen was a difficult process requiring cleaning, trimming and carving. Special feathers had to be selected and often only two or three feathers from one goose could be used. A slit is made at the base of the shaft for the ink to flow to the tip and the tip must be kept very clean for quality writing.

Skill and practice are required when writing with a quill pen. The touch must be light and the hand must be slanted. The quill holds the ink until light pressure is applied. If kept clean, the pen improved as a writing tool.

Ink was made with indigo that was taken from the galls of oak, and sometimes nut trees. The juice from berries was also used. Colonists often used soot that came from burnt lamp oil. It was mixed with gum or glue and molded into sticks which could be mixed with water for writing with the quill pen.

To recognize the difficulty in writing with a quill pen, one can understand why young men were often sent to "writing" schools because it was very important to write a "good hand."

RECIPES FROM THE COLONIAL HEARTH

Hoe Cakes (or Johnny Cakes)

Scald a pint of milk and add 3 pints of Indian meal.

Add half a pint of flour. Add molasses and shortening, work it up and bake before the fire.

Brunswick Stew

Put 2 cut up squirrels in a large pan with 3 quarts of water. Add one large onion, and one half pound of lean ham that has been cut into small pieces. Simmer for 2 hours.

Add 3 pints of tomatoes, 1 pint of lima beans, 4 large potatoes, 1 pint of corn, salt and pepper. Cover and stew softly until done.

Baked Beans

Place 1 quart of dry beans into soft water and let set overnight. In the morning, wash them out and put them in a pot with enough water to cover them. Let them simmer on the fire until tender, then wash them out again. Put them into an earthen pot with a little pork that has been scalded. Add a little molasses and bake for 5 or 6 hours. If you use a brick oven, it is best to let them stand overnight.

Hasty Pudding (Indian Pudding)

Boil 1 quart of milk add to it 2 gills and a half of corn meal, 7 well-beaten eggs, a gill of molasses, and a large piece of butter. Bake it for 2 hours.

Do you remember this verse in Yankee Doodle?

"Fath'r and I went down to camp
Along with Captain Goodin,
And there we saw the men and boys
As thick as Hasty puddin'."

THE BREAKFAST OF HASTY-PUDDING.

Peas-Porridge

Put a quart of fresh green peas into a quart of water with a little mint and a little salt. Let them boil until the peas are tender. Add some beaten pepper, a big piece of butter rolled in flour. Let it boil a few minutes; then add 2 quarts of milk and let it boil for a quarter of an hour. Take out the mint.

Note: a "gill" equals a half a cup or 4 ounces.

THE ORIGIN AND MEANING OF THE TERMS "OLD GLORY," "UNCLE SAM" AND "YANKEE"

"OLD GLORY"

March 17, 1824 was the twenty-first birthday of a young sea Captain of Salem, Massachusetts, William Driver. On that day his mother presented him with a beautiful American flag that he quickly named "Old Glory."

Old Glory accompanied young Driver on every sea voyage he made until he retired in 1837 and moved to Nashville, Tennessee. So meaningful was this flag to him that he displayed it from his home on every special occasion.

When Tennessee broke from the Union in 1861, Captain Driver hid Old Glory inside his bedding. However, when the Union soldiers marched into Nashville in 1862, Driver proudly carried Old Glory to the capitol and raised her to the big, blue sky.

Before his death he presented Old Glory to his daughter with the words, *Mary Jane, this is my ship's flag, Old Glory. It has been my constant companion. I love it as a mother loves her child. Cherish it as I have cherished it.*

The flag was later donated by his family to the Smithsonian Institute in Washington, D.C where it remains under glass.

"UNCLE SAM"

A meat packer by the name of Samuel Wilson, in the city of Troy, New York supplied barrels of beef to the U.S. Army troops during the war of 1812. The barrels were stamped "U.S." meaning, "for the United States" but the soldiers began referring to the barrels as "Uncle Sam's." This reference was picked up by a local newspaper and "Uncle Sam" became the nickname for the U.S. Federal government.

Sometime in 1860, a political cartoonist, Thomas Nast, created an image of Uncle Sam with a white beard and a stars and stripe suit that appears on posters today. (Thomas Nast is also credited with the modern image of Santa Claus, and the donkey and the elephant to symbolize the Democratic and Republican parties.)

"YANKEE"

No one seems to be sure of the origin of the term "Yankee." One commonly used explanation is that William Gordon, in 1789 published a history of the American Revolution where he tells of a Massachusetts farmer by the name of John Hastings who used the term as an adjective meaning "excellent." This was in contrast to a derisive use of the word earlier. The song *Yankee Doodle* was written as a mockery of the troops but was later turned around by the troops to display national pride.

There are other unverified versions that include: the word having been found in a letter (1758) by the British General George Wolf as a term of contempt for the colonial troops in his command, or even as a nickname used by the Dutch settlers.

Although we may never know the true origin, the term today usually refers to Americans native to New England or "Northerners."

FASCINATING FACTS ABOUT
THE CONSTITUTION

1. At the time of the writing and signing of the Constitution, America's population was four million people and today it is 320 million.[6]

2. The Constitution went through many revisions and drafts, but it was written in 100 days from May 25, 1787 to September 17, 1787. The delegates met from 10:00 a.m. until 3:00 p.m. six days a week. During this convention the delegates took a 10-day break.

3. James Madison is considered to be the "Father of the Constitution" because of his prolific work on the document. He was a major contributor to the writing of the Constitution.

4. James Madison was the only delegate to attend every meeting of the Constitutional Convention. He also kept careful notes on the proceedings. These notes were kept secret until his death. These and other important papers were sold to the U.S. government in 1837 for $30,000 and were later published in 1840.

5. George Mason is considered the one primarily responsible for the Bill of Rights. He developed the Virginia Declaration of Rights in 1776, which was largely influenced by the English Bill of Rights and the Magna Carta.

6. Since the inception of the Constitution, the House of Representatives has introduced over 11,000 amendments, but only 33 have been sent to the states for ratification. Only 27 of the 33 proposed amendments were approved by the state conventions and have become part of the Constitution.

7. Adding another amendment is the only way to repeal an existing one. This has happened only once when the 21st Amendment was added to repeal the 18th Amendment, which dealt with the prohibition of alcoholic beverages, thus ending Prohibition.

8. A proposal was made during the proceedings of the Constitutional Convention that the American army be limited to 5,000 soldiers. George Washington sarcastically agreed only if the opposing army had no more than 3,000 soldiers.

---

[6]   Population Clock – http://1ref.us/ei

9. The word "veto" is from the Latin and actually means "I forbid". The President actually lives up to this meaning when he refuses to give his approval to a bill.

10. The decisions made by the Supreme Court are of national importance. All other courts are subject to the rulings made by the Justices. The Constitution also gives the Supreme Court the power to determine whether or not the federal, state or local governments are acting within the Constitution's authority. The Supreme Court can judge whether a President's action is constitutional.

11. The decisions made in lower courts may be appealed and questioned, while the decisions made by the Supreme Court are final and cannot be appealed to another court. Even though there are thousands of requests for rulings to be made by the Supreme Court annually, less than 150 are actually heard at the bench and ruled on by the Supreme Court.

12. James Madison showed his dedication to the task of writing the Constitution by arriving three months early and putting together a blueprint for the Constitution.

13. The Constitution was signed on September 17, 1787 by 39 of the 55 delegates. The average age of the signers was 44. Three of the delegates refused to sign the Constitution. They were Edmund Randolph, George Mason, and Elbridge Gerry. They refused because it contained no formal statement on the rights of the citizens.

14. The only Presidents to sign the Constitution were George Washington and James Madison.

15. All public officials may be impeached if they fail to carry out their responsibilities. Public officials include Supreme Court Justices.

The U.S. Constitution is the oldest and shortest written constitution of any major country of the world with 4,543 words in the original, unamended document.

16. The U.S. Constitution is the oldest and shortest written constitution of any major country of the world with 4,543 words in the original, unamended document. This includes all the signatures of the signers. If the 27 amendments were included, the Constitution would then contain 7,591 words.

17. Our Constitution, especially the Bill of Rights, was based on several "freedom" documents which included the Magna Carta (1215), the Petition of Rights (1628), the Writ of Habeas Corpus (1679), and the English Bill of Rights (1689).

18. The four pages of the original U.S. Constitution are now located at the National Archives Building in Washington D.C. where it is preserved in a protective glass case that is filled with argon gas. It is framed with titanium and is kept at a constant temperature of 67 degrees Fahrenheit and at 40% relative humidity.

19. The full Constitution is only displayed once a year, on September 17th, which is the anniversary of its' signing.

20. The U.S. Constitution has influenced many countries of the world and has been copied innumerable times.

21. The reason why the Constitution continues to endure after more than 200 years is because it has successfully protected the rights of the people. In addition, the document reflects different opinions and philosophies. It shows that people were willing to work together and put aside private agendas to develop something for the good of all the people.

22. Through a proclamation by President George Washington and a Congressional resolution, Thanksgiving was established on November 26, 1789 to declare a thanksgiving in honor of the Almighty's care of America in assisting them in achieving independence and the establishment of a Constitutional government.

23. After some discussion on how to address the President, the Senate proposed that he be called "His Highness the President of the United States of America and Protector of the Liberties". However, the Senate and the House of Representatives finally compromised and decided on simply "The President of the United States".

24. Congress proposes new amendments to the Constitution. Half of the House of Representatives and half of the Senate must agree on them. Two-thirds of the state legislature must ask Congress to have a national convention on a proposed amendment. For an amendment to be rati-

fied, three-fourths of the state legislatures must vote to approve it and three-fourths of the states' ratifying conventions must agree.

25. Thirteen of the fifty states can block an amendment and can keep it from becoming part of the Constitution. A proposed amendment is given a time limit by which it must be ratified. If it fails to pass during that time, it is blocked. Approval and ratification of the amendment is considered as final.

26. The Constitution requires that a census be taken every ten years. If a state's population changes in size, then the number of representatives from that state are changed proportionally.

27. The President serves as the leader of our country and he makes sure that the government runs smoothly. He ensures that the laws are enforced and obeyed. As part of his Presidential oath, he promises to preserve, protect, and defend the Constitution.

A BRIEF SUMMARY OF THE CONSTITUTIONAL AMENDMENTS

AMENDMENT I: Guarantees freedom of religion, speech, and of the press. People are given the right to meet peaceably and to voice complaints to the government.

AMENDMENT II: Guarantees the right to keep and bear arms.

AMENDMENT III: Sets Conditions for housing soldiers in peace time.

AMENDMENT IV: Guarantees the right to privacy. Limits the power of the government to search and seize property.

AMENDMENT V: Provides protection from being held for committing a crime unless you have been indicted correctly by the police.

AMENDMENT VI: Guarantees a citizen to a fair trial, a fair jury, and an attorney, if desired by the accused.

AMENDMENT VII: Provides for the jury trial in civil lawsuits beyond a cost of twenty dollars.

AMENDMENT VIII: Prohibits excessive bail and fines, and cruel and unusual punishment.

AMENDMENT IX: People hold more rights than those listed in the Constitution.

AMENDMENT X: Powers that are not given by the Constitution to the central government, or forbidden by the states, are reserved for the states or the people.

AMENDMENT XI, 1798: A state cannot be sued by citizens of another state or foreign country.

AMENDMENT XII, 1804: Establishes Presidential election procedures.

AMENDMENT XIII, 1865: Abolishes slavery.

AMENDMENT XIV, 1868: Forbids laws that unfairly deny citizens' rights and guarantees equal protection under the law to all.

AMENDMENT XV, 1870: Forbids depriving citizens the right to vote because of race or color.

AMENDMENT XVI, 1913: Authorizes an income tax.

AMENDMENT XVII, 1919: Prohibits the manufacture or sale of liquor.

AMENDMENT XVIII, 1919: This amendment banned the sale and drinking of alcohol in the United States. The only amendment repealed from the Constitution.

AMENDMENT XIX, 1920: Gives women the right to vote

AMENDMENT XX, 1933: Sets time of Presidential and congressional terms to begin in January.

AMENDMENT XXI, 1933: Repeals the Eighteenth Amendment.

AMENDMENT XXII, 1951: Bars any President from serving more than two 4-year terms.

AMENDMENT XXIII, 1961: Gives residents of the District of Columbia the right to vote.

AMENDMENT XXIV, 1964: Outlaws the payment of taxes as a voting requirement.

AMENDMENT XXV, 1967: Rules for the succession of a President if he/she cannot complete the term.

AMENDMENT XXVI, 1971: Lowers the legal voting age to eighteen.

AMENDMENT XXVII, 1992: Establishes rules for varying compensation for senators and representatives.

To keep resources clean, concise, and easy to update, all Web addresses in this book have been assigned a shortened version using the YOURLS 1ref system. For instance: "http://this_is_an_example_of_a_very_ long_url/192837/can-you-make-it-shorter.com" would be shortened to "http://1ref.us/mis" Please note that none of these addresses end with a period. Any periods at the end of a short address are there only to indicate that it is the end of a sentence.

BIBLIOGRAPHY

Ackerman, Bruce. "The Living Constitution." Harvard Law Review 120, no. 7 (2007): 1737–1812. http://1ref.us/ej. Accessed Feb. 26, 2011

Agency, Catholic News. "Interpreting the Constitution and Voting for President: Catholic News Agency (CNA)." *Catholic News Agency*. Web. 26 Feb. 2011. http://1ref.us/ek.

Alba, Bonnie. "'Living and Breathing' vs. Original Intent." Renew America. Feb. 5, 2009 http://1ref.us/el. Accessed Feb. 26, 2011

Alexander, Mark. "A 'Living Constitution' for a Dying Republic." Patriot Post (blog). http://1ref.us/em. Sept. 16, 2005. Accessed Feb. 26, 2011.

"Amendments to the Constitution of the United States of America." *Ashbrook Center for Public Affairs at Ashland University*. Web. 07 Mar. 2011. http://1ref.us/en.

Anderson, Kerby. "The Declaration and Constitution: Their Christian Roots." Probe Ministries. May 27, 2003. Accessed February 25, 2011. http://1ref.us/cl.

A Perfect Union: America Becomes a Nation, A Teacher's Guide. National Constitutional Center, 2006.

Baldwin, Chuck. "The American Revolution Revisited." *NewsWithViews.com -- Where Reality Shatters Illusion*. Web. 18 Mar. 2011. http://1ref.us/eo.

Barton, David. *Original Intent: the Courts, the Constitution & Religion*. Aledo, TX: WallBuilder, 2008. Print.

"Bill of Rights." *National Archives and Records Administration*. Web. 02 Nov. 2011. http://1ref.us/eq.

Bradley, Bev. "Vocabulary of the US Contitution." *Quia Web*. Web. 4 Nov. 2011.

Brooks, Jack. "Constitution: Foreword and Historical Notes." 24 June 1992. Web. 2 Nov. 2011.

Brunell, Evan. "If I Ruled on Progressive v. United States." http://1ref.us/er. Accessed September 22, 2010.

"Chapter 2. The Lessons of Constitution Making." *The Claremont Institute*. Web. 07 Mar. 2011. <http://www.claremont.org/publications/pubid.574/ pub_detail.asp> (site discontinued).

"Charters of Freedom - The Declaration of Independence, The Constitution, The Bill of Rights." *National Archives and Records Administration*. Web. 14 Mar. 2011. http://1ref.us/es.

Chin, Jonathan, and Alan Stern. "The Constitution in the Flesh." *Oracle Thinkquest*. 1997. Web. 2 Nov. 2011.

Chin, Jonathan, and Alan Stern. "The Living Constitution." *Think Quest*. 1997. Web. 1 Mar. 2011.

"Citizens for Principled Government — Justice Souter Retirement Frames Constitutional Question of Original Intent vs. Unchecked Judicial Activism" *Citizens for Principled Government*. Web. 26 Feb. 2011. http://1ref.us/et.

"Civil Rights, 1954". http://1ref.us/eu.

"Constitution Day, September 17." *Center for Civic Education*. Web. 04 Nov. 2011. http://1ref.us/ew.

"Constitution Day." *The Claremont Institute*. Web. 07 Mar. 2011. http://1ref.us/ ex (site discontinued).

Davis, Kenneth C. *Don't Know Much about History: Everything You Need to Know about American History but Never Learned*. New York: HarperCollins, 2003. Print.

Diaz, Mario. "The Death of the Living Constitution." *Concerned Women for America*. 6 Aug. 2009. Web. 01 Mar. 2011. http://1ref.us/ey (site discontinued).

"Do We Have a Living Constitution." *National Center for Constitutional Studies – NCCS*. Web. 01 Mar. 2011. http://1ref.us/ez. (site discontinued)

"Dred Scott Case: The Supreme Court Decision." http://1ref.us/f0. Accessed September 13, 2010.

Feldmeth, Greg D. "Articles of Confederation vs. the Constitution." 31 Mar. 1998. Web. 4 Nov. 2011.

FaithFacts.org. "The Bible and Government" *Biblical Principles: Basis for America's Laws*, Web. 25 Feb. 2011. http://1ref.us/cm.

FaithFacts.org. "Biblical Principles for America's Laws" Web. 25 Feb. 2011.
    http://1ref.us/ep.

"Few Rules for New Constitution Day Requirement | Inside Higher Ed." *Inside
    Higher Ed | Home*. Web. 04 Nov. 2011. http://1ref.us/f1.

"Firstamendmentcenter.org: Religious Liberty - Overview." http://1ref.us/f2.
    Accessed March 18, 2011.

Foner, Eric. "Our Living Constitution." Web. 25 Feb. 2011.

Garvin, Peggy. "The Government Domain: Back to School for Constitution
    Day 2008 | LLRX.com." *LLRX.com | Legal and Technology Articles and
    Resources for Librarians, Lawyers and Law Firms*. Web. 14 Mar. 2011.
    http://1ref.us/f3.

Hamilton, Alexander, James Madison, John Jay, and Lawrence Goldman. *The
    Federalist Papers*. Oxford: Oxford UP, 2008. Print.

History News Network. Web. 26 Feb. 2011. http://1ref.us/f4.

Kroll, Woodrow. "Center for Bible Engagement." *Center for Bible Engagement
    - Home*. Web. 25 Feb. 2011. http://1ref.us/f5.

Learn About the United States (U.S.) Constitution & More | Constitution Facts.
    Web. 04 Nov. 2011. http://1ref.us/f6.

Levington, Kristen, and Brenan Center for Justice. "Defending Our Living
    Constitution | Civil Liberties | AlterNet." *Home | AlterNet*. 17 Mar. 2008.
    Web. 01 Mar. 2011. http://1ref.us/f7.

"Liberty and the Constitution." *Welcome to The Future of Freedom Foundation*.
    Web. 18 Mar. 2011. http://1ref.us/f8.

"Living and Breathing" vs. Original Intent." *SmallGovTimes.com*. Web. 04 Nov.
    2011. http://1ref.us/f9.

"Living Constitution - Conservapedia." *Main Page - Conservapedia*. Web. 28
    Feb. 2011. http://1ref.us/fa.

"Living Constitution." Web. 1 Mar. 2011.

"Living Constitution." *Wikipedia, the Free Encyclopedia*. Web. 01 Mar. 2011.
    http://1ref.us/fb.

Maltz, Earl. "Implied Powers." http://1ref.us/fc. Accessed September 7, 2010.

National Constitution Center: Home. Web. 14 Mar. 2011. http://1ref.us/fd.

"News: Few Rules for New Constitution Day Requirement - Inside Higher
    Ed." *Home - Inside Higher Ed*. Web. 18 Mar. 2011. http://1ref.us/f1.

Observing Constitution Day." *National Archives and Records Administration*.
    Web. 04 Nov. 2011. http://1ref.us/fe.

"Originalism vs. the "Living Constitution"" *Disputations and Meditations*.
    Web. 01 Mar. 2011. http://1ref.us/ff.

Primary Monitor. "Welcome to the Living Constitution, Justice Scalia"
    Primary Monitor Blog. 27 June 2008. Web. 1 Mar. 2011.

Regents of the University of California v. Bakke". http://1ref.us/fg. Pearson
    Education, Inc., publishing as Pearson Prentice Hall, 2005.

"Roe v. Wade Decided January 22, 1973." http://1ref.us/ds. Accessed August 9,
    2010.

"Scalia Slams 'Living Constitution' Theory – Politics | Republican Party |
    Democratic Party | Political Spectrum – FOXNews.com." *FoxNews.
    com – Breaking News | Latest News | Current News*. Web. 01 Mar. 2011.
    http://1ref.us/fh.

Skousen, W. Cleon. *The 5000 Year Leap. 28 Great Ideas That Changed the
    World*. Malta, Idaho: National Center for Constitutional Studies, 1981.

"Supreme Court Hallmarks." Web. 17 Mar. 2011.

Taylor, Jr., Earl. *5000 Year Leap & Making of America Study Guide*. Malta,
    Idaho: National Center for Constitutional Studies, 1994. Print.

"The Articles of Confederation – The U.S. Constitution Online –
    USConstitution.net." *Index Page – The U.S. Constitution Online –
    USConstitution.net*. Web. 04 Nov. 2011. http://1ref.us/fi.

"The Constitution Explained – The U.S. Constitution Online –
    USConstitution.net." *Index Page – The U.S. Constitution Online –
    USConstitution.net*. Web. 17 Mar. 2011. http://1ref.us/fj.

"The Constitution Explained – The U.S. Constitution Online –
    USConstitution.net." *Index Page – The U.S. Constitution Online –
    USConstitution.net*. Web. 02 Nov. 2011. http://1ref.us/fj.

"The Constitution of the United States." *The U.S. National Archives and
    Records Administration*. http://1ref.us/fu Web. 4 Nov. 2011.

"The Living Constitution." *Harvard Law Review*. Web. 01 Mar. 2011.
    http://1ref.us/fk.

"The Making of the U.S. Constitution." *Library of Congress*. http://1ref.us/ft
    Web. 4 Nov. 2011.

"National Constitution Center: Constitution Day." *National Constitution
    Center: Home*. Web. 04 Nov. 2011. http://1ref.us/fl.

"The Philadelphia Horror Story." *The Claremont Institute*. Web. 07 Mar. 2011.
    http://1ref.us/fm.

"The Roots of Religious Liberty." *America – Engaging the World – America.
    gov*. 22 June 2008. Web. 18 Mar. 2011. http://1ref.us/fn.

"The Signers of the Constitution." *The U.S. National Archives and Records
    Administration*. http://1ref.us/fs Web. 4 Nov. 2011.

"ThisNation.com--Features of the Constitution." *ThisNation.com-American
    Government & Politics Online*. 25 Feb. 2011. Web. 25 Feb. 2011.
    http://1ref.us/fo.

"ThisNation.com--The Constitutional Convention." *ThisNation.com-
    American Government & Politics Online*. 25 Feb. 2011. Web. 25 Feb. 2011.
    http://1ref.us/fp.

"ThisNation.com--United States Constitution Quick Facts." *ThisNation.com-
    American Government & Politics Online*. 25 Feb. 2011. Web. 25 Feb. 2011.
    http://1ref.us/fq.

Thompson, Charles. "Plessy v. Fergusson: Harlan's Great Dissent". University
    of Louisville Louis D. Brandeis School of Law, 2010. http://1ref.us/dn.
    Last modified: Fri Sep 17, 1999.

Whittington, Keith. "How to Read the Constitution: Self-Government and the
    Jurisprudence of Originalism | The Heritage Foundation." *Conservative
    Policy Research and Analysis | The Heritage Foundation*. Web. 26 Feb.
    2011. http://1ref.us/fr.

american family association

The mission of the American Family Association is to inform, equip, and activate individuals to strengthen the moral foundations of American culture, and to give aid to the church here and abroad in fulfilling the task of the Great Commission.

American Family Association (AFA), a non-profit 501 c (3) organization, was founded in 1977 by Donald E. Wildmon, who was the pastor of the First United Methodist Church in Southhaven, Mississippi, at the time. Since 1977, AFA has been on the frontlines of America's culture war. The original name of the ministry was National Federation of Decency but that was changed to American Family Association in 1988.

In 1991 AFA started a new division called America Family Radio. With the first radio station going on the air in 1991, now AFR has over 185 radio stations in over 30 states, AFA also operates its own news outlet called One News Now. ONN broadcasts hourly newscasts on all of the American Family Radio stations along with publishing stories daily at the website, onenewsnow.com.

Along with radio and news, AFA activates Christians through weekly emails that are sent to over one million of our most faithful supporters. In these emails which we call Action Alerts, each individual is able to contact Fortune 500 companies that are advertising irresponsibly or even call their Congressman on legislation that AFA supports.

Today, AFA is led by AFA President Tim Wildmon, and it continues as one of the largest and most effective pro-family organizations in the country with hundreds of thousands of supporters.

If you would like to find out more about our work and how you can get involved, please visit our website, afa.net

Tim Wildmon
President, American Family Association